THE TRAINS DON'T STOP THERE ANYMORE
The Life Story of a Footballing Nomad

MIKE LEWIS

To Nick

Very best Regards.

Mike Lewis

VERTICAL EDITIONS

www.verticaleditions.com

First published in the United Kingdom in 2007 by
Vertical Editions, 7 Bell Busk, Skipton,
North Yorkshire BD23 4DT

www.verticaleditions.com

ISBN 978-1-904091-20-2

Cover design and typeset by HBA, York

Printed and bound by the Cromwell Press, Trowbridge

CONTENTS

To Glenys, for being who you are

1

WEDNESDAY'S CHILD IS FULL OF WOE

Wednesday 14th May 2003 started encouragingly. Sunlight pouring through the bedroom window, the discovery of half a pack of smoked bacon that had become hidden in the fridge behind the butter and some fresh bread. What more could a man ask for? Little did I know that within an hour of awakening that this day was going to be the mother of all red letter days.

It was only later that same evening as I was walking home from Heavitree Police Station in Exeter at 10.30 pm having spent 11 hours there, that I afforded myself the luxury of a wry smile as I took the short journey to my flat. I remembered that through my 64 years on this planet most of the major events in my life had occurred on a Wednesday. Family deaths, career opportunities, a life-threatening car crash at 18 years of age and I distinctly remember losing my virginity on a Wednesday night. Earlier that particular evening together with my girlfriend, I had watched Manchester United play a European match on a 14 inch black and white TV. Fortunately her landlady was out for the night so we slipped into her lounge to watch this epic. The four bottles of Mann's Brown Ale consumed watching the game with my girlfriend gave me enough confidence – and hopefully lead in my pencil – to later test out 'the equipment'. It was a disaster. I wish I hadn't bothered. What a let down! Subsequently, when relaying that event to my mates I told them a completely different story of course. Many years later I received a phone call from my publisher on a Wednesday saying that he was happy to publish this story. Wednesday 30th May 2007 was the date set aside for my sentencing after charges were brought after a four year investigation into my horrendous 11 month tenure as Vice-Chairman of Exeter City Football Club. To this day I treat the advent of Wednesday with some trepidation!

A phone call from my close friend Glenys in Swansea at 8.30 am on that fateful day in May 2003, made my heart miss a beat. Members of the Devon and Cornwall Fraud Squad had visited her property (where I was a lodger) for the purpose of a house search. The search was for any documents relating to matters at Exeter City Football Club. Her call was to tip me off that they were probably going to visit my residence in Exeter. Sure enough, within 15 minutes of her call I received a knock on the door. There, standing before me, were two plain clothed policemen and a woman. The senior officer thrust a pink search warrant into my face. He said he was following up a complaint from a third party suggesting financial irregularities had occurred at Exeter City Football Club. The possibility of a charge of conspiracy to defraud creditors by virtue of reducing a former director's loan by £100,000 and allegedly trading whilst insolvent were the reasons for the search and questioning. Later when charges were brought, they were extended to include obtaining a pecuniary advantage by virtue of claiming that I had access to substantial funds. I was told that I had to accompany these officers to the police station where I would be asked a series of questions in an effort to shine some light on the complaint that had been made.

I subsequently discovered that the co-owner of the club and his wife had also received a visit. Glenys in Swansea received a visit at 8.15 am. I received a visit at 8.30 am. John Russell the co-owner of the club and his wife received a visit at 9.00 am. There was a 45 minute difference between the three visits, which goes to prove that even the most structured organisations such as the police are quite capable of cocking up their timings! Still, 15 minutes' warning did not give me enough time to pack, jump on one of the boats moored across the road from my flat and set sail to freedom!

Perhaps I had watched too many episodes of *The Bill*. These guys had mastered 'Police speak' to a fine art. 'We are led to believe...certain persons have made a complaint...anything you say...' and finally, '...you will accompany us to the Police Station where further questioning will take place...' How bloody tiresome.

At the police station I was introduced to the custody officer. Endless forms were completed and details entered on his computer. He asked me to remove my belt, tie and any valuables that I carried, plus my shoelaces. Shoelaces? Why? My bewilderment magnified tenfold when I was instructed to take off my shoes *outside* the cell that was going to be my 'new abode' for a while. If I had left the laces in my shoes they would have been 'parked' outside the cell for the entire period of restraint! Anyway, even if they were not removed what could I do to hurt myself with shoelaces that had seen better days and were only 10 inches long? With an 18 inch neck and a maximum of 20 inches between the two laces there was no way I could endanger myself. Now maths was never my strong point but a simple calculation would reveal that two shoelaces x 10 inches = 20 inches. One neck measuring 18 inches would leave just two inches for the purpose of hanging oneself. Doesn't work, does it? Give a man enough rope and he will hang himself, but with two inches? Never.

I was banged up in a filthy cell that had blood splattered walls, filthy toe nails scattered around the floor, a toilet that had not been cleaned for days, coupled with a ledge that supposedly was used for the purpose of rest or sleep (or in my case to sit for hours and ponder what the hell was going on). A one and a half-inch thick mattress covered this ledge that certainly did not react kindly to my 17 stone being placed on it. The compulsory visit from a custody officer after six hours of containment was welcomed. I needed to talk to another human being even if it was with laughing boy himself.

'How we doing then?'

'Oh I'm fine, any chance of a full English?' No, that wasn't my response, but what did he expect, I just felt that he was going through the motions and didn't really care too much about me or any other persons placed in custody.

Quite early on in my adult life I became familiar with police mentality. I joined the special constabulary at 18 years of age and thoroughly enjoyed the Thursday evening shift walking the streets of my home town of Newport. The regulars were miffed that we amateurs were pinching their overtime (as they saw it). Any hint of serious crime and I made my way to the nearest blue police box that normally occupied a place on the corner of a main street. Using the black phone that nestled inside of the top compartment of the box I was able to get straight through to the main police station and within minutes the regulars would be there taking over matters and in the process pushing the special constable to one side.

I solved just one crime during my 19 months as a special. On my beat down Commercial Street, I had to pass what would now be called a mini market. As I strolled past the front door I noticed a trail of what looked like water emanating from the letter box and careering down the street. I followed the trail and within 20 yards I found two lads aged about 12 sitting with their back to a motorcycle shop window and sinking their teeth into slices of water melons. As I stood over them, they dropped their melons and tried to run off. I caught one of the boys and after questioning I discovered that the blighters had used a bamboo pole with a sharpened end to spear the melons stacked near to the front door. They drew the melon up to the letter box and used a knife to slice it small enough to pass through. Ingenious I thought. After what could only be described as a gentle ticking off I sent the lad packing.

Back in my cell in Exeter what the laughing boy did get from me was request to be moved to a cleaner cell. Bloody hell, that went down like a lead balloon! Very reluctantly I was moved to a slightly cleaner cell.

At 5.00 pm some six hours after my arrest, I heard the slat being drawn across the cell door and a lady who looked as if she had been press ganged into her role of domestic, shouted, 'Tea or coffee?' I asked for tea. She grunted and explained that she was serving coffee and that tea would take 15 minutes to make. I never saw a cup of tea.

Sleep was impossible. The ledge not quite big enough for my 6 foot 1 inch frame coupled with the constant noise of fellow prisoners crying out with pleas ranging from a demand to see their solicitor to an animal-like scream from a female inmate insisting that they bring her man to her cell immediately. Was this really happening to me? Had I died the night before and was this the equivalent of hell? I often tried to imagine what hell would be like as the likelihood of going upstairs to the pearly gates was a very thin one indeed taking into account the credits versus the debits that I had accumulated in God's log book. During the long wait before questioning, many thoughts swept through my mind. Some relating to the reasons I was detained under custody. Other thoughts were more focused. For instance, the helter-skelter ride of life I had lived. These included family matters with two divorces and a desperate sadness felt for my two daughters, Karen 34, who never saw too much of her dad during her early years as he was always at the 'Football Club' and Faye, then 15, suffering a similar fate, being the victim of the separation of her mum from her dad at a time when youngsters are sensitive to change. Heaven knows how she coped with that. Guilt came rushing through and irrespective of the issues that had put me in this hellhole there was no escaping the heart wrenching feeling that I was a desperate failure. As you will discover on your journey through this book, there was fun, laughter and moments of sheer ecstasy, but the present moment was scary and I could not see a way forward.

The well-rehearsed 'good cop, bad cop' syndrome was about to unveil itself as I was eventually led downstairs from the cell to the interview room. After 10 hours in the banger it was a welcoming sound to hear the jangling of a heavy bunch of keys nearing my cell door that hopefully signalled my release. The interview room was half the size of the cell I had just left. I was confronted by two CID officers. Immediately it was possible to identify who was going to present his questions in the softly, softly mode and who was going to dispense with first name terms and attempt to make me give answers to questions fired at increasing speed hoping that I would reveal some interesting detail that they could note and use at a future date. Wanting to be helpful, I answered as best I could. The 10 hours in the cell had the desired effect as far as the coppers were concerned. It's a good tactic to make a prisoner sweat a little before questioning, when all he wants to do is go home. I refused their kind offer of legal representation on the basis that I felt that I could answer any question they put to me. On reflection I was probably wrong to 'go it alone'. In fact later when I did receive professional advice I received what could only be described as a 'bollocking' for not being represented at the interview. I wanted to get out of there as quickly as possible and I must confess that the thought of a Chinese takeaway on the way home got my juices going as I had not eaten for 12 hours.

The interview took two hours. It seemed that the two policemen were struggling to pin any charges on me and they seemed to run out of steam. On being told that I could go home I picked up my shoelaces, belt and valuables from the custody office near the rear door of the station. It seemed perfectly reasonable that I should leave by that door as that was the way I came in. The request to leave by the same door to avoid the plethora of cameras and radio journalists together with the local scribes was met with strong resistance. Oh No! The boys in blue wanted their moment of glory. Knowing that the media had been waiting outside most of the day looking for quotes and pictures of Mike Lewis and John Russell was far too good an opportunity to raise the profile of the Devon and Cornwall Constabulary and they were going to make certain that we left the building by the front door. The media circus had begun and little did I know that it would last for over four years.

On leaving via the front door the media were there in force. Flashing cameras, microphone sticks thrust into my face and scribes ready with their notepads. The stampede for an interview resembled the type of activity that I imagine takes place outside a London nightclub when the press get word that a C-list celebrity is about to leave in a dishevelled and pissed up state. But this was Exeter after all, so I tried to be helpful and give the press something that was definitely going to hit the front page of the Exeter Express and Echo the following day. They had their job to do and they had all been ably assisted by the police who obviously had tipped them off as to when and who was coming out first. My philosophy about the media has, never changed. They cannot be beaten so I can at least get them to print some of the things I want to say rather than ostracise them.

I never bothered with the Chinese takeaway. I was released on bail, left wondering what was going to happen next and I was asked to return to the same police station three months later.

You will be forgiven for wondering how this qualifies for an 'early call off the bench' as a book opener. I felt that my story in part, needed to draw attention to the very serious position this beautiful game will soon find itself in now that a precedent has been set. No more can clubs continue to trade using the futile excuse, 'We are only technically insolvent'. My case has brought an end to that escape route. Now, the moment a Chief Constable receives a complaint that the club(s) on his patch may be trading whilst insolvent, he will be obliged to take action.

As time marched on from 13th May 2003 to February 2005 when a summons was administered, many events occurred that changed my whole belief about our justice system. This is not sour grapes on my part as I was well prepared to receive whatever sentence was handed down. No, it is simply that the system is such that unless you have an IQ of at least 140 and the ability to correspond at A Level English standard then you are, my friend, well and truly done for. I have written dozens of letters to the CPS, the police and the Court for Human Rights in an effort to highlight not only the futility of this case but the damage it has done to me in these twilight years of my life. It's all about successful prosecutions as far as the police and the CPS are concerned. Sod the defendant.

Adam Crozier when he was the Football Association's CEO declared that the majority of Football League Clubs were technically insolvent. Being technically insolvent is akin to being partly pregnant. In the event of an investigation, many clubs will have to admit that they too have been trading whilst insolvent. That is precisely the accusation placed against Russell and myself. Imagine the consequences should the Chief Constable of Manchester receive complaints concerning 'trading whilst insolvent' from creditors serving Stockport County FC, Bolton Wanderers FC, Wigan FC, Bury FC, Rochdale FC, Oldham FC, and who knows, perhaps Manchester United FC if Mr Glazers' plans go belly up! Pop across the Pennines to Yorkshire and add to that list York City, Scarborough, Bradford City, Leeds United, Barnsley, Doncaster Rovers, Rotherham United and the two Sheffield clubs then you have two counties containing at least a dozen clubs who may be trading whilst insolvent.

Who 'blew the whistle' on us? The main complainant was Uri Geller supported by Bernard Frowd, the ex-chief executive of the football club. It's ironic that Geller pushed and pushed to get us to employ his friend Guis Rivaud in our commercial department. Rivaud was, at the time, a manager with Virgin Records in Barnstaple. I interviewed him to keep Geller quiet and surprisingly Rivaud not only came across in a very positive way, but had spent some considerable time laying out his plans for the commercial development of the club should he be appointed. This was all positive enough stuff which led me to offer him the position of assistant commercial manager. But this energetic smiling Frenchman was not all he seemed. Within a few weeks he was caught spying in the office.

Rivaud, with typical French arrogance, was asking far too many questions outside his remit. This made many members of staff suspicious and curious as to his motives. Early one morning he gained access to the accounts department. It transpired that he was looking for the 'gate' book. This book contained the record of admissions and money paid in for every home game. Little did he know that the information he was seeking had been on the accountant's desk the whole of the day before and was not particularly sensitive information. His anger at being detected by the office cleaner who, thankfully, immediately informed John Russell and myself that not only had he caught Rivaud pouring over documents on the accountant's desk, but that he saw him sat up in the new stand on his mobile phone for half an hour after being caught. I pulled him into my office and in front of a witness asked him what he was doing going through accounts. He denied the activity so I suspended him on the spot and subsequently sacked him when more evidence of his spying became known. He remonstrated as expected, but within a week of being fired, he wrote asking for his job back stating that he wanted desperately to work with the club. No wonder the French are ridiculed by so many Brits.

At this point it is sufficient to say that for 18 years I considered Geller to be a close friend. How sucked in can a person be? Geller used the 'life or death' parallel when the press asked him within minutes of that fateful game being finished on May 3rd, just how he felt. His reply given in front of the cameras as tears were falling down his face was totally crass. Geller, speaking on radio and in national newspapers, compared the loss of league status for the club to that of the other lowest point in his life when, during the 1967 war in Israel, he shot dead a Jordanian soldier. To compare that to the loss of status of a football club is beyond comprehension. To put this footballing tragedy into perspective it ranks only second in disaster terms to that of the club being wound up altogether. However, it was never a matter of life or death as the club was quite capable of returning to League status and missed out by one point in season 2004–2005.

A TV programme entitled *On Holiday with the Gellers* shown on Channel 4, in August 2003 only confirmed what thousands of people have felt for some time. The programme was filmed in Croatia. Geller with wife Hannah, daughter Natalie and her boyfriend plus Geller's manager Shippy, visited Croatia taking in Dubrovnik and Split. A classic scene was filmed at the top of a bell tower inside an ancient Church. Geller, head in hand and using all his mind power, revealed to viewers that he was going to try and make the huge church bells ring. They rang four times. His delight was obvious as he rushed downstairs and looked straight down the camera lens exclaiming, 'I've done it, I've done it'. His balloon was immediately pricked when he was informed that the bells normally ring four times at four in the afternoon. Then, as if to compound the felony, he looked across a street in Dubrovnik saw this little dog with its owner and shouted, 'My mind is receiving a signal from your dog, he's 7 to 9 years of age isn't he?'

'No,' replied the owner. 'He's two'. Exit stage left!

Geller's loyalties have stretched from Reading FC to Newcastle United then on to Norwich City, the England team and now the Israeli national team. His relationship with Michael Jackson helped Exeter City FC to attract this megastar to the city for a guest appearance. Geller can never be thanked enough for that remarkable achievement, but was he standing at Michael's side during his trial in 2005?

I have pulled no punches in my effort to hopefully make this book interesting and provide a window opener to the sick, hypocritical, jealous and greedy world of football. It is a world that I was part of for 27 years and regretfully was a party to some of those frailties. There were large helpings of laughter too. Being a firm believer that laughter can have a very positive effect on a person's wellbeing, I have tried to ensure that a constant thread of humour runs through this book as it has in my life. I hope the reader can smile and perhaps chuckle at some of the crazy situations I experienced. The ability to laugh at myself was always the escape route when times got hard. Tears and laughter are not always a million miles apart in the pantomime world we call football. It is a wonderful game that our country handed down to the rest of the world. It has formed a global collective band embracing all nations. Now the beautiful game can be seen from the beaches of Rio to a piece of scrubland in Ghana. In my opinion, the game has been tarnished and almost destroyed through corruption. However it still remains the most popular sport in the world.

Professional football in the UK is in for an almighty shake up with more and more clubs struggling to stay alive. Meanwhile the Premiership looks down with a sympathetic smile at those in their nadir, pulls up the anchor and sails away into their financial zenith.

Who is to blame? In a minor way I suppose I helped this decline by sitting at boardroom tables with various clubs allowing players and managers to have their own way. Loyalty in the game is in short shrift and that goes for directors, players and managers. Sadly, 95 percent of footballers in the lower leagues will happily walk away from their 'beloved' clubs to take an extra £10 per week elsewhere. For players in the Premiership and

Championship, just add a few extra noughts to that figure.

Can I give you an example of misplaced loyalty? Steve Flack a veteran striker at Exeter, having spent nine years there was considering his future very carefully in the summer of 2005. His contract had come to an end. The club quite rightfully offered him a new contract on lesser terms. Flack, never slow in coming forward (pardon the pun) suggested that as he had already signed a pre-contract agreement with Tiverton Town for the new season as an option would take a £10,000 reduction in his pay at Exeter on the basis that they would grant him a testimonial match in the new season for staying at the club for 10 years. The testimonial would probably raise far in excess of the £10,000 shortfall on his new offer, so he would lose nothing at all, but would be seen by many fans as being a hero for staying another season and taking a wage cut.

Flack, always first to bang the door down if his wage was not in his bank on the last day of each month, was very lucky in my opinion to be offered a contract at all! Every time I saw him play I was left in wonderment as to how a limited player like him could command a wage of any kind playing football. It was Flack, who was accused by a number of fans, that he cost the Grecians their third division place by virtue of having missed a sitter from two yards out during the game at Cambridge in the relegation season. Exeter was 1–0 up at the time and well set to 'close the door' on Cambridge had Flack tucked his chance away. Heaven knows how he missed. The law of physics would suggest that it was harder for him to put the ball over the bar than to tap it over the line. A win that day would have placed the Grecians comfortably above the other relegation candidates.

Am I cynical? Yes of course I am, but with good reason. On the basis that football has already put regular support by nature of paying at the turnstiles outside the reach of the working man. Gates will continue to decline whilst the game at the Premiership level will continue to be subsidised by money from TV who broadcast match after match. Meanwhile, the clubs in the lower levels are feeling the squeeze, many will be forced out of business and more footballers will join the dole queue. Most footballers are takers, not givers. In fact starry eyed directors are as much to blame for this. They have their favourites and will 'break the bank' to keep their Johnny, Brian or Dean 'who hasn't put a foot wrong all season Chairman'. Yes you will hear of some players making a community contribution by visiting a local hospital or children's home but do you realise that they are contractually obligated to spend some time each week carrying out these duties? I once took the entire Reading Football Club first team squad down a disused mine shaft. One senior player commented, 'Did men actually work down there for hours at a time?' On another occasion back in 1985 when we were putting the final touches to a trip to Spain, a 34-year-old player asked if he needed a passport! Perhaps this is the reason that many players turn to booze and gambling when their playing days are over as they have never been prepared for the time when they have to take that giant step into the real world.

Directors and chairmen must take their fair share of the blame too. When a manager asks his board for an extra player or two that will either help the club make that promotion push, or take them out of the relegation zone, you will see directors relishing the opportunity to impress the manager by supporting his cause. If I had £10 for every time I heard a manager say in a board meeting: 'Chairman, if I had a wide man (read central defender, striker, goalkeeper, full back as is the case) then I would guarantee you promotion/avoid relegation'. At that point, my bank balance would be in a healthy state. Shamefully, as directors we bought these empty promises knowing that failure to comply with his demands would give the manager a wonderful opportunity to 'get off the hook' if matters got worse. With wide open arms the manager would exclaim to the media that money was not available and he would have to work with what he had. What he had was the squad he put together at the start of the season when he promised so much!

Unfortunately the game does not encourage loyalty. Two defeats on the bounce and you will hear directors discussing who the new manager should be. Flip that one on its back for a moment and we will see an endless procession of managers who having declared their loyalty to their present club have left to seek their fortune elsewhere.

I have been a part of this circus for 27 years and I am not particularly proud of some of the actions I have made. I made classic blunders on the way to the top, worse still I compounded the felony by making more blunders on the way down! I wonder how many of those questionable decisions were made on a Wednesday?

2

WHEN INNOCENCE
WAS BLISS

I was unwanted as a baby. My real mother would have readily had
an abortion had it not been for the sheer disgrace it would have
caused her at that time. The embarrassment at nine years of age
when I discovered that Molly and Albert were not my real
parents was extremely difficult to deal with. I was a war baby and
joined the ranks of many other bastards who were the results of
wartime flings. My real parents were called Dot and Fred. I knew
Dorothy as my 'Auntie' until the truth was revealed. It made me
curious as a young child when the best birthday and Christmas
presents always came from Auntie Dot. That curiosity
disappeared the moment I knew the truth. Perhaps it was her
way of compensating. I will never know.

My real father, Fred, appeared only once after hearing that I
had a serious car crash at the age of 18. My pride and joy was a
powder blue Standard 8 bought from my Uncle Roland who
specialised in restoring old pre-war Rovers and changing them
into beautiful sports cars. He also kept a few post war cars and
the Standard 8 was one of them. There was an inherent fault with
these cars. They used Bendix brakes and the whole system was
operated via lengths of thick wire cable. If the brakes were not
adjusted properly the front offside would engage momentarily
before the back nearside, thrusting the car into a dangerous
swerve. Whether this fault caused the crash, I will never know.
Something happened at the bottom of Charles Street, Newport
and after being hit by a shale lorry; both me and my pride and joy
were sent crashing through Woolworth's window. During the late
1950s, Lorries transported shale to the new steelworks being
built at Llanwern near Newport. It was a well known fact that
cowboy drivers would drive their lorries for 24 hours a day before
handing over to one of their mates. They even shared one

licence. It was claimed that the driver who pushed my car 50 yards up Commercial Street was asleep when the accident occurred.

On returning from hospital after a few days having thankfully suffering from concussion and cuts and nothing more serious, Fred saw the newspaper article reporting the accident and came to my house. My adoptive mum would not let him into the house. Understandable though that was, I still find it sad that I never stood eye to eye with my real dad.

I have a half brother. His name is Keith. He is a fine drummer and ironically I used to boogie the night away to the music of his group at the tender age of 17. We never met despite the fact that he was only 10 yards away at times bashing out drum riffs to accompany his group in their efforts to emulate Cliff and The Shadows or Elvis.

My adoptive parents, Molly and Albert, did their very best and my childhood was quite a happy one. A brother or sister would have been nice, but these were the post war years with both money and food scarce. An extra mouth to feed was out of the question. Dad was a crane driver on Newport Docks. At his funeral, one of his work mates sidled up to me and asked me if I knew that Albert held the record for loading a ship. Apparently at the latter stages of the war he was asked to work a double shift during which time he loaded thousands of tons of high quality coal that had been transported by rail from Merthyr, Aberdare and the Rhondda Valleys to the Alexandra Docks in Newport. 'He could drop his grab on a pin head,' was the expression used by his former colleague. Mum stayed at home and did the housework (usual at the time). She made twice weekly excursions to the local shops and visited a whist drive once a week.

My memories of the Second World War are few and far between. I do however distinctly remember the presence of an Anderson shelter shared with Mr and Mrs Richards from 161 Bassaleg Road, Newport. I remember the general excitement that arose from the discovery of an unexploded bomb nestling in the overgrowth of a field opposite our house. In later years I was told by my father that it was probably one of many offloaded bombs that the German planes had to discard if they could not find their targets. Offloading their bombs enabled them to get home. The steelworks at Ebbw Vale some 18 miles away were difficult to find as the works were nestled in between two valleys making it difficult for the bombers to locate. The release of their cargo meant that Cardiff and Swansea took a hammering before the planes turned for home.

The Richards' had a son called Brian who, for a reason I never discovered, was always referred to as 'Peachy'. Now Peachy was quite a lad. He was eight years older than me which meant that when I was 10, he was old enough to have sampled some of the bad elements of life. Beer, fags and probably women all got their fair quota via Peachy. One night, when Molly was down the whist drive with Mrs Richards and Albert was on a late shift at the dock, I was left alone. I had strict instructions not to answer the door if anyone called. Those orders were quickly ignored when I saw Peachy drift across the front window (we had a bay window in our semi-detached house). He yelled through the letterbox, 'Let me in Mike, I want to show you something.' His delight in showing me his packet of 10 Turf cigarettes could not be contained. Even at 18 years of age it was still considered to be too young to smoke. That pleasure was reserved for 21st birthdays.

As Albert smoked like a trooper, there was no need to open windows or doors in order to remove the smell of stale smoke. Peachy lit up a cigarette and lit a second cigarette and handed it to me. Christ, what an experience! He was smoking like a docker and I wondered how many other packets of Turf he had dragged his way through. I turned green after the first drag. Well it wasn't so much a drag as a minute intake of breath and a sharp cough. I managed not to be sick until after Peachy had returned home. Mother returned at 9.30 pm, father at 10.30 pm by which time I was in bed. Now this was a Thursday. The reader must be marvelling about my wonderful memory. It was nothing to do with my memory really. The whist drive was always on a Thursday night. Normally a Thursday evening was the worst day of the week for me because the same futile argument would take place between Molly and Albert. It was so common that I can recite its content even now.

Albert: 'Have you been to that bloody whist drive again?'

Molly: 'Yes, why?'

Albert: 'How many times have I got to tell you that I do not want you going to that place again?'

Molly: 'Just because they hold it in the Conservative Club.'

Albert: 'Bloody Conservative Club. People will think I married a Tory.'

Molly: 'What's the Labour Party done for you?'

At this point it was time to put my head under the blanket.

What followed was not nice and words were used that were completely foreign to me.

Molly and Albert shared the same house but lived independently of each other. His interests were mainly a bet on a horse and a swift couple of pints on the way home from work, and of course his football. The gambling reached such a critical level at one point that I remember Molly issuing a threat that it had to be the horses or her. This was not the type of threat anyone issued to a docker!

Thursday night was pay night and Albert handed over what he felt was the appropriate amount of money needed to keep the home going for another week. Molly always remonstrated and inevitably made a comment that she wanted to see his pay slip. To my knowledge that never happened.

As no decorating was ever done and minor repairs were normally bodged by Albert, it became incumbent upon me to try and learn some basic skills. At 12 years of age, the best I could manage was re-fixing a window latch and nailing on a draught excluder (a piece of thin rubber sufficed) to the bottom of the front door. The offending gap was in danger of letting in more fresh air than when the door was fully opened. That chilling wind tunnel of a draught that found its way into the main room was the cause of all the family's colds according to Molly. She had a rather simple, limited, medical outlook that centred on the need to keep off cold walls to prevent piles. Her mantras were, 'Wrap up warm otherwise you will catch a cold', and the one that I never fully understood was, 'Don't jump into a very hot bath because you'll faint.' Now the logic seemed fair enough, but the reality was something quite different. Our hot water never reached a temperature that made it really comfortable enough to sit in. The four inches I was allowed at a lukewarm temperature meant that I wanted to get out of the bath within minutes of entering it. The explanation was attributed to the war and how families were limited to how much water they could use and that the temperature was controlled by an outside agency. I pictured this command control based somewhere in Newport where the Big Controller lowered the temperature of any householder should they go beyond the limit. It wasn't too many years later that I worked it out for myself that it was a simple case of the boiler being knackered!

I am being rather harsh as Molly suffered from Albert's inertia and neglect for many years. She could hardly be blamed for the lack of heat in the bath. So, I did my best, but it wasn't good enough. Screws magically worked their way back out of hinges, paint ended up streaky with huge channels sticking out like mountain ranges on a global map. However, in my vain attempts to patch things up, I came across a most important discovery: the Oxo tin. Toolboxes as such did not exist and unless a family had a garden shed for tools, another container had to be found. The most popular residence for tools was under the staircase. In Albert's case the container was a wicker basket straight off the front of his Raleigh bike. This became the home for a screwdriver, a chisel, hammer, two files, a hacksaw, a tyre repair kit and some multi-coloured wool that always smelled of oil. It was also (I'm getting excited writing about it) the home of an Oxo tin. The first O, part of the x, and the last o were still there to be seen; the remainder consisted of shiny tin caused by years of regular opening and closing and being cosseted. Believing that this tiny tin contained something of use such as screws and nails, I lifted the lid off and to my amazement I found a bundle of money wrapped up in a rubber band. Large white fivers provided the outer wrapping for ten bob notes. Remember that this was 1953 when £20 per week was a king's ransom of a wage. I counted 12 fivers and six ten bob notes. In total there was £63. Guilt suddenly enveloped me and I quickly put the notes back and closed the lid of the Oxo tin. Oxo will appear later in the book in an entirely different context. Molly bless her, went to her grave ignorant of the fact that a small fortune lay hidden under the stairs.

On the many occasions I heard Albert rummaging under the staircase, I had a good idea that he was taking money out of his Aladdin's Cave! Was this his gambling fund? Was the money savings for a good holiday? Who knows, I never examined the contents of that tin again. Temptation was there, I admit. As I grew more reliant on the tools in the tool basket, I tried to shut out of my mind the fact that a fortune was close at hand and how Molly could have used some of it to provide some little extras.

159 Bassaleg Road had a large sitting room come dining area. When Molly and Albert were out, I repositioned the two armchairs at one end of the room and swung the utility sideboard around 90 degrees to form a goal at the other end. I managed to play both teams at once and used the best leftover balloon from Christmas as my football. Men of my age talk about volleying and half volleying an old tennis ball against a wall, claiming that it was

this practice that gave them good control when later they played with a full size football. I did graduate to a worn out tennis ball, but for me that balloon, with its tendency to swing in the air due to the gale force wind coming into the lounge before the modifications were made to the front door, made it difficult to time my shots. This was Wembley and Somerton Park all rolled into one. I was Stanley Matthews one moment and Ted Ditchburn the next. What a pity that we lose the ability to play out our dreams as we grow older. Or do we?

I could never identify with Subueteo. I loved the green cloth that formed the pitch, the goals with nets, but seeing players rolling about on a round base never hit the target with me. The ball was far too big and the stick that was glued to the goalkeeper and stuck out the back of the net for the purpose of control never seemed realistic enough to make for a good game. However I learned how to adapt this game by replacing the swaying players with marbles. Somehow over the years I had acquired a small wooden ball that was in precise proportion to the goals. A big marble occupied the goal and the smaller marbles represented the team. The line up was always the old fashioned 2 – 3 – 5. I had accumulated dozens of marbles through being the marble king for a week beating off neighbourly challenges from Geoffrey Gwilliam and Michael Russell so I was able to form a blue team, a red team and an all colour variety. Games were played as follows: the marble was flicked in the normal way, but only to propel the ball in the required direction. Once the 'player' had struck the ball he was immediately replaced in the original position. I became accomplished to the extent that my hands were moving over the pitch at such a speed that had Russ Conway or Winifred Atwell popped in they would have been amazed at my dexterity. (Both these entertainers were piano players selling millions of records at this time.) I played great games, invented a league and constructed floodlights using the huge 12 volt battery that served as the power supply to my radio. Mind you, by the time I had hooked it up to the homemade pylons I would have been served better with a box of matches for light!

During the summer, the side alley, which measured a good 18 yards long by 3 yards wide, became Wembley, Somerton Park and Lords all rolled into one. A worn out tennis ball was the treasured possession that served these occasions well. I played a form of solo cricket using 3 feet long sticks that Albert brought off the docks to use as supplementary firewood. I got to three of them before they were snapped in two ready for incineration. They were my stumps. I forget how the scoring system worked but somehow, miraculously, England always beat Australia by an innings, with Freddie Trueman taking all the wickets. Then one day disaster struck. Michael Russell (more commonly known by his so-called mates as Fatty Russell) came to play. He lived at 135 Bassaleg Road, so the walk past 12 houses to reach 159 not only took him 20 minutes because of the weight he was carrying, but also meant that he always arrived at my house desperate for a drink of water or a glass of pop out of a bottle that had the most intricate sealing system. The owner needed a degree in engineering to master it. The bottle had a rubber seal attached to a thick wire clasp. This particular afternoon he brought with him his latest birthday present, a full size cricket bat. Well, the way I played cricket down the alley did not require a bat, as runs were scored on the basis that the further my bowling missed the stumps the more runs were attributed to the 'batsman'. With some reluctance I let Fatty place his huge frame in front of the stumps and I bowled at him. After four swipes of the bat, and the ball coming back off the wall at a great speed, he took the confident view that he should come down the wicket to the next ball and catch it on the volley. Well he was 100 percent successful. He cracked that ball 20 feet up into the air and with utter dismay I watched as it hit the kitchen window of the Clarke's house next door. There was no breakage, but the spin on the ball took it straight into Mr Clarke's strawberry bed. Oh my God! Now to say that grumpy Clarke was obsessed with his strawberry bed would be a total understatement. He bloody well worshipped his strawberries. Every summer Mrs Clarke would make a public announcement that Harold would be picking his strawberries shortly and according to how big the crop was likely to be, he would decide if there were enough left over for his immediate neighbours to share. Isn't that bloody sad? It was a nice gesture, but really rather sad as my dad Albert had planted strawberries years previously, gave them no loving care or attention and still managed to produce buckets full of the most delicious variety much to the annoyance of Mr Clarke.

Cricket was drawn to a close with my precious tennis ball tucked under a strawberry plant. Fatty went home, I went indoors and when Molly asked why we had finished playing I at least had the guts to tell her what had happened, even if my

'bottle' didn't extend to knocking on the door of 157. I never saw
that ball again. The next time I became acquainted with a sphere
like object that could be used to play a game was when I was
given a 15 panel Pakistan made football, complete with lacer.
Now anyone reading this book that happens to be over the age of
50 might just have an inkling of what is to come. Remember the
lacer, that long thin metal rod with an eyehole at the end that
would have looked more at home in an operating theatre? It took
an eternity to feed the leather lace through the eyeholes of the
leather outer casing. Then that final pull through meant that you
were only minutes away from using the ball. Excitement nearly
got the better of me as I passed the lacer through the last hole
then weaved it back under the lace work and tied a small knot
pushing the knot under in between the leather outer and the
bladder. Magic. The bladder inside was fully blown up with its
neck tucked away safely just below the intricate weave of leather
string. What an achievement! That same instrument clumsily
used could also signal deep despair. With one more eyehole to go,
in went the lacer, but this time at the wrong angle and the hissing
of escaping air would bring tears to my eyes. Another visit to the
tool box, out came the tyre repair kit, French chalk, glue, a patch
covered with that wonderful sticky substance that never let you
down and soon the patch was applied to the hole in the bladder.
You will appreciate of course that the visit to the toolbox under
the stairs had to be timed to be made when Albert was in work.

Fortunately, so popular had the Pakistan football become that
every kid seemed to have been given one for Christmas. It was no
great sadness to use someone else's ball for a session, but my
pride had taken an almighty knock, as I was always confident of
conducting that simple lacing task satisfactorily and not stare
forlornly at a deflated ball muttering whatever profanities I had
acquired at this early age.

Hold a discussion with anyone who ever played with a laced
up football and I guarantee that they will immediately point to
their foreheads and in doing so relate the occasion they too were
either knocked out or had stitches inserted. Modern day players
don't know they are born.

By the age of ten my love affair with football was cemented for
life. Albert, shifts allowing, would take me to most of the games
at Somerton Park to see Newport County play. The ritual was
simple. A bus ride from west Newport to the east side meant a

change of buses at the market place terminus. The total journey time took one hour. On the odd occasions that 'Football Specials' were used, the time reduced to 40 minutes. They were very odd occasions because the specials were only put on when it was estimated that a big crowd would turn up for a game. Newport County hardly ever qualified for this 'special' provision!

I remember that sartorial elegance had no place at this football ground in the early 1950s. The war had not long ended and clothes were plain to say the least. Men would dress in thick woollen trousers, a jacket with leather elbows, a waistcoat and boots rather than shoes. Most men wore flat caps, apparently bought from the same shop and they all seemed to smoke. The blue haze that drifted across the pitch was the result of cheap ciggies such as Woodbines and Turf being smoked at an alarming rate. The more discerning supporter sucked at his Capstan, Senior Service or 'roll your owns'. The blue haze was matched by the white steam that spewed out from trains on the main Paddington to South Wales line that ran in close proximity to the Beechwood end of the ground. At times it was impossible to see the game as the billowing clouds of smoke enveloped the pitch. This event gave the wags an opportunity to shout, 'Send a few more trains down, we can still see the buggers playing'.

Little 1,500 tank class pannier shunters used to crawl along the siding track even closer to the Beechwood end. The track stood some 10 feet above the fence so the drivers and their mates were able to lean out of their cabins and see the whole pitch. Inevitably, a cluster of engines would congregate on the occasion of a league match and only leave when their superintendent walked along the track presumably asking them why there was a delay in sending the wagons further down the siding. The trains don't stop there anymore. Somerton Park became a housing estate in 1991. Dear old County play in a Municipal Stadium now and are in the Blue Square Conference Southern League.

On the rare occasion I drive over Somerton Bridge and look down at the railway tracks, my mind drifts back to those golden days. Thousands poured over this small bridge to enter through a paddock gate, drop down the 20 steps to the lane that curved around for 30 yards to the turnstiles where men paid two bob or a shilling for a kid to enter their own theatre of dreams. I remember the sound of laughter was prominent at most games. Players taking a throw in near the pitch perimeter fence would often wink or make a crack such as, 'Give us a drag on your fag mate.' Occasionally if the ball shot into the crowd it took ages before the ball was returned. The player about to take the throw in became exasperated, until he heard a wag cry out, 'Keep it under your coat Charlie, we've seen enough,' then a broad grin would envelope the player's face. It's a pity humour seems to have disappeared from the modern game.

My hero was the County centre forward, Reg Parker. Like today's kids with their idols, I tried to emulate him when I trotted out to play. The only real similarity between us was the flowing blond hair that we both shared.

Albert had his own 'spot' on the terrace. Later on in life when I was able to go to games unaccompanied, I made that spot my own. My spot was the seventh railway sleeper back at the railway end with my left foot touching the bolts that were once used to attach the sleeper to the railway track. This was not a good idea at the time as the left sole on my shoe was always the first to go and my mother could hardly afford to have it repaired, even if it was only the one shoe. Should a visitor from another club mistakenly stand on that spot, they quickly shuffled along when told that the spot was reserved for a home fan whose father occupied that sacred territory for 40 years.

Somerton Park became my spiritual home. Postponement of a home fixture was a personal disaster, the weekend destroyed. Defeat had to be taken on the chin because it was such a regular occurrence. Little did I realise at 12 years of age that one day I would be on the staff at the County. Back then, my dream was to play for them. That dream never materialised, in fact I stood a better chance of playing for Cardiff City at the age of 17.

3

MY FIELD OF DREAMS

My secondary school was blessed with excellent rugby players. Several went on to play for Wales. The school also played soccer but the game was given a lower priority. As I missed out on my 11 plus, I was sent to a secondary modern school. Brynglas Secondary Modern (if there was anything modern about the converted convent, I never found out) stood high on top of a hill overlooking Newport. The distinction between secondary modern and grammar schools and the stigma attached to those who had failed the dreaded 11 plus did, in most cases, leave an indelible mark on the personality of those who 'failed'. I felt it, yet after the first term in the secondary modern when I was offered a place at Newport High School, I turned it down with the consent of my parents. Apparently I had just failed the 11 plus by a short head and was on a reserve list for a place in the grammar school. Looking back, that decision was probably one of the worst I made. More bad calls came very much later in life which begs the question: Do we ever learn from our mistakes?

I did manage to hold onto a few friends from my pre-secondary school era. Kenny Grainger was one of those, although he was more of a peripheral friend than a close buddy. Kenny innocently commented one day as we sat in the field opposite our houses thoroughly enjoying the potatoes we were baking on our own little open fire, 'Hey Mike, our PE master knows you'. Hell, I was hoping to keep that fact a secret. 'Trig' (as he was known) was living with my real mother some 300 yards from my adoptive parents' home. Trig was a tough cookie, strong as an ox and the author of several books covering the subject of physical training and excellence.

Dot and Trig stayed together from 1943 to 1960. Their house was the last on a row of semi-detached houses on the Gaer

Estate. The side of the house faced a wide open expense of land known locally as the golf links that led down to the main Newport to Cardiff Road and overlooked Newport Docks. Now Trig's full name was Tregertha and for reasons that were difficult to understand, a few of the neighbours thought that he was German, not realising that in fact his name was of Cornish origin. During the Second World War an amazing story developed that suggested that Trig was going up to the side window of his house every night carrying a lamp and guiding German bombers into Newport Docks! The house had a panoramic view of the large docks situated some three miles to the west and was a target for the bombers. It was an absolutely crazy suggestion. It was hardly surprising when Trig found out what was being said by neighbours that he turned to the bottle and hardly ever left home apart from making the journey to school and back. Nearer the truth was the suggestion that Whitson Court some four miles out of Newport that housed German officer prisoners during the war was used as a landmark for German bomber pilots when navigating towards Newport Docks. It seemed that the prisoners put their spare time to good use by using every conceivable device to guide their bombers in.

At Brynglas I sat next to Ernie Beaver, who to this day will never forgive me for copying the whole of his music exam paper and getting better marks than he did. We remained good friends for 55 years, and on the occasions we met, he never failed to remind me of my indiscretion. Sadly Ernie was diagnosed with pancreatic cancer in December 2005. He passed on in March 2006. Over the lengthy period of our friendship we never lived in each other's pockets. I believe that our respect for each other blossomed because of this factor. I never had a brother. Ernie filled that gap. Having lost my parents, grandparents and all who preceded me, Ernie stood out as my nearest 'relation'. His highly successful career in fruit machine manufacture facilitated financial security. Without exception a visit to his home was enjoyable. I always came away feeling privileged to have spent time with him and his lovely wife Annette. His serious illness managed to bring home to me the frailty of life, the folly of worrying about matters that cannot be change or altered. How bloody futile is the pursuit of material happiness?

At the age of 12 I had been a regular visitor to Somerton Park where Newport County played and I had a good understanding of the game. Whether I could play it or not came under scrutiny when school Form A played Form C one wet and windy afternoon on a council pitch at Shaftesbury Park. 'Dog' Thomas was our sports master at the time and he took charge of events. 'Lewis, you play centre half, Bennett, you play on the left wing. Have we got a goalkeeper?' He enquired. Goalkeeper was never a popular position and this was clearly demonstrated by the unwillingness of any of the Form A kids to put up their hands and volunteer for action between the sticks. 'Okay, I'll pick one for you. Beale you go in goal.' Now Beale was not the most alert of individuals at the best of times. His rather sleepy, laid back disposition did not lend itself to being stuck between two posts that must have appeared miles apart to him! Ernie Beaver played in defence and I can remember how delighted he was to see that his 'enemy' Eric Jones was left out of the starting line up altogether.

Jones sat behind Ernie in class and for a reason I found hard to understand, he detested Ernie. Ernie came from Jewish stock and Eric's dad had been injured fighting in the Second World War. Perhaps Eric got a little confused over this issue. I do remember him taunting Ernie with cries of, 'Jew-Boy-Jew-Boy,' the moment the teacher left the room. These taunts were accompanied by a thumping of his fist on Ernie's back. I would turn around and tell Jones to find someone his own size, hoping beyond hope that he did not turn his attention to me. I was an only child for goodness sake, and not suited to rough and tumble.

Teams selected, we lined up against Form C. Oh my God, Tommy Young was lined up to kick off for them. Now in those days the centre forward was marked by the centre half, so it was Tommy against Mike. No problem there as I was aware that Tommy Young didn't play football. Tommy's claim to fame was that he wore the mantle of the full time school bully. A few weeks earlier he had taken a knife to my throat in the gym shed during break and threatened me with a slash across the Adam's apple if I didn't pass the Test. What bloody Test? I soon found out as I was pushed to the edge of The Woods. I knew all about The Woods because many a kid had to be taken to hospital with a broken nose or smashed leg having attempted to survive the Test. Now it was my turn. If by the time pupils had started their second year and managed to avoid The Woods and Tommy Young, then they were either very lucky or off sick from school for long periods of time. My number was up. I stood looking down a one in four gradient and tried to establish the best way to negotiate the dozens of trees that awaited my arrival. Confused and frightened, I did something rather stupid. I turned around, looked Young straight in the eye, and said I would prefer to have a knife fight with him rather than take the Test. Whether or not it was the sheer cheek of the suggestion or the fact that Tommy wasn't quite sure how to handle this one I will never know. However to my surprise, he agreed. Back to the gym shed I trudged with him and his three 'oppoes' as they are called in Wales. Out came his sheath knife and his mate produced another knife and gave it to me. With my bowels about to go into auto drive, Tommy looked at me, drew his knife and thankfully at that precise moment Dapper Roberts the gym teacher opened the shed door and barked, 'Get out all of you, haven't you heard the bell?'

Desperate to make an early impression with Dog Thomas I decided to give it my all even if that meant physical contact with Tommy Young. It was well into the first half with Form A going two up when Tommy came storming towards me with the ball at his feet. He had no intention of dropping a shoulder to slide past me to the left or right but came straight at me. Giving myself an angle, which just might have suggested to the bull-like warrior approaching that I was giving him enough room to pass, was a very brave ploy. Just as he stabbed the ball to my left and was about to bring it under some form of control I pounced. A lunge forward with both feet aimed at the ball meant that both player and ball were taken out cleanly. In today's game this assault would certainly have warranted a red card. Tommy fell on top of me and to my dismay uttered the following words, 'You'll fucking pay for that Lewis!' Bloody hell I was back to living in fear. As I climbed to my feet I was aware that the form master was looking at me.

'You'll do for the school team Lewis.'

At that moment I thought, 'Bollocks to Young and his threat'. I was destined to play for the school team. This was the first step on the ladder to fame. Or so I thought.

I made the team and, more importantly, stayed in the team. The team was unbeaten during the 1955–1956 season and we played in the Newport & District school cup final at Somerton Park, the home of my beloved Newport County. All my dreams had come true. The day of the game came and I was due to report to the ground at 5.00 pm for the kick off at 6.00 pm. The same day I received an invitation to go for a ride with Jeffrey

Gwilliam. His father, Des, was one of a few people who had a car and his gleaming Rover saloon parked outside his house was so immaculate that it seemed a shame to take it out on the road where it might attract mud and dust. I told Mr Gwilliam that I needed to be back home by 3.00 pm in order to get to Somerton Park. He assured me that he was aware of this fact and promised to get me back in time. To this day what happened next still sticks in my throat. I knew that Jeffrey was slightly jealous about me playing at the County. Fatty Russell had told me so. We returned from the ride at 4.45 pm. I was in a desperate state. Dad, who was coming to the game with me, was anxiously waiting at the front door. We ran to the bus stop, as the Gwilliams made no offer to run us to the ground. I made it to the ground 20 minutes before the kick off. There was no time to savour the feeling of sitting in the home dressing room (Brynglas had won the toss and our opponents St Andrews had to take the visitors' dressing room). There was no chance for me to pick the space underneath the magical No. 9 that was my hero Reg Parker's peg. No, I sat under the number 11 peg. That belonged to Beriah Moore the bald left winger. Dog Thomas was not happy and said that he was about to give my number six shirt to John Everson, the first reserve. This was ionic really because John went on to play professional football. I never earned a penny from pulling on the boots.

We played out a 0–0 draw and shared the cup. Brynglas retained the cup in school for six months before passing it on to St Andrews for the remainder of the year. All I can remember from my own performance was a massive kick up field that put our centre forward into a good goal scoring position. He then blasted the ball onto the main railway line behind the goal. No engines parked there that day.

I was amazed at the size of the pitch. It was vast, very sandy and nothing like I expected. Albert sat next to a County player who kindly came along to see if there was any worthwhile talent on display. Billy Shergold was his name. He played in the number 10 shirt and was very small to the extent that his black and amber shorts almost reached his bootlaces.

'Tell your lad to keep playing and don't give up hope,' he commented to Albert. That was about the kindest comment he could make given my poor performance.

4

IF ONLY I HAD A RIGHT LEG

The opportunity to try out with Cardiff City in 1960 as members of the 'old' first division came about during what I would describe as my one and only purple patch as a centre forward. I notched up 42 goals in season 1959–1960 in the Newport & District League and it was no real surprise that I attracted attention. My hope was that it was the County who might be interested. I was wrong.

I joined a local team called Gaer United the previous season. As I was someone with advanced views of how even local teams should organise themselves and be self funding, I was given the job of finding a sponsor for our kit. Where better to start than with the local sports shop? I went along with some level of trepidation to meet the owner of Gilesports in Skinner Street, Newport. My aim was to obtain some kit for the following season. Henry Giles, now deceased bless him, but leaving behind a very successful chain of sport shops, met me with a smile and a firm handshake. He said that he had received dozens of requests over the years for sponsorship and was not really interested. Looking back at that meeting, I now understand why I eventually took the commercial route in the game. Not wanting to be pushed away by Mr Giles, I came up with another suggestion that *did* interest him. The suggestion came off the top of my head and to this day I cannot explain how I confidently persuaded this shrewd businessman to let me have some kit. I remember the conversation as if it was yesterday.

'Mr Giles, why don't we put your company's name on our shirts? In addition we could change the name of our club from Gaer United to Gilesports.'

'Would you really do that?' he asked.

Not having the authority from the other members of the committee, I hesitated. Then I shook hands on it. I had heard the

31

expression 'close the deal' used in many different contexts and felt this was my opportunity to do just that. Out went my right hand, Henry Giles met it with his and the deal was done. Then the doubts flooded in. Could I persuade the other committee members that this was a good deal?

The next committee meeting was three days later in the local pub. I had sweated and stayed awake at night worrying about whether the deal would be rejected making me look like a fool. Consequently I approached this meeting with some level of anxiety. In the meeting, I added a few white lies to a little psychology. I explained that I had already approached Mr Giles of Gilesports and said that I wanted to put to the committee the possibility that I could always return and offer him another pioneering deal. The deal might mean changing the club's name for instance. (In my quest to weigh up whether or not my destination on leaving this planet would be heaven or hell, I guess this little episode put a tick in the wrong box!). The committee loved it and couldn't wait for me to return to Gilesports and 'tie up' the deal.

We completed the 1959–1960 season winning the Championship of Division Two of the Newport and District League. We also got to the League Cup final by winning the semi final against Maesglas United, our bitter enemy. We played the semi final on a beautiful playing surface at the Whiteheads' Steel factory sports ground in Bassaleg just outside Newport. This was 300 yards from my home. Most of the iron and steel companies in the area provided better playing surfaces than the dear old County could ever afford. With 10 minutes to go and the score standing at 0–0, I received the ball from our skipper, John Brunnock. I was on the right hand side of the pitch and I crossed the half way line, put the ball on the favoured left foot (that's a joke as my right foot was only for standing on) and cracked a 35 yard shot into the left hand corner of the goal. Reg Parker would have been proud of that one! We kept our lead and as I left the pitch, John Brunnock said that a guy from Cardiff City asked for my name. Little more was said and we waited for the final one week later. In the final we were due to play Bassaleg United at Rexville (the home of Southern League Lovells Athletic). The score was 0–0 after 90 minutes, and as we didn't play extra time, we shared the cup. My own performance was mediocre to say the least.

On leaving the ground with three other players I was aware that someone was following us. At that time scouts could not directly approach amateur players. I knew this, so it came as no surprise to see this gentleman in a trilby hat and grey mackintosh beside me asking through the corner of his mouth if I wanted to play for Cardiff City. After the initial shock I was surprised they were interested in a 6 feet 1 inch gangly centre forward with no right foot, a first touch that was better than a pass and who was not exactly from the Pelé school of close touch control. I did possess an ability to head the ball well and score the odd amazing 35 yard goal. He then asked for my address, scribbled it down on the back of a fag packet and swiftly walked off.

I received the letter inviting me to attend Ninian Park twice a week for training a few weeks later. At the time I was working as a clerk in a local brewery. I needed to shoot off at 4.30 pm on Tuesdays and Thursdays to catch the train to Cardiff in readiness for the training session that started at 6.00 pm. For six months I made the journey and every inch of it was a sheer delight. Could I possibly be on the first step of the ladder to becoming a professional player? My hopes and aspiration were killed stone dead in a two-minute conversation with the coach after a training session some months later. He said that he felt I was not good enough for the First Division. Being kind, he told me that I had a good left leg (the expression 'peg' was not even born back then) that I was very good in the air, but lacked awareness. He reminded me that I only used my right leg for standing on. However, he had written a letter recommending me to the manager at Newport County. I rushed home with the letter close to my chest and showed it to Albert my adoptive dad, with great anticipation and excitement. Albert took one look at the letter and said that I must stay at the brewery and not risk playing football for the County as it was a dubious career. Also the County was having serious financial problems, and anyway it wasn't a real job. To this day I have never really forgiven him for preventing me going to the County and perhaps becoming the latter day Reg Parker.

After being rejected by Cardiff I returned to Gilesports who, at the time, were romping away with the league due in some part to the fact that their kit was immaculate. White shirts, Gilesports emblazoned across the front, blue shorts and red socks. We had four sets of everything and went out on the field at least a goal up due to our apparel. Opponents sneered at us before the kick off and we were accused of being posers. They soon came to realise that the flashy lads in their immaculate gear could play a bit too.

It was November and having waited weeks for a place in the team I finally got the call. Why the delay in my return appearance? Our manager Jack Ritter who was my boss at the brewery was the kindest and fairest man I ever met. He would not replace the lad who had done well in my place whilst I was at Cardiff just because big ideas Lewis had returned to the scene, so I had to wait for someone to be injured before I could get a game. Remember substitutes were not allowed in the early 1960s. Eventually I got my call and made my way down to Tredegar Park Newport, pitch number 7. Our opponents were Bedwas Colliery. Their team consisted mainly of miners who had come off the Saturday morning shift to play football in the afternoon. My team mates decided to pin a huge gold star which declared 'Ex-Cardiff City' on the lavatory door of the dressing room. That's where I was forced to change into my kit.

I never found out who informed Bedwas Colliery that I had just been rejected by Cardiff City, but whoever it was needs to be sure that we don't ever bump into each other as I have an old score to settle. What occurred on the field of play was nothing short of thuggery. I was kicked and pushed and sworn at. Cries such as, 'Fuck off back to Cardiff, Lewis,' and, 'So you think you can play eh?' coupled with, 'You will be lucky to walk off this pitch today!' were ringing in my ears. It was the worst 90 minutes of football I can remember. In case you are wondering, I didn't retaliate. It is futile to kick a swarthy 5 feet 8 inch miner with coal dust ingrained on his face in the bollocks or go over the top. This is in case the victim decides to take retribution in the car park after the game! At 10 stone soaking wet I would have proved no match for a mining monster.

I still turn out for charity matches convinced that I can still 'turn it on'. The truth is that apart from taking the odd free kick, corner kick, or goal kick when the keeper is struggling to reach the edge of the his own penalty area, my contributions are very limited. When I told the club doctor at Exeter City back in June 2002 that I was going to play in a charity match at the age of 61, he delivered me a look of shock and surprise. I was four stone overweight and about as mobile as an 84 year old granny pushing her trolley around Tesco. Not to mention the fact that I was a heavy drinker to boot. He must have thought to himself, 'What is this man trying to achieve?' Yet do we ever give up on the dream? Heaven help us all when the day should come that we shed our childlike dreams and accept that we are too old to participate anymore in these make-believe fantasies.

5

COWBOYS, CLOWNS AND COUNCILS

Between the years 1963 to 1972, I worked for the National Children's Home (NCH). I was given the responsibility for all fund raising events in Wales, a job which prepared me for my future career in football. Events called 'Festivals of Youth' would herald the finalisation of collections by children who had collected all the year round in their schools and churches. As part of the event the home would provide an entertainer. Two of these entertainers in particular spring to mind. They were known as Percy Edwards 'The Birdman' and Cal McCord 'The Cowboy'. At the time, Percy Edwards was still a big name, although not at the peak of popularity due to the plethora of new TV entertainers. Percy would stay at my home for the duration of the events held in Wales which would normally cover a period of 10 days. Karen, my young daughter was enthralled as Percy would make bird sounds from behind curtains and cupboards in our new home.

As we needed to inspect the venues before the evening's entertainment, Percy and I often arrived just before lunch. That meant that after our inspection we had several hours to kill. Inevitably, weather permitting, Percy would ask me to drive him out to the countryside so that he could 'talk' to the birds. I used to find an isolated country lane, park the car, turn the windows down then wait for Percy to perform. He claimed that he had over 1,000 different types of bird sounds in his throat. We sat in silence waiting for any bird to respond to Percy's call. Amazingly, birds would not only answer his call, but came within a few feet of the car, tilting their heads in wild curiosity searching for the source of the call. Sometimes they would sit on the bonnet of the car staring through the windscreen. Not only could Percy identify the bird, he could describe each species in great detail.

Percy was also able to reproduce animal sounds such as lions, elephants, gorillas and crocodiles. Children attending the presentation evening would stare wide-eyed as these amazing sounds roared out of his mouth. Unfortunately the same attentive state from the kids was not the case when Cal McCord performed. The poor man had progressive arthritis in his hands making his gun slinging, and in particular his lasso act, fall well below par. The last time he performed for the NCH was in a hall in Pontypridd where the kids did not take prisoners. The previous year I took along Cyril Jackson the clown. As part of his grand entrance I had to assist in filling a small container concealed in his bowler hat with paraffin, set it alight then rush on to the stage to quickly announce his arrival. The entrance door he used to negotiate the small staircase leading to the stage had a restricted framework and as Cyril passed under the door with his bowler hat spewing flames, the top of the door frame caught on fire. The kids loved it. The hall superintendent was not quite as amused as he tried desperately to extinguish the flames that had now started to encroach onto the paint on the wall above the door. Cyril went straight into his act and played *Keep the home fires burning* on his tenor sax. The kids were far more interested in the fire fighting prowess of the caretaker than they were of Cyril's antics. Cyril left the stage after five minutes.

One year later after dropping his six shooter several times, Cal decided to turn to the ropes for salvation. The plan was to lasso a child sat in the back row of the hall. Unfortunately the huge rope caught on the wall lights almost ripping them from their fixings. The kids held their sides in laughter. Cal got angry instead of joining in with the fun. But after all, how many times do you see a lasso act in Pontypridd? The NCH was never allowed to use this venue again.

In 1970 I was elected to Newport County Borough Council having won the Alway Ward seat for Labour. Because of my work with the NCH I took a keen interest in Social Services and became Vice-Chairman of the committee. In the local government reorganisation in 1973, all councillors in Newport had to make a choice. They had to decide whether to stay as a County Borough Councillor or to seek election as a County Councillor. Newport's main activities such as Education, Social Services and Planning were to be passed over to the new County Council of Gwent. I decided to stand for the County Council in my home ward of Malpas, Newport.

Having successfully won the seat with a comfortable majority for the Borough election, I was curious as to how the new County Council of Gwent would operate with some of the ex-Newport County Borough Councillors joining in with a majority of old Monmouthshire County Council members. The distribution of Chairmanships seemed to be in the favour of the old Monmouthshire members. I was given a number of interesting responsibilities including the Chairmanship of the School Governors for those schools in my ward. The little primary school attended by my daughter Karen was a stone's throw from our new Wimpey Dorma House bought for £4,750.

In an effort to make an early impact with the other Governors, I asked the head of my daughter's school what was her priority in terms of needs. She was quick to point out that the school gate leading on to the pavement next to a busy road had no protective fence. Pupils could run out of the gate straight into the road. I took the matter to the school's committee on the County Council. Some three months later, workmen started to erect a 30 foot long, 3 foot high, metal fence much to the delight of parents, teachers and the headmistress.

I was at home one night when I received a call from my friend and fellow County Councillor Ken James. Ken lived but half a mile away from my home and suggested that we meet in the local pub to chat over some Council business. The pub was situated directly across the road from my daughter's school. After discussing Council matters, we were invited by a couple of regulars to take them on in a game of pool. Ken was a good player, so in the accepted tradition we stayed on the table until we were defeated. After six games and as many pints of beer, we retired just as the landlord was closing shop. The car park to the pub was on a steep gradient and the sharp right turn taking me back to my home meant that my car would momentarily be at an acute angle with the nose much higher than the tail. That night, or should I say, early morning as the pool game had gone on a bit, a heavy frost had descended. As I accelerated to climb over the ridge of the junction, the car shot forward like a bullet and in the process demolished the first 12 foot of the new fence. My head went through the windscreen, glass splintered on my head and for what seemed an eternity I sat there in a complete state of shock. Reversing off the demolished fence, placing the car in first gear and slowly heading for home with the accompanying sound of the screech of metal on metal, was a small miracle in its own right. Stepping out of the vehicle outside my home and at the same time wiping blood from my face, I was shocked to find that the bonnet of the Vauxhall Victor had an indentation in a 'V' shape measuring a good six inches deep!

The next morning I carried out my normal fatherly duties and walked my daughter to her school. The lollipop lady who, only 24 hours earlier had congratulated me on my successful efforts to provide the life saving fence, was in a rage. She pointed across to the tangled mess and used words to describe the culprit that were not for the faint hearted. I groaned and shook my head being unable to speak properly because of my swollen mouth. As I turned to walk back to my house she shouted after me, 'Good God Councillor Lewis, look at you. Have you been in a fight?' The Chairman of the Public works committee was not at all pleased when I explained the circumstances surrounding the demolition.

At about the same time I helped a new Labour Party colleague to win his seat on the Borough Council in the same Ward. With a two year old baby, a new house, steady job and a political role to play, this was hardly the right time to engage myself in an affair. Unfortunately that was exactly what happened. My brief fling with the wife of the new Councillor I helped to elect, almost led to tragedy as he caught me with his good lady in their home one night and took a shot gun to me. She had warned me to get out of the house as her husband raced upstairs, but bravado (or more like stupidity) engulfed me as I tried to show the lady how brave I was. Fortunately, he chased me out of the house with the barrel of his gun pushed in my back. The affair surprisingly fizzled out shortly after that! Some years later he was elected to Parliament as an MP where he still sits.

As a period in my life, the early 1970s were full of interest and intrigue and some huge regrets. But nothing could have prepared me for what was to become an even more dramatic and exciting period from 1976 to 1984.

6

THE SLINGS AND ARROWS AND MORE COWBOYS

Somerton Park, Newport was my theatre of dreams. Although joyous moments were few and far between, it didn't seem to matter. This was my spiritual home. It was a place where I could stand and admire the efforts of the £10 maximum a week footballers, even if those representing the home side were normally inferior to those visiting the ramshackle ground. I never looked at the flapping tin sheets that clung to the rotten batons running along the roof of the stand, or at the ripped and torn club flag hanging pitifully from the main stand thinking, 'What a disgrace'. No, this was my home ground, as poor as it was, and the only football club that mattered to me.

I greatly respected Keith Saunders, the club secretary at Newport County. He had gained a reputation for being an institution in the town. So with a little trepidation I met him at the club after I had received an invitation from Cyril Rogers, the legendary Chairman of County, to discuss taking up a role as commercial manager. The outcome of the meeting was positive although the offer of £50 a week and 10 per cent commission on all raised income did not fill me with excitement. What did excite me was the prospect of working for 'The County'. Leaving behind a secure job with the National Children's Home really did not come into the reckoning as football was where I wanted to be.

Keith was for all intents and purposes the equivalent of the modern day chief executive. Despite the daily erosion of my long held belief that anyone working for the County could have no faults, this man was, in his own way, a colossus with a giant crack down the middle making him susceptible to criticism. Prior to my arrival, he had spent 30 years at the club. Not only had he experienced every conceivable event that could occur in a struggling outfit like the County, he had remained loyal to successive Chairman and directors. Imagine how diverse in make up and personality they were! He was a survivor even if survival meant that his liking for a drink or two increased over the years as the pressure mounted. Even allowing for the increasing dependence on drink, how he survived was a small wonder. Hardly a week went by at Somerton Park when we were not faced with a crisis of one sort or another. Keith used to remind me that the moment the bloody referee blows his whistle for the start of the new season, the grass decides to give up and die and with it our hopes for the season.

Come with me on a trip back in time. Picture the scene. We're at Somerton Park, Newport in the autumn of 1976. It is a Tuesday night on 27th November. The club has a home game against Halifax Town. A gate of 2,901 turned up for this bottom of the table encounter. How can a game played in the autumn with 28 games left be a bottom of the table encounter? Well County's record over the last few seasons was similar to Halifax's record and the description fitted perfectly. We had already drifted away so far from the rest of the teams in the division that it was going to take a miracle to enable us to climb to safety.

Keith, on the other side of a couple of double rums, sat in his office at 6.45 pm when a visitor arrived. The visitor was no ordinary visitor but a man clad in a navy blue uniform with a black cap emblazoned with the letters SWEB (South Wales Electricity Board). He clutched a pair of wire cutters. Just after the man's arrival I found myself walking past Keith's office. His office had an open hatch in the wall that allowed onlookers to peer in and observe any visitors present. Without too much difficulty a passer by could hear what was being said. Keith spotted me walking past and beckoned me to join him. I walked in and immediately sensed that the atmosphere was very tense. Keith seemed ready to explode. The veins on his face stood out like purple tributaries. His hands trembled and his eyes popped out of their sockets. The SWEB man's face had turned crimson too. Note the careful description of colour. Any visit to Keith's office was always going to be colourful! Keith had come to a part in the conversation that brought him to his feet. The tirade that followed should have been recorded for posterity and used at management courses when the lecturer had reached the point where he was extolling the 'do nots' to his group during lessons on diplomacy. Saunders screamed, 'You go anywhere near those floodlight cables with your bloody clippers and I'll put you in hospital!' The SWEB man retreated and was never seen again.

Okay there was an unpaid bill for £230 for electricity but this was Newport County for Christ's sake. No floodlights meant there would be no match therefore there would be no revenue and this meant closure. Rumours suggested that Keith was a pretty mean amateur boxer. This was never confirmed, but no one argued the point and the SWEB man was not about to find out.

On one occasion in 1960 when the County were playing an FA Cup game against First Division Spurs at Somerton Park, the Chairman received a visit from a policeman in the boardroom 15 minutes before kick off. Pulling the Chairman to one side, the copper explained that there was a problem at one of the turnstiles and could he accompany the policeman to the scene of the incident. Imagine the Chairman's surprise when he discovered that the main cause of the confrontation was the secretary, Keith Saunders, who had grabbed a spectator by the throat and was shouting at him, 'If the turnstile operator says you gave him a fiver then don't come here claiming you gave him a tenner!' It is believed that the same promise of a hospital visit given to SWEB man was also made to this unfortunate visitor to the County that day.

I, like most others, never really got close to Keith as he was very much his own man. He was married with one daughter Janice, but I never met anyone who had met his wife. At times it seemed that not only had life passed him by, but that he never really enjoyed the experience anyway. The hangdog look that covered his face suggested that here was a man not entirely at peace with himself. Perhaps the drink helped. Every simple request was met with a huge sigh as if the business of football had become very tiresome for him. However, when fuelled by his daily ration of large rums and a few pints down the Black Horse he came into his own. It was a joy to listen to him answering a call from an outraged creditor. A famous sport shop in Newport supplied the County with kit, balls and training gear. The company was a family business and prided itself on good service. Even allowing for the fact that the County owed the supplier a vast amount of money at any one time, they were patient like so many other local traders who were involved with their soccer club. It is frightening to think of the devastation that would have been caused if local traders ran to the County Courts every five minutes to push the club for payment. Soccer has not changed much in that respect. It is sad to see club after club in the new millennium entering into administration or offering national and local creditors a settlement of 5 percent. In most cases the local traders grin and bear it because they do not want to be the people who put the final nail in the coffin of their club. This particular call from the sports supplier seemed to one of desperation as they had waited an eternity for settlement. Keith kept repeating, 'Yes I understand. Yes, I understand'. He then moved up a gear and cut to the chase. 'Well, how much do we owe you at the moment?'

'£2,500 apparently,' was the reply. This was a lot of money in 1976. There was silence for a few moments then this blockbuster.

'When the Chairman comes in I'll ask him to sign a cheque for £50. Will that satisfy you for the time being?' I didn't hear the answer to that suggestion, but there was no mistaking Keith's indignation to the supplier's response. 'Who do you think we are? Bloody Manchester United?' was his retort.

We were playing Darlington on a Friday night. I am not sure why, perhaps it was due to the fact that the Welsh rugby team had a match in Cardiff on Saturday. The morning started well apart from the weather. Rain lashed down on Newport for several hours. Now Somerton Park at that time could not claim to be a ground that dealt with rain very well. In fact a few light showers and the pitch resembled a large pond. If it rained constantly, then the pitch became a lake that was quite capable of taking boats with a shallow draft! As commercial manager it was not my area of concern as to whether or not the pitch was playable, but as a lifelong fan I wanted every game to be played whatever the weather. It was in this context that I dared to ask Keith his opinion on the ground's fitness, half realising what the answer might be. I felt that I was enquiring about his personal wealth, his sex life or whether he farted in bed, so deep was the hurt that the question inflicted upon his face. Perhaps it was the pain of having to constantly repeat the same answer to the question that he had been asked a thousand times or more over the years. 'There's no problem with the pitch and we are not asking for an early inspection,' was the stock reply. As I saw it on this particular day we had more chance of playing a water polo match than a game of soccer. It was no illusion. I had seen two seagulls on the pitch the last time I looked.

My gentle enquiry as to whether or not we would be staging a football match or not really didn't deserve the onslaught that followed.

'What the fucking hell do you know about Somerton Park? You've only been here five minutes and anyway it's a quick drying pitch. Once the tide has gone out it will dry out and we will need to *put* bloody water on it later.'

At approximately 12.30 pm on the same day I just happened to be in Keith's office listening to his concerns about the manager's performance. The manager in question was Jimmy Scoular. Jimmy was in the middle of a bad run and Keith thought that it was time for a change. Now Keith didn't have much time or respect for managers apart from one. The exception was Billy Lucas. Billy was inevitably called upon when the club was on the slide, to the extent that he was known locally as LucasAid! Keith was about to use his usual closing comment on Newport's succession of managers which usually went along the lines of, 'They come here, say they can work the bloody oracle with no money to spend, then within a few weeks start moaning about the pitch, the dressing room, the directors, me and anyone but their bloody self!' At this point, Jennifer, Keith's secretary, shouted through the hatch that Mr Bates (not his real name in case he is still alive) the match referee had arrived early to make a pitch inspection.

'Pitch inspection,' yelled Keith, 'what's he talking about?'

Mr Bates from Bristol entered the room. 'Just thought I would come over early to inspect the pitch because of all the rain we've had over the last 24 hours.'

'Look,' said Keith, 'it's up to the home club whether or not we have an early inspection. Anyway, Darlington are well on there way by now.'

'Well in fact Mr Saunders,' said Bates, 'they have stopped off in Birmingham and are waiting for my report before travelling any further. As I've not been here before, will you join me as I inspect the pitch?'

'I'm very busy ref, but in case you can't find it, just turn left out of my office, left again and it's straight in front of you'.

This was an example of how Keith won friends and influenced people. Mr Bates left hastily.

Ten minutes later a rather bedraggled referee with his black wellies covered in mud entered Keith's office once again. 'I'm going to phone the League and tell them I have called the game off Mr Saunders.'

I looked at Keith and wondered what other armoury he had apart from the threat of putting people in hospital. Was Mr Bates about to suffer from a new, hidden form of attack?

'If we don't play tonight ref, we won't be able to pay the players this week,' came his feeble response.

'Not my concern,' replied the ref.

'What do you mean "not your concern", what will happen if Newport County go out of business? You won't have so many games to referee, will you?' I could see the logic in that statement but it did little to impress the ref. Keith, using an even softer mode, said, 'The moment the tide turns in the Bristol Channel the water level on the pitch drops and within minutes it will be as dry as a bone'.

The referee, also softening up a little, commented, 'I'll tell you what I will do. I will leave it until 2.30 pm and do another inspection.'

If only the story had stopped there. Keith asked me to take the ref down to the Black Horse and get him sandwiches and a drink. He said he would follow on as soon as he had made a phone call. Anyone entering the Black Horse was hit by the football theme that provides much of the environment of this homely pub. Mr Bates had no idea that the previous landlord was in fact Mr Billy Lucas (as in LucasAid) and that Billy had left a rather unique feature in his public bar. The ceiling was painted depicting a football pitch. Somehow he managed to magnetise the ceiling so that it could take Subueteo players resplendent in their various team colours. Bates' eyes popped out of his head when he was told that Mr Lucas used this ceiling when he was training the team. He used a long teacher's cane to move players around on the ceiling. By now Mr Bates had consumed two pints of Brains Bitter (not a drink to take lightly) accompanied by ham sandwiches with pickle, all having a calming effect on him. Keith arrived almost on cue and lined up a further three pints of beer. For some reason the conversation at this point took a decidedly favourable turn. The ref explained that he was only doing his job. In response to some rather pointed facts of life from Keith, such as the facts that Birmingham to Newport was only an hour by coach and that Darlington might just as well carry on with their journey. He also invited the ref to look out of the bar window so that he could see the trees swaying in the pub car park suggesting that the infamous Bristol Channel wind was starting to build up.

'Can you get some volunteers to help clear the water should there be any left on the pitch at kick off time?' asked Mr Bates.

'No problem ref,' replied Keith and at the same time giving

me a huge wink. How does he do it? I pondered to myself.

Keith's refusal to give in to anyone that threatened the existence of the County was a rather unusual attribute. He was no real lover of the game, didn't really understand it, but he was Mr Newport County. He easily commanded respect because he carried his frailties around with him for everyone to see. So what if he drank himself silly? So what if he swore inappropriately? So what if he wore the same suit for weeks on end? So what if he smoked 40 a day? He was Keith, the man who knew everything there was to know about this tin pot club. He alone, at times, had kept the door open for business. On one occasion he pleaded with a police sergeant at Newport Police station to release a recently signed player who had the misfortune to find himself in custody the night before a big game. Keith succeeded in gaining the player a reprieve on the condition that the player was returned to the Police station immediately after the game!

I was rather pinning my hopes on the Darlington game going ahead as we were due to have our first ever match sponsor that night. Mr Collingbourne the coal merchant very kindly offered to donate one ton of coal to the person with a lucky draw ticket number. He didn't want to attend the match himself, but arranged much to everyone's surprise, to deposit the one ton of coal in hundredweight bags on the side of the pitch. He even agreed to deliver the coal to the winner's address. The most miserable swine I have ever met won the coal and stated that he did not use coal at home. I asked if he would donate it to a worthy person who did use coal like a pensioner for instance. But he would have none of that. I never bothered to find out what happened to his prize. Thankfully it disappeared before the next Speedway meet two days later.

But back to the weather. By now Mr Bates had consumed four pints of the devilish Brains brew and was ready for action. There was no way he would not referee a game that night. What could go wrong now I asked myself? It didn't take too long to find out. On returning to the ground, a call across the car park from Bill on the main gate alerted us to the fact that the Darlington coach had arrived. I could hear the sound of a bellowing voice (presumably their manager) exclaiming that there was no need for the lads to get off the coach as he had looked at the pitch and had reached the conclusion that it was totally unplayable. Well was he in for a surprise. We played the game, lost 2–1, but at least we had the wages for the week.

Change, of any kind, was always a difficult proposition in Keith's mind, so when I suggested that a little bit of pre-match entertainment would not go amiss he gave me a long hard stare that suggested I was off my bloody rocker. He told me to forget it as they had tried that 10 years earlier and one of the police dogs in the display got away from his minder and ran amok causing the lone bobby on duty at the ground that day to enter into a forlorn chase! I pleaded my case on the basis that anything that could attract even a few dozen more fans was worthwhile. He listened intently. Admittedly, the proposition was not one of my best, but the display I had in mind was free after all. I took the view then as I still do that 90 minutes of football should be front, middle and back surrounded by entertainment as there is never a guarantee of the quality of the football. Earlier that week a group of men had come to the ground and explained that they lived and worked in Bristol (just 40 minutes away using the first new Severn Bridge crossing) and at weekends they used their farm as the venue for their hobby, playing Cowboys and Indians. They asked if they could use the pitch before a game to demonstrate how well they could re-enact Custer's last stand. They wouldn't use live ammunition. This was a pity because we could have disposed of one or two players off the payroll plus a director or two! The Indians fired arrows with blunt ends. There could still be some damage I thought, but I kept that to myself as this was beginning to sound interesting. The Cowboys and Indians would bring straw bails and need just 20 minutes to re-enact the battle. It was brilliant; I could build up the event in the local press, invite hundreds of kids to the game and swell the coffers. Keith, in his best imitation of a Frenchman with his bottom lip rolled up and his palms turned skywards, was totally unimpressed by the idea.

The disaster that occurred on the day of the event still makes me shudder. It turned into a right bloody fiasco. The local press had given the arrival of Cowboys and Indians to Newport the press that it deserved and the kids started to flow into the ground well before kick off. Bradford City was the visiting team and was not exactly enjoying the best of good fortune on the field of play. The County was, once again, fighting to keep out of the bottom four. At 11.00 am Keith was on the other side of a few drinks. He smiled his knowing smile that seemed to indicate that something might go terribly wrong with Lewis' plans.

'Has General Custer turned up yet Mike? Someone said they saw Indians in town, but they turned out to be waiters from the

Lahore Indian Restaurant,' was Keith's only comment. Swine!

I asked General Custer and Laughing Cloud to be at the ground no later than 12.30 pm so that straw bails could be put in place with the groundsman's approval. Well, 12.30 pm came and went, so did 1.00 pm, then 1.30 pm. I wondered what had happened. The teams warm up at about 2.30 pm and they need most of the pitch. At 1.55 pm a tannoy message announced that I was wanted at the front gate. There to my utter dismay was Ken, the chief steward, with his back to the corrugated-sheeted gates holding back the burgeoning doors trying to prevent anyone coming through. 'I've got 20 bloody Indians out here saying that they should be allowed in. They say that you know all about it.'

The fact that I went through the whole operation with the grounds staff at 11.00 am that morning, including the part where they escorted the Cowboys and Indians off their individual buses through to the pitch, had completely escaped Ken's memory. Mind you he was 79 years old. 'Ken just let them in,' I said wearily. Through they came in magnificent splendour. Sitting Bull was easy to identify as he measured six feet six inches, had a stomach that went on forever and he carried a huge bow. I counted at least 20 arrows in his quiver. As they made their way to the side of the pitch, Laughing Cloud peeled off and told me that it was very windy coming over the Severn Bridge and that they had manage to cross but the Cowboys were left on the Bristol side of the river and couldn't cross until the wind subsided and the bridge was re-opened. Laughing Cloud came up with a suggestion that seemed to represent the only way we were going to minimise this cock up. 'Mike, I'll get the Indians to do a war dance around the bails of straw encircling the centre circle. When the lads arrive we'll go to another part of the ground and turn our backs on the bails whilst the cowboys take up their places inside.'

I must have looked like Basil Fawlty at this point. My mouth was wide open and I had staring eyes and an overwhelming feeling that I would rather be dead. After what must have been 30 seconds, I responded, 'Let's go for it'.

Time was marching on, and I did promise the manager that all activities would be completed by 2.50 pm. It was now 2.25 pm, and having gained the permission of both managers to keep the display to the edge of the centre circle allowing their players to warm up, I seemed to be in with a slim chance of survival. At 2.35

pm another tannoy message asked me, 'Would Mike Lewis go to the front gate urgently?' It couldn't be, could it? Unfortunately it was. Ken stood with his back to the corrugated gate preventing the Cowboys from entering.

Finally the cowboys got into position. All we heard was the chanting of Indians, the blasts from shotguns and bloody smoke everywhere. The straw bails had been penetrated by over zealous Indians and straw was strewn across the playing surface. The show moved on to a climax where cowboys were lying all over the straw bails clutching arrows to their chests. Indians were standing with one foot on the 'dead' bodies then going into a dance of victory, moving to every corner of the stadium. It was at this point that I saw Keith poking his head out of the player's tunnel and beckoning for me to join him. There he was with the match referee, officials, players and managers ready to step out for the kick off.

'Mike, the referee's not very happy. He wants to take the teams out. It is five to three you know.' Of course I knew the time.

The kids loved the battle and were cheering the Indians when I took it upon myself to go to the centre of the pitch and yell at the cowboys, 'Get off the pitch now.' I chased the Indians off the pitch and the kids in the crowd were hysterical with laughter, yelling, 'Shoot him!' To his eternal credit Keith never mentioned the day again. We lost 1–0.

Months later we launched a hot air balloon off the pitch linking the idea to a competition asking fans to guess how far the balloon would fly before landing. The tickets sold like hot cakes. I took a call from an old lady who said what a great idea it was and she wished the club well. Then she asked me what time the balloon was coming back so she could come down to the ground and see it land! What do you say?

After lift off, the balloon crashed into the hillside at a place called Machen. It had travelled 5.7 miles in a straight line. Tim Matthews, a fervent supporter of the club and a member of the executive club, had said that if he could go up in the balloon then he would give us £200. Well there was no debate really. The pilot agreed that Tim could travel with him. Once again there were difficulties with the timing as the wind was blowing in a northerly direction and the balloon had to clear an 80 foot floodlighting pylon, so maximum height was needed quickly. That meant that the ground crew had to restrain the basket until sufficient height had been gained. This operation took a little time and once again the teams were ready to take to the pitch for kick off. The pilot, with other matters on his mind, had obviously forgotten about his paying passenger. Dutch courage had engulfed Tim to the extent that he was guzzling down his fifth large gin and tonic in the bar when I pulled him out and on to the field and just managed to shove him in the basket as the last guide rope was released. I don't think that the pilot was very amused to see a tipsy vice-president being poured into his cradle. Little did Tim know that we had rigged up a radio mike on board and everything that he said in the balloon was sent back through the tannoy system at the ground. We simply wanted the pilot to tell the crowd where he was and how the flight was going. Tim, upon realising that he was now airborne and peeping over the edge of the basket to see at least 200 feet between him and the ground, screamed out, 'Fucking hell, get me out of here!' Fortunately the pilot had the good sense to turn off the radio mike after that little outburst. To his eternal credit Keith never mentioned that day again. We lost 3–1.

It is a simple matter of fact that in the lower divisions, particularly in the second division or, as in this case, the old Fourth Division, priorities were not always in the right order. Wages had to be found if possible and some of the utility bills met if only to keep the absolute necessary services operating. To accommodate these payments, items such as ground maintenance and supporter comforts including bars and toilets and car parking facilities were sacrificed. Included in the list for certain would be the floodlights. Except for the absolute necessity to change bulbs when the floodlights had been reduced to 50 percent of their capacity through popping out, nothing else was serviced. This meant the occasional failure of the lights when they were requested to come on 30 minutes before a game, or the loss of a complete section if a fuse decided that it had come to the end of its useful life.

We were at home to Rochdale one dark November evening. The crowd, a magnificent 1,881, had witnessed a sordid affair on the pitch with the County losing again. Keith sat in his office putting the final touches to the referee's and linesmen's expenses before depositing the remaining money in the club safe. He rang me and asked if I would pop into his office. He wanted moral support. In his office at the time was Alan Williams, a loyal supporter of 30 years standing. He stated that he was an electrician by trade and would be only too pleased to investigate the problem with the lights.

'What's it going to cost?' enquired Keith.

'Nothing at all Mr Saunders but something needs to be done as you can hardly see play in the corners of the pitch.'

I was beginning to wonder what my role was going to be in this little scenario. It soon became obvious.

'What can you do to them?' asked Keith.

'Well, perhaps Mr Saunders it is simply a matter of turning the lights to a better angle.'

'I bloody knew it the moment you came in. You're a bloody smart arse. You can't turn the lights just like that.'

'It's a simple task Mr Saunders.'

'Look chum, I've had a bad day and I could do without this. Those pylons have been set in concrete for 15 years, now piss off and leave me alone.'

I accompanied the loyal supporter out of the office and explained that the secretary wasn't on his best form.

Football was driven by people like Saunders who knew the regulations and who to speak to if there was a problem. It normally won hearts and minds of those running football. He hated players and reckoned they were all on the take, but he gained their respect because he was an honest man and would not suffer fools gladly.

The final story about Keith was when he showed me a letter one morning that had come from Mike Thomas, the club's bank manager at Barclays. It came straight to the point. Unless the club could deposit £50,000 within 24 hours, the bank would foreclose. Keith was not perturbed and asked me to help him to get that particular week's wages out before any possible foreclosure. Now I did feel pretty nervous about the idea and more so when he explained the plot. I was to go to the bank with the wages cheque (do you remember those old cheques? They were almost the size of an A4 sheet of paper), wait until the girl with the ginger hair was free and take the cheque to her, look her in the eyes and wait for her to start talking about the County as her fiancé was a season ticket holder. As soon as she opened up about the County, slip the massive cheque with the breakdown of monies on the reverse side through the grill, start talking to her again the moment she checked the breakdown and started to prepare the wages. It worked a treat. The money was placed in a blue canvas bag and I quickly returned to the club and hopefully an ecstatic Keith.

On returning to Keith's office at the ground I found him deep in conversation with the bank manager. On putting down the phone he said, 'He's not very happy Mike, I told him that I tried to stop you presenting the cheque but you didn't get the message at the bank.' We managed to survive a little longer, but the next episode involving the bank was straight out of a Laurel and Hardy film. Keith had gone to pick up the wages. His secretary, Margaret White, rang my office to say that he had broken down at the bank and could I rush over there immediately? What was I to think? Was he curled up prostrate on the floor of the bank or what? No, it was his car that had broken down. Fortunately I had a towrope in the back of the Vauxhall Victor I was driving. Keith's 1962 Corsair was parked outside the bank unable to move. I attached the towrope to one of the few parts of his car that I felt would not come away on the first tug and slowly we moved away. We managed to reach the right hand turning that was to take us over the second steepest hill in Newport. As we approached the junction with cars racing down on the other side of the road, I was aware that Keith was not too confident about this towing exercise as he kept putting his foot on the brake. I got out and walked back to him explaining that the moment there was a gap in the traffic coming towards us I would pull us across quickly. I managed to get to the turning of the road we wanted to enter, but Keith decided that he was not going to get his car across. He could see a car on the horizon coming at a rate of knots towards us. He kept his foot jammed on the brake pedal. Now bear in mind that there was a 10-foot towing rope between us and as it obstructed the side of the road the oncoming driver was approaching, it made this a dangerous manoeuvre. Before I could climb out of my car and release the rope, the oncoming car was at a standstill with its bumper resting gently on the towrope. I got the blame from a hysterical Keith on the basis that I did not judge the speed of the oncoming car and should have not made a move. We negotiated the climb up the hill successfully, but then it all went wrong. I could feel the tension in the towrope all the way down the hill as Keith was very nervous and kept jabbing his foot on the brake. Turning the final bend before the safety of a flat road 100 yards away, I was aware that the tension had disappeared completely and that Keith's Corsair was nowhere to be seen in my rear view mirror. Stopping the car and racing back up the hill I was confronted by Keith waving his fist at me as he climbed out of his car which had crashed into a wall.

'You were going too bloody fast! I couldn't keep up with you.' To this day I wonder what on earth was going through his mind when he made that statement.

On hearing that I was departing Somerton Park for Tottenham Hotspur, Keith was genuinely sad. The news came on the same day that County Manager, Colin Addison, was offered the post of assistant manager to big Ron Atkinson at West Bromwich. Colin and Keith had a love-hate relationship. Colin ran around the club frenziedly whilst Keith had a laid back approach to everything. This meant there was a natural incompatibility. At my last board meeting I remember the Chairman of the club asking Colin why were there problems with the previous Saturday's trip to Northampton.

'Well Chairman,' said Colin, 'The pre-match preparation left a lot to be desired if I am honest.'

'Why, what happened?' asked the Chairman.

'I asked the girl in the office to book Warwick Castle for a pre-match lunch. Well she did just that. She booked Warwick Castle. We arrived at Warwick Castle together with hundreds of foreign visitors and were shown to the mediaeval banqueting suite where we had our chicken legs and mead. Chairman, it was impossible to keep all the lads focused as there was a lot of activity going on around us with serving wenches and noisy visitors. The girl should have booked our regular stop off in Warwick at the Warwick Castle Arms, in Warwick High Street where we should have had soup and sandwiches, not the bloody castle.'

One occasion that will stay with me forever was the time that I met Elton John. He was the Chairman of Watford back in 1977 and after an evening game at Watford when they entertained the County he asked me about the financial state of the club. He disappeared quite suddenly and on his return handed over 10 LPs, all signed by the great man and asked that I put them to good use. His 'man' stood at his side, then handed me a jug of cash that amounted to £340, the proceeds of a collection Elton had organised when he held an impromptu 'concert' in the supporters' club after the game. Gestures like that are never forgotten.

An intervention by George Kitson the former player and trainer and a regular visitor to the Blackhorse to catch up on the gossip, proved to be a turning point in my career. George had served the club for many years, never whinging if the club could not pay him, as he was black and amber through and through. Occasionally, I would accompany Keith to the pub for a quick sandwich and a pint. On this particular occasion, George sat in the lounge studying the race card in the *Daily Express* (George was a bit of an old Tory and he was reminded of it on many occasions by red blooded left wingers that knew of his political leanings). George came over to Keith and me and handed me a piece of paper that he had ripped out of that day's *Express*. It read *'Tottenham Hotspur Football Club require a Bingo Manager as part of its Commercial staff. Apply in writing to ...'*

'You should apply for that Mike, you've set up the new bingo card here and now we have a lottery making a lot of dosh.'

At this particular time, football was enjoying a freak success on the back of new legislation that allowed clubs to offer £1,000 in first prize money for Gaming Board registered lotteries. I investigated the possibility of the County launching a scheme and it seemed viable. We were selling 15,000 £1 tickets a week and the financial fortunes of the club were changing drastically by virtue of the introduction of £250,000 new money per annum. But, did I want to apply for a job in London selling bingo tickets, even if it was with the great Spurs? I decided, tongue in cheek, to send in an application on the 7th April 1978.

7

FROM FOURTH TO FIRST WITHOUT KICKING A BALL

On 19th April I received a letter from Geoff Jones, the secretary of Spurs, thanking me for my application. The letter contained a paragraph that made my day. It read as follows: '*We have decided on re-consideration to create the post of Commercial Manager at Tottenham, and we will be holding initial interviews here later this week. If you wish to pursue your application perhaps you will kindly telephone me on the above number with a view to fixing an appointment this coming Thursday the 13th instant.*' I rang, trying to sound sophisticated by losing my heavy Welsh accent. I was worried my accent would do nothing to further my application, as my mum told me that the Cockneys laughed at the Welsh because of their singsong accent. My appointment was to be Thursday, April 13th 1978.

Richard Shepherd, a well known Welsh football commentator-journalist and author of the histories of Newport County, Cardiff City and Swansea City, worked with me at Newport County during the period 1976–1978. He was my programme editor. I shared my excitement about my interview at Spurs with him. Richard very kindly let me borrow a book entitled *The Glory Game* written by Hunter Davies. Hunter had been given permission to spend a whole season with the Lilywhites and this led to him writing a great book about the real Spurs. He not only covered matches but also covered the club as a whole. He wrote about the dressing room on a match day, the club offices, the training ground plus the opportunity to meet and discuss matters with the board of directors and management. After the quickest read of my life, I caught the train to London filled with these Hunter Davies visions and backgrounds of the senior people at the club. I was capable of giving a thumbnail description of every member of the board. I expected that others on the interviewing list had done the same. It became apparent later on that in fact they had not.

I prepared for the biggest day of my life. I wore my best suit, conservative tie, polished shoes and a new shirt that felt so uncomfortable that I really wanted to rip it off! I took the Underground to Tottenham Hale followed by a short walk to White Hart Lane. I looked at the old building that occupied the front entrance to Spurs at the time. There was a pub on the left and an old Victorian building to the right of the front gates, which I assumed accommodated the club's offices. After a deep breath I walked into the reception area to be met by a lovely middle aged lady who gave me a huge smile, asked me how far I had travelled and offered me a cup of tea. I later discovered that she had been at the club many years and that her name was Mrs Wallace. I never asked what her first name was because even in the mid 1970s at Tottenham Hotspur, it was not done to refer to anyone by their first name until you had known them for 30 years! I passed on the offer of tea as my stomach was churning in nervous excitement and I was anxious to see if any other candidates where already there. I went through a couple of thick oak doors and into a reception area about the size of a typical doctor's waiting room. There was bench seating fixed around the wall and a small section on each side was occupied by four other guys who I imagined must be the other candidates. I recognised two of them, they were Ray Ellis from Exeter City and Dudley Kernick from Stoke City.

Dudley was buoyant. I imagine his mood was dictated by the fact that he had the reputation of being football's highest paid commercial manager at Stoke City. For that reason I wondered why he was here. Ray was very quiet. Perhaps the magnitude of the situation was hitting him as it was hitting me. I was numb. My mind was a jungle of thoughts and I had a total incapacity to place matters in any sensible order.

Suddenly Dudley opened up a conversation. 'What are you guys going to ask for?'

Ray was first to respond, he said, '£12,000 a year plus a car.' The other two remained silent.

'What about you Mike?' asked Dudley.

Was he setting me up or not? In order to sound ambitious and creditable I said £10,000 would do me plus a car and a bonus. My salary at Newport was £4,500 I guessed that the 'ceiling' would be in and around the £10,000 mark.

'You've got to be joking,' said Dudley, 'I'm asking for £35,000 plus all the fringe benefits.'

Ray Ellis gave me that knowing look that suggested Kernick was probably attempting to wind us up.

Ellis was called at 1.30 pm followed by one of the unknown candidates at 2.30 pm, Kernick at 3.30 pm; I was next at 4.45 pm. I imagined that apart from the occasional departure and arrival of managers, staff stayed at Spurs for long periods. Later I found out that this was true. Mrs Wallace had been at the club for 40 years, Geoff Jones had been there for 20 years, his assistant Peter Day had been there for nine years, the groundsman for 23 years, and unbelievably the Spurs first and reserve teams starting the 1978–1979 season contained 17 players out of 22 who had come through the ranks. Today there's no doubt that the proportions are reversed.

I believed that being last to be called for interview was not a good omen. After the interview, the other candidates had left by another door. This denied me the opportunity to at least gauge the look on their faces as they departed White Hart Lane. Perhaps the more elderly directors would be sleepy and tired of asking the same questions and listening to the same weary answers so late in the afternoon. I was escorted up to the oak panelled boardroom by Mrs Wallace and as I climbed the stairs I kept subconsciously repeating to myself, 'Cool head, cool head'. The huge boardroom table was surrounded by 12 chairs, of which five were occupied. At the top sat Chairman Sydney Wale, on his right was Vice Chairman Charlie Cox, to Wale's left was Arthur Richardson and sat next to him was his son Geoffrey Richardson. Geoff Jones, the club secretary sat two seats down from Richardson Junior. I tried to compose myself, but in an off putting way, I found myself analysing every word spoken by a member of the board and fitting it into the word pictures conjured up by Hunter Davies' book.

Mr Wale opened the interview by welcoming me to White Hart Lane. He then asked me to outline the reasons I applied for the job. Several questions by the board followed interspersed with comments by dear old Charles Cox who had gained the title of commercial director overnight. This appointment was the first of its kind at Spurs. Mr Cox, obviously very conscious of the fact that he needed to be seen *and* heard as the director in charge of commercial activities addressed me with a startling opener. 'Mr Lewis, we don't want White Hart Lane turned into a circus with lots of those adverts around the ground and all that sponsorship stuff. We have a good 5p-bingo ticket that is selling well at the moment so could you concentrate on that if given the job?'

It was time for some quick thinking. 'Well Mr Cox [I think he was impressed that I remembered his name from the formal introductions earlier on], I feel that football is changing and the need to examine every opportunity to bring extra finance into a club should not be missed.' He nodded approval but little did he know that my response to his question was intended to hit home with young Richardson. It was he who stated in the Hunter Davies' book that perhaps it was time for a revolution in the game, and that gate receipts alone could not guarantee a club's survival even at the highest level.

'Tell us about Newport County Mr Lewis. What have you achieved there?' This question came from Richardson senior.

At that point I asked if I could produce some evidence of my success at Newport. The surprised reaction from the board as I spilled out programmes, lottery tickets and photos taken of ground advertising made me wonder if previous candidates had either not bothered to support their application in this way or that they simply talked the talk. Richardson Junior seemed to approve of my initiative by uttering, 'That's enterprising. We haven't seen anything like this before'. The pictures of puny but clean 8 feet advertising boards hung around the pitch and a sample of a new £1 lottery ticket about to be launched by the Mayor of Newport in three weeks time, plus an award winning programme, all seemed measly evidence of what I had produced at little Newport County. For what seemed an eternity they muttered amongst themselves with Mr Cox seemingly nodding in approval.

The final question when it came was only to be expected. What was I looking for in terms of pay? This was put to me rather embarrassingly by the Chairman who was obviously uncomfortable with being given the responsibility of introducing such personal matters. It was years later that I understood his reticence. I discovered that he was a very gentle person uneasy about discussing such matters as salaries.

'£8,500 plus a commission and a car, Mr Chairman.' I know, I bottled it.

The interview was over and I left the boardroom 35 minutes later in the belief that I acquitted myself pretty well, but what I would give to go straight back in there and do it all again.

On 25th April a letter arrived from Spurs. It had three folds down and one across making it very difficult to open in one go. It was an indication that 'The Great Spurs' had not co-ordinated envelope size with A4 paper. As I read from the top my heart began to sink.

'Following your recent interview here I wish to advise you that your application ['Here we go,' I thought] *is receiving further consideration.'* It went on. *'This matter is being discussed at our board meeting later this week when a decision as to our choice for the position will be made.'* I quickly calculated that the meeting would be two days later on 27th April. I didn't sleep much over the next two nights. No letter on Friday or Saturday. Monday morning's post brought nothing. I started talking to myself. It was the kind of subconscious conversation where I answered my own questions. My inner conversations were working overtime. 'Kernick's got the job. Shall I ring Ray Ellis? What about giving Geoff Jones a ring and say, "Look Geoff, time's moving on I need to know". How will I respond when asked by my colleagues at the County when they ask the inevitable question "Got the job Mike?"'

I couldn't sit down and work so I jumped in the car and drove to see Mrs Stickland, my favourite lottery agent. Now when I say favourite, I should explain that she was not a friend but simply the best ticket seller we had. She sold 2,000 tickets a week on a regular basis. Of these, 600 were sold at the Maindee Bingo Hall on a Tuesday night, and the remainder were bought by her. Why did she do this? It was because she magically covered the cost of the tickets through her winnings. My visit to her home in one of the poorest parts of town did not produce the desired effect. Instead of hearing her say, 'Give me some more tickets,' I was met at the front door with her bellowing, 'Fuck off Lewis and take these bloody tickets with you!' The problem was that she always had enough winners in her personal bundle of 1,400 to give her a profit, until this particular week. It did cross my mind that it was rather unusual for her to 'hit the jackpot' every week, but as her tickets represented 30 percent of total sales, it was not beyond the realms of possibility. I was not prepared to lose my best customer. Returning to her front door I could hear her three Alsatian dogs going berserk. She opened up and immediately I was jumped upon by these savage hounds. I was not bitten, but covered in slimy excretions from their mouths.

'Do you want a cup of tea Lewis?' Her genteel tones rang in my ears. I refused the offer on the grounds that the last person to take a cup of tea off her was our manager Colin Addison, and he had been sick for days after!

I soon uncovered the mystery. The previous commercial manager at the club planted winning tickets in her bundle every week. Not always the top prize but certainly enough to cover her outlay. This was in the time when you could come to a friendly arrangement with your ticket printer and he would print the winning bingo numbers separately and put them in a brown envelope that he would attach by sellotape to the side of the cardboard box used for delivering the tickets to the club. After I took over, because of the large number of tickets purchased by Mrs Stickland, it was some time before she failed to scoop a big prize.

Some months later at a meeting of commercial managers I gathered that the seeding of winning tickets was common practice.

I lost Mrs Stickland as an agent two weeks later when once again she threw 1,400 opened tickets at me. After a very quick discussion with the printer, a return to the norm was established and winners came in from all over the district. This scam came unstuck at Newport's ex-commercial manager's new club when the groundsman ripped open a huge parcel that he thought was for him only to find 10,000 tickets plus the 'magical' extras strapped to the outside of the carton.

At 3.00 pm that Monday afternoon, Geoff Jones rang me from Tottenham. He waffled a little and I believed that this was a pre-cursor to his delivering bad news but his next comment was one I shall never forget. 'Michael, the board would like to offer you the position you applied for, at the salary you requested, and would like you to start in May.' What does a simple 'thank you' mean in response to that news? I wanted to jump a train and hug every person that made this happen, that was how overjoyed I was. However, the only person I could contact immediately was George Kitson, he of the newspaper clipping. Off to the pub I raced and there he was, head buried in his *Express*. He greeted the news with joy. I thanked him for putting me on the trail and bought him a whisky chaser.

Spurs had one game left in the 1977–1978 season. They were in the second division, uncommon territory for them, but they held second place behind Southampton. The last game was Southampton away. A draw would put them back where they belonged in the old first division. Southampton was already promoted. Was I to join a famous club in the second division or in the first? From the kitchen of my home in Newport, I listened to every second of the commentary on the radio. It ended 0–0 and I was on my way to First Division Tottenham Hotspur as their first commercial manager.

I travelled to London the Saturday before I started work, having arranged to meet Charles Cox at the club for a guided tour.

8

SPURS ENTER THE NEW FRONTIER

I purposely arrived early at Tottenham Hotspur and obtained the ground man's permission to go out into the arena. I stood and stared at the vast stands. Looking up at that massive cockerel on top of what was the old East Stand I was completely transfixed.

Somerton Park, Newport with its little main stand, cracked terraces, Portakabin offices and its general appearance of decay, had been my workplace for two years and I loved it. Here, as I looked skyward from the centre circle, was a stadium that had experienced everything. Great European battles, the awesome sight of Blanchflower, Mackay, Jennings, Greaves, Smith, Gilzean, Hoddle, and soon to be graced by the artistry of Ardiles and Villa followed by Klinsman and Berbatof. I wondered if I had bitten off more than I could chew. How would the fans take to the idea of the club appointing a commercial manager? Did the great Tottenham Hotspur need a Welshman with some clever ideas of how to attract kids by putting on a shambles of a Cowboy and Indians show as pre-match entertainment? Just how big a jump was this from the fourth to the first division? Would they expect too much from me? Was I up to the job? Great comfort and relief enveloped me as these thoughts were racing through my mind as from behind me I heard Charles Cox say, 'It's a great club Michael and we know that you will handle it with care'. He went on to tell me that gradual change was acceptable, but I was not to fill the ground with advertising hoardings as they had experimented with that idea before and the Oxo sign behind the Park Lane goal, was to use Charles' words, 'A target for our centre forward Bobby Smith', who he claimed, tried to aim at the O in Oxo every time and goalkeepers had sussed him. To my question, 'Which of the 'O's Mr Cox?' I never got an answer and upon reflection it was a smart-arse question to pose.

Soon I was able to move my family to Hertford, just 20 miles from White Hart Lane. It was the start of a new era and one that was to surpass any expectations I might have had. The roller coaster ride was about to begin.

Back in Wales the *South Wales Argus*, a Newport based paper, covered the story of my purchase of a £25,000 detached property in Hertfordshire. Having left my new Wimpey Dorma house in Newport that cost £4,750, this was indeed a massive jump. I made this investment on the back of an expected commission inserted in my contract to the tune of 2.5 percent of the commercial turnover. The existing turnover in 1976 from a department that dealt with bingo tickets and very little advertising in the match programme was £55,000. At Newport I was able to turnover £270,000 in my last year, so the commission offered at Spurs was attractive if I performed. Granted, it gave me serious problems within 12 months! But I'll reveal more about that later.

After my first three weeks I attended my inaugural board meeting. The board as they had done for years, met for tea in the afternoon, examined the agenda and invited senior management to attend when the directors were ready. Because commercial interests did not seem to rank very highly on their list of priorities, I sat waiting in my office until 7.30 pm to be called up. This was after Keith Burkinshaw, Geoff Jones, the club accountant and the shop manager had all been dealt with. Looking back I now have a certain admiration for those gents sat around the boardroom table at Spurs discussing issues such as the quality of the sandwiches in the boardroom. It reflected a certain quaintness that has long gone. Or has it? I was not unduly concerned about the boardroom pecking order as I felt that I had to 'earn my spurs' first, then I would have a legitimate right to request a move up the ranks. Armed with a commercial attack plan that would see the coffers swell almost instantly, I bounced into the boardroom.

'Settling in okay, Michael?' was the Chairman's opener.

'Yes Chairman, I'm very excited about the commercial future of the club and can't wait to instigate schemes.' Now that remark on its own would normally stir some directors at other clubs to sit up and take notice. It would possibly awaken those who had had enough after four hours sat around a table in a stuffy room. But it didn't work with the directors of Spurs. It got no bloody response at all.

'If there's anything you want to know or any help we can give, don't be afraid to ask,' commented Sydney Wale.

My mind was bursting with ideas. Of course there were matters that I wanted clarification on. For instance, could I start match sponsorship? Could we launch a new lottery? Could I produce a bigger and better match programme allowing us the opportunity to have more advertising? Could I talk to agents about ground advertising? Now was not the time to lay these matters before them. I returned to my office neither deflated nor exhilarated, but numb, just bloody numb. I had 15 minutes to give my report and many hours after worrying about the apparent apathy that I faced. I called Geoff Jones and asked him what he thought.

'Mike, that's how it is, they'll spend two hours with Burkinshaw, 30 minutes with me, stop for more tea and sandwiches, then suddenly realise that you're still waiting to be called up.' At least this was consistent with the picture that Hunter Davies painted.

At that moment I took a decision. They *were* going to give me more time in board meetings because I would present a written report for the next meeting that would blow their balls off. I planned to fill the stadium with advertising, introduce match sponsorship, launch a new lottery and take Spurs into a new era. From the team manager down to the senior management staff, there was an urgent need for cars. I mention this because there is no other matter guaranteed to upset management at a football club than that of the provision of cars. Where the board draw the line and who has what type of vehicle has led to mutiny at many clubs. I made a good contact with HR Owen, a London based quality car supplier and they provided the appropriate new cars in return for guest appearances by players at their respective functions. This matter was not taken to the board (as suggested by Geoff Jones) as it might take an eternity to finalise. Instead I rang Charles Cox, the commercial director, and not to put too fine a point on it, I put a gun to his head.

'Mr Cox, staff moral at senior level is very low. Promises have been made and broken. Can I run this past you?' I was on fairly safe ground when it came to discussing motor cars as Mr Cox had been a Rolls Royce executive. After putting the car scenario to him his response was as forecasted.

'We can't have our best people upset, go ahead Michael, get the cars.'

When the new cars arrived en bloc from Owens (three Austin Princess' and two Rovers), I was gob smacked. HR Owen had really come up trumps. Geoff Jones and Keith Burkinshaw received the Rovers. The most pleasing sight, however, was to see Geoff Jones climb into his. He was like a dog with two dicks. I had made a friend for life, although for the first three months he would not attempt to put the car in his drive at home as he was not sure this could be achieved without scraping the wings.

A lottery was launched. The department that had been administered by two ladies whose main job was to check the bingo sales became bursting with energy overnight. New, excited lottery agents were only too keen to visit the club to pay in their collections. One such visitor was Len Duquemin the famous ex-Spurs centre forward who sold our tickets from his shop near the ground. Returns were now growing by the day and money was pouring in. Extra batches of scratch cards (the vogue at the time) were ordered and we needed three reps on the road and one extra person in the office. Within six months, sales had grossed £220,000 netting the club £95,000. By the end of my first 12 months we employed eight full timers and 40 part timers just to handle the lottery. Even I had underestimated the status that working for Spurs as an agent brought to an individual.

Then, as the summer was slowly slipping by and our attentions turned to the new football season, I received a visit. There was no appointment in my diary to see the man from Mills and Allen (part of the Pearl and Dean Empire and best known for their advertising in cinemas). However, instinct suggested to me that he was worth seeing. Perhaps it was his Canadian accent that attracted me. He introduced himself as Joe Doyle. He was resplendent, wearing a Stetson and walking like a cowboy. Within seconds of being invited to sit down he asked if he could light up a cigar. Being impartial to the odd Hamlet or two, I had no objections to the request. He asked if I had a three point plug and said that if it was convenient he could give me a film show. I gave him half an hour.

'How much do you want for your ground advertising sites?' asked Joe.

Shit! I hadn't expected that one as I really thought that Mills and Allen wanted to simply sell the sites on a commission basis rather than control the ground. I hastily recalled a conversation I had with one of the girls in the office. She had informed me that last season we earned £9,000 for the four ads on the ground much to the chagrin of Mr Cox at the time. 'We'll probably sell them ourselves,' was my feeble response.

'I'll give you £75,000 for the ground and we will do all the production,' continued Joe.

I will never be the best negotiator. I tend to rush in, shake hands and move on, leaving decisions to pure instinct. This was different. 'It's worth more than that.' I said with a straight poker face desperately trying to conceal my excitement.

'Mr Lewis, I have come here today to offer you £75,000 the same as Arsenal. Anything over and above that figure would have to be approved by my Chairman and there is no guarantee that he will agree to that figure.'

'Will you run £90,000 past him then?'

£90,000! What was I saying? Was this the beginning of 'the circus' I had promised Mr Cox I would not introduce? We got our £90k but not before some fun and games along the way. Unknown to Joe, our Canadian friend, Mills and Allen had engaged my best friend Ken James to advise them on outdoor advertising. Ken was aware of the discussion between Mills and Allen and Spurs and asked Joe if he could attend the meeting with me to sign and ratify the contract. Ken's stance was that he would purely observe, but would take the opportunity to look at the periphery of the ground to see if there was any mileage in Mills and Allen and the club arranging poster sites facing the High Road. Joe agreed and I hosted lunch at the club's restaurant where the contract was to be agreed. I signed the contract later in my office.

Ken and I had known each other for 20 years and during that time we had joined forces politically by becoming County Councillors in the same ward in Newport. We were regarded as the 'boys about town' as our whole approach to the election was based upon having some fun along the way. Our slogan 'Remember the names – Lewis and James' rang out for weeks in the Malpas ward of Newport. On one occasion whilst converging into a shopping area one Saturday morning with the roof top speaker ringing out this trite slogan followed by a plea that their vote would not be wasted, we pulled into a lay-by to gather breath. Some shoppers stopped, pushed their hands through the car window to shake us by the hand and wish us well; others walked past and turned their heads in the opposite direction thus suggesting that their political allegiances rested elsewhere. All was well until I stretched back in my seat and commented, 'I don't know about you mate but I'm fucked.' What was terribly wrong with that comment, you may ask? The comment did truly reflect the wear and tear of three weeks' non stop canvassing. The problem was that we had forgotten to switch off the PA speaker. Ken looked at me; I stared at him, then we rapidly started the motor and drove away. The following evening in our local, just when we thought that the *faux pas* had gone unnoticed, Vic the Greek, a good friend and supporter, said that he had heard the remark as he was coming out of the butchers and could not believe what he was hearing. I was returned to office with a majority of 345 votes and to this day I wonder if that majority could have been a tad higher if my indiscretion had been avoided.

Back at Spurs, Ken and I had a pre-lunch meeting before Joe arrived at the club for lunch. We talked for a while about old times then decided that as the contractual talks had gone so smoothly perhaps we should give Joe a little last minute surprise. On the basis that he would, at some time during this lengthy lunch, want to relieve himself, we decided that on his return from the loo, Ken and I would appear to be in a heated discussion about the real value of the site. As Joe sat down I would tell him that my board were not happy with the money being offered.

We put our plan into action. Looking at Ken's forlorn face, Joe asked him what was wrong. Ken explained that the club was not going to sign the contract as it stood as they had it on good authority that Arsenal had in fact been offered £100,000. Joe started coughing and spluttering and asked if he could have a large brandy. After the third large one, Joe regained some control over his emotions and started to explain what it would mean to him if he didn't take a signed contract back to his office. Once again he promised that the Gunners were not to receive a penny more than the Lilywhites.

'Mike, please go and phone Ken Friar at Arsenal and ask him exactly how much I have offered,' Joe pleaded. Friar at the time was the secretary at Arsenal and handled most day to day matters. Just at that moment, Ken James, his attempt to stay po-faced weakened and he confided in Joe. We ordered more brandy and signed the historic contract.

Sadly Joe passed on a few years ago. My final memory of the man was helping him into a taxi at White Hart Lane after *that* lunch after I had prised him off the church railings that provided his only means of support. God bless you Mr Doyle.

The contract with Mills and Allen proved to be very successful for both parties, but the success was not always easily achieved. It might seem that matters like keeping advertising boards clear of obstruction would be an elementary task. It's not easy when attempting to keep photographers from obstructing boards. Memories of my run in with Monty Fresco, the chief photographer with the *Daily Mirror* at the time still fills me with despair. The occasion was the FA Cup 6th round game against Manchester United at White Hart Lane. A total of 51,800 attended the game which ended in a 0–0 draw. Spurs lost the replay 2–0 four days later. For the game I had issued groundsheets to be handed out to all the accredited photographers including their 'spokesperson' Monty Fresco. The purpose of these groundsheets was to allow photographers to lie on their bellies, thus preventing them from covering the ad boards as they sometimes did when sat on their tiny stools. Monty confronted me before the game and told me in no uncertain manner where I could put the groundsheets. I put the case for the club, which in fairness to him he accepted. The groundsheets were never used as I slowly came to the conclusion that my plan was hastily cobbled together and needed much further consideration.

The following Friday was 31st August, my birthday. It saw the *Daily Mirror* run a story by Kevin Moseley that covered the whole charade and commented that, *'the order came from Mike Lewis the club's commercial manager. The photographers refused to comply with his instruction. Mr Lewis appeared on the touchline during the game using language that has got some supporters ejected'*. Moseley added, *'It left a nasty feeling that one of the great clubs lowered themselves to a money grabbing attitude'*.

Looking back I must confess that it was a crazy idea and the press boys were entirely right. Monty and I moved on and when we bumped into each other at subsequent games no hard feelings prevailed.

Spurs were regarded as mean and careful with their money. That mould was well and truly broken in the summer of 1978. It was world cup year and Argentina lifted the coveted trophy beating Holland 3–1 after extra time in the final in Argentina. In their team for 75 minutes of the final was a little feller called Osvaldo Ardiles. Included in the squad was Ricardo Villa, a good friend of

Ossie's. Ossie was a hero in his homeland along with Mario Kempes because they both displayed their own level of skill, which had not been seen for four years since the departure from the international scene of players such as Cruyff. England had nothing like it. When he joined Spurs, Ossie fitted in well, although Ricky found it difficult at times to hold down a regular first team place. He made up for his absence by the remarkable ability to waltz through defenders and look threatening inside the box when called on to play. The reader is probably 20 steps ahead of me by now and at a guess I would say that you are remembering that Ricky Villa goal against Manchester City in the FA Cup Final replay of the 1980–1981 season. I'll tell the story about that goal a little later on. What most people are unaware of is the trauma around the signing of these two world cup stars. Let's go back to the summer of 1978. My greenhouse of an office tucked away overlooking the car park at Spurs had so many windows that I could have grown tomatoes in there! My desk could only be placed in one position and that happened to be just in front of the window that caught the afternoon sunshine. This therefore turned my room into a sauna. It was almost 7.00 pm and I had just put the phone down after a conversation with Vernon from Adelaide who rang me every week and asked just two questions. What was the weather like and what could I see from my office window? His interest in Spurs was frail to say the least. He was a retired sheep shearer and spent most of his time in a Hotel in Adelaide getting absolutely smashed on the proceeds of his pay off. On being asked why he rang Spurs so regularly he replied, 'Jees, Mike, they sounded like cowboys to me when I looked at the soccer teams in the UK and that was good enough.' Not bloody cowboys again I thought!

'It's warm Vernon and I am looking at terraced houses that are squashed together. I can see cobbled streets and an ice-cream van surrounded by kids.' It was absolute bollocks but that's what he wanted to hear.

'Just as I imagined. Got to go Mike, the old back's playing up a little and I need to rest before I start another session.'

The phone rang again. This was not unusual as all the office staff had gone home and the telephone system went into a loop mode. This was so that if anyone was left in the club they could answer the call. 'It's Keith here, Mike [no not the Newport Keith but Burkinshaw]. Can you get hold of the Chairman for me I've tried and tried but the phone is not being answered?'

That afternoon the Chairman's wife had called into the offices, did the rounds of the management staff and alerted them to the fact that Sydney was having dinner at home that evening. His guest was Ted Willis, later to become Lord Ted Willis. The Chairman was not to be disturbed whatever the circumstances and this was the reason Keith could not contact him. I passed this information on to Keith who was not very happy and retorted, 'If I can't speak to him the deal's off'.

What deal? I didn't ask, but said that I would try myself, even if it meant that Mr and Mrs Wale would be very displeased with me. I did detect an echo on the line as I spoke to Keith and that at least gave me an idea that he was abroad and possibly about to sign a player. I tried in vain to contact the Chairman. So, I rang Keith on the number he gave me which was some 11 digits long. I passed on the news that I could not raise the Chairman.

'Look Mike, you probably don't know this but I'm trying to sign Ardiles. The board have given me the approval to spend £250,000, but he will not come on his own. He wants his mate Ricky Villa to come with him. Now Ricky's going to cost £150,000 and I need to know whether the club can stretch to the extra. Ossie's playing hard to get and will piss off in the next hour and sign for another club. They're queuing up to sign him.'

'Do *you* want to try again Keith?'

'No fuck it Mike, you try.'

I tried again. To my equal delight and horror Mrs Wale answered the phone. She sounded exasperated. Before I could get a word in she asked me if I understood what she had said earlier in the day. It was like being back behind my desk in school being rebuked by the teacher for talking in class. 'But, Mrs Wale it's urgent Mr Burkinshaw needs to speak to the Chairman.' There was silence and the sound of the phone being picked up.

'Michael this is very inconvenient,' he said in a voice that suggested that he was in the process of enjoying a fine dinner with Ted Willis. It sounded like Ted was providing the very best of company.

'Chairman I would not have bothered you, but Keith is pulling his hair out and he is calling from abroad.'

'Oh! *You* know where his is then?' Sydney said in a rather patronising way.

'Yes, and I also know about the problem he has.'

'Tell me about it quickly.' I relayed the story and asked if he would take a call from Keith. He said he would not, but would ring me in half an hour after he had spoken to the rest of the board to put the proposition to them.

I imagined that by now Ted Willis was in on the scene and that Mr Wale was getting some enjoyment in breaking the news to him. Perhaps the disruption of dinner was not quite so bad after all. Ted was a fervent fan of the club and I imagined that he was just as excited as Sydney about the prospect of Ossie playing for the team.

Exactly half an hour later, Sydney called back and uttered the immortal words, 'Tell Mr. Burkinshaw to go ahead.'

Ossie and Ricky entered into the new era at Spurs.

Keith Burkinshaw hated player's agents to the extent that when Ossie and Ricky arrived in England he asked me to look after them. I pointed out to Keith that it would compromise my position at the club if I represented players. He said that the board was comfortable with the idea. I did my best to represent the players. Sponsored cars were no problem, but sponsored houses! What the hell Keith promised them in that hotel in Buenos Aires I had no idea. We managed to get a great deal on two detached houses in Broxbourne. They were next to each other and this pleased both sets of families. Ossie at the time was driving a sponsored Jaguar, once again courtesy of HR Owen, and Ricky had an Austin Princess. Why Ossie fancied the E-Type I could not imagine. We needed to put two cushions on the driving seat so that he could see over the steering wheel! John Holloway, the chief salesman at HR Owen and provider of the vehicles, had a very acute sense of humour. He suggested that on the day of delivery of these cars to the ground that he would bring up an old Ford Prefect kept at the showroom at HR Owen. It was in immaculate condition. He parked the old Ford Prefect outside my office with the E-Type hidden around the corner. John and I escorted Ossie to the Ford Prefect and handed him the keys. Now who was fooling who? Ossie sat in the car without comment, started it up and drove around the car park bringing it to a halt in exactly the same spot it had started from. On climbing out he said, 'Thank you,' to John and proceeded to walk back into the club offices. John and I exchanged glances and without any comment John rushed after Ossie and started to explain the joke. Ossie, totally unperturbed, came back into my office and waited for the E-Type to be driven from around the corner. As Holloway was outside organising the transfer, I asked Ossie if he knew what was going on.

'Mike, I saw the Jaguar parked in the street when I came in.'

When handed the keys of the Jag, Ossie said that he preferred the Ford Prefect asking John if he could have the keys back. The last laugh was on HR Owen. John Holloway sadly passed away at an early age and the club subsequently lost contact with HR Owen.

Ricky Villa was the quiet one. Ossie liked to socialise in the full sense of the word, so it was no surprise to me that a few weeks after his arrival I received a call from a policeman in the early hours one morning. He explained to me that Mr Ardiles wanted to speak to me as there was a problem with the car.

'Mike the car's gone bang. Can you help me?'

'Look Ossie what do you mean the car's gone ... no never mind, put the policeman back on the phone.'

'Look Mr Lewis, if you can get here and take Mr Ardiles home then all well and good. The car's on the top of a roundabout and it is not driveable. Make it as quick as you can as he needs to be removed from the scene if you understand me?'

As Ossie jumped into my car the policeman poked his head over the driver's window and said, 'I'm a season ticket holder at Spurs Mr Lewis, he's very lucky'. Message understood and within 10 minutes, Ossie was wrapped up in bed.

Both Ossie and Ricky were great ambassadors for the club. Ossie delighted fans up and down the country. There were claims, mainly from the soccer writers, that he and Ricky would not be suited to the wintry conditions and they would struggle to play in the UK. Nothing was further from the truth. Ossie weaved his magic and not only became a hero at White Hart Lane but was well respected throughout the leagues. In his first season he appeared in 46 out of 51 fixtures. This hardly suggested that he could not manage British conditions. He thrilled fans at lower division clubs such as Swansea and Altringham. To this day, Swansea fans remember their captain Tommy Smith kicking Ossie up in the air within 10 minutes of the League Cup first round game at the Vetch on 6th September 1978. Before the game, Ossie enquired about Tommy Smith's title as the hard man of football. Ossie commented that Smith would have to catch him first! Catch him he did.

Players are always up to the latest prank and any newcomer is fair game. His team mates convinced Ossie that he would need to take his passport with him on entering Wales and show it to the 'passport control' officer on the Severn Bridge! Ricky, in my opinion, was an equal player to Ossie but was never given a long enough run in Spurs' first team to cement his place. He played in 28 of the 48 games in his first season. Ossie's English was very good. Ricky initially struggled with the language and became the victim of many a 'set up'. The first of these was upon his arrival at the club. A club official sent to bring Ossie and Ricky from the airport decided to explain to Ricky in a slow, purposeful manner, how to greet English people. He said that the shaking of the hand was compulsory, accompanied by the words, 'Hello wanker'. On his first visit to my office to meet the staff, I was blown away by the very courteous manner in which Ricky was conducting himself. The girls were putty in his hands. He immediately put his English to the test.

Before he could get to the second lady waiting to shake him by the hand I had hustled him out of the office. Some weeks later when we sat quietly discussing his off the field of play activities with the help of his mate Ossie, he turned to me and said in his very best pidgin English, 'Me get the bastard who sit me up.'

9

THE STARS COME OUT AT WHITE HART LANE

I am not the bravest person in the world. I will fight like hell for friends and relatives, but when it comes to defending my own corner I am a little short on what it takes. Don't ask me why I'm like this as I haven't a clue. It will take a good psycho-analyst to fathom that one out. Having said that, I am especially proud of my British Parachuting Association certificate, membership number 161565. This battered and torn piece of paper, which is cherished I might add, is a little proof that I can rise to the occasion, or rather fall from grace! How did I get it? My honest answer to that question is simply that I got pissed as a fart after a long matchday at the club and agreed to have a go at that dropping out of the sky lark.

I had invited the Green Jackets to perform a 'drop in' at White Hart Lane with six of their ace parachutists. Bob Dowling was their leader. He and I got on well. The display before the game was magnificent. It would have qualified for a jump of perfection had it not been for the loss of the youngest member of the team. Thankfully he didn't kill himself, but came very close. He was number three out of the aircraft that was circling the arena. Those of you who are acquainted with the ground will know how tight the houses and a school are to the stands. This was the first time that a parachute drop had taken place at a London football club, so it was no surprise when they missed the drop zone. This young lad of 18 streaming down at 30 miles per hour had to make a very important decision as he was making his approach to the arena. At 100 feet it became obvious that he was not going to make it onto the pitch, so he decided to overshoot and land in the club car park. This was achieved by sliding down the back of the roof of the East Stand and gently dropping into the car park. Bear in mind that the display was at 2.45 pm with crowds pouring in and the car parks rapidly filling up. He landed on the roof of a car, gathered in his chute and ran around to the sponsor's suite. He was half way through his first pint of lager before the other five had finished their arm waving to the crowd in appreciation of their wonderful reception.

After the game, Bob, on the back side of seven rapidly consumed pints of lager, pulled me to one side for a chat and suggested that six members of staff at the club could be trained for a jump free of charge as long as the proceeds went to a charity. This was a wonderful gesture from Bob. As Graham Dene, the former Capital Radio DJ and Princess Diana's favourite presenter was with us that day; it seemed appropriate that the radio station's favourite charity 'Help a London Child' should be the beneficiaries. We undertook four nights of training at the club with Bob taking us through various exercises such as the parachute landing preferences, which the parachutist had to decide some 200 feet above the ground whether to fall and roll to the right or the left. The exit position from the aircraft was also discussed and it seemed to me that the worst seat in the aircraft was that of the co-pilot as the person occupying that seat would be first out.

The 25th October 1983 was in my diary as the day of the jump at Thruxton Airfield near Andover. A small coach transported us from Tottenham to Thruxton on the morning of the 25th, to carry out our jump. We had raised over £2,000 in sponsorship with one wag giving me £100 together with the words, 'I'll give you another 50 if you hit the drop zone'. Drop zone? What did he know about it? Apparently he had served in Cyprus with the Army Parachute regiment and had completed 280 jumps. His parting shot sent a shiver down my spine. 'You're all fools, bloody fools. No one in their right mind should jump out of a plane unless they have had at least six months' training.' There was to be a personal hitch however. Bob had asked those of us over 40 years of age to bring a doctor's certificate in order to validate the insurance cover. Now, honestly I really did ask the club doctor for a certificate, but his response was not in a favourable one. 'You must be mad, go and play golf you silly bugger, I'm not signing your death warrant.' I decided to bluff my way out of that one by ignoring the subject on arrival at the airfield.

Two girls from the office, the assistant club secretary, two security men and I made up The Parachute Team and we were pretty gung ho about it too. On arrival at Thruxton we were ushered into a Nissen hut and given the last drilling, mainly on safety measures such as what to do if the chute got tangled up with the tail plane of the aircraft. The answer is to stay there until the jumpmaster crawls along the fuselage and cuts the chute free. Then count to 10 and pull the reserve chute. There's nothing to it really. Should a parachute get caught up in electricity lines and a farmer rushes over with an aluminium ladder, it's best to simply holler, 'Fuck off!' There's nothing to it really. If the main chute doesn't deploy, wait until 500 feet from the ground and pull the reserve chute. There's nothing to it really. Should the jumper drop into a tree and hang 20 feet off the ground, don't try and release the harness as it's possible to turn turtle and fall on the head with severe consequences. Stay there until one of the ground crew climbs a ladder to help re-visit terra firma. There's nothing to it really. Perhaps I have an over active mind. When the instructor was going through these hazards I was thinking the following: If I get caught up with the tail plane and my 16 stone drags behind the aircraft, will that give the pilot a problem? The answer is yes, in fact. If I was not cut free I would bring the plane down. Christ! Secondly, how will I know when I am 500 feet off the ground? The answer was when the plane is climbing to prepare for the drop; the jumpmaster will count – 100 feet, 200 feet, 300 feet, 400 feet, 500 feet, and so on. This little exercise will ensure that the parachutist is totally aware of the height they are at. Now, when cows in the field are starting to look like miniature models at 400 feet, they look no different at 800 feet so how the hell is anyone going to be able to judge 300 feet off the ground from 500? There's nothing to it really. Next it was the reserve chute drill. It went something like this: left hand over the reserve kit strapped to the midriff, right hand over the piece of equipment that contains the gunpowder, or whatever it is that propels the reserve chute out at 600 miles per hour, then left hand over right and pull the cord which extends from the right hand side of the equipment. There's nothing to it really.

Bob, having demonstrated the procedure, without pulling the cord of course (who would be so silly as to engage the reserve chute inside a Nissen hut?) repeated the instruction several times. Just at this point, almost as if Dr Curtin had sent a telepathic message to him, Bob walked across to me and asked for my medical form. Two others were over 40 and he had already collected their forms. I really thought that I had got away with it and that Mr Dowling had forgotten the need for paperwork. I confessed. Bob growled at me, carrying the intensity of a Sergeant Major, 'You 'aint going anywhere Lewis.' I pleaded with him to let me go, conscious of the fact that a little tiny bit inside of me was hoping that he would keep to his word and retire me to the bench. He insisted that I continued the drill as he would get me to come down to Thruxton the following week and carry out my jump.

Bob was immovable. There was no way was I going to get my wings that day. Then he came up with an idea. He said the girls were fine and up for it, one of the security guys was okay but the other one was suffering and had already spewed up in the toilet. The club's assistant secretary was in no state to continue. I have never witnessed before the many changes of colour a face can take on inside a few minutes. He went from red to white to grey in five minutes. My role (suggested by Bob) was to entertain them by cocking up the reserve chute drill. Bob explained that he would go around all the other jumpers one by one and go through the reserve drill leaving me till last. He would ask me to conduct the reserve drill as instructed but with one important deviation. At the point when he yelled, 'Left hand, right hand, don't pull!' I was to pull the reserve chute lever. This last instruction was imparted to me in a whispered tone under his breath so that the others could not hear.

The other five having done a perfect practice run stood in a circle waiting for me to complete my turn. Bob stood in front of me in a rigid form without a smile or a blink of the eye. 'Mike, reserve chute drill please.' Right hand, left hand, and then with a shaking hand I pulled the cord. The resulting explosion, albeit not on any Richter scale, was nevertheless frightening. The hut filled up with the orange canopy and all I could hear was Bob shouting, 'You fucking idiot Lewis, Christ there's always one.' As I gathered in the chute on my hands and knees I looked up to see the others pissing themselves with laughter. It did the trick.

In order to keep up the pretence and not let the others know that I was out of it, Bob asked me to get kitted up and join them in the Land Rover to go to the airstrip. As the jumpers left the Land Rover one by one to take the short step to the awaiting aircraft, Bob shouted at me to get out and go and take my place next to the pilot. 'But Bob I'm not jumping today am I?'

'Just get out and get in the aircraft.'

I can only describe the feeling that rapidly crept through my body as a feeling experienced by a man on death row who is marched down to the execution room, only to be stopped at the hang room door to be told that he had won a reprieve. Then, on his way back to his cell the Governor turns to him and says it was only a joke, turns him around and marches him back to the execution suite. My mind was blank, not only that, I was the one that was to sit next to the pilot where normally a door is positioned. For parachuting purposes the door had been removed. I sat 12 inches from an open space looking down at the fast disappearing ground. This position meant that I was to be first out. I sense by now that all you want to know is how it went. My parachute descent record card reads as follows. *'Mr Lewis was very confused about his exit position and did a perfect somersault. He landed 300 yards from the drop zone.'* The drop zone was a white cross painted on the ground.

For some reason I had forgotten one of the more important instructions that had been crammed into my mind over the last six weeks of training. This particular instruction was simple and I should have remembered. Whist I was hanging on the wing strut with my left foot on the metal pad attached to the side of the aircraft and awaiting the jumpmaster's bellowed order to, 'Go!', we were constantly reminded not to push ourselves off. The natural aerodynamics of a plane travelling forward at 90 miles an hour and being released of an object hanging onto its wing strut does not require any help by virtue of same object pushing away! Look, can I say in my futile defence that training on terra firma is fine, but when hanging onto a flimsy wing strut some 2,500 feet up, it is a very different proposition and there is the slightest of tendencies to forget some of the detail. Guess what happened? I pushed, and the consequence of such an action became very apparent almost immediately. Looking up from the harness to the parachute to check that deployment had occurred, I was shocked to find that the lines were entangled to the extent that they were hanging together like strands of spaghetti forcing me to perform pirouettes in the sky. I took 20 turns to the left followed by a slightly less number to the right as the lines gradually returned to their normal configuration. By now I was sailing to earth, albeit a long way from the drop zone. The feeling was one of excitement coupled with some trepidation as I saw the model cows slowly becoming life sized. I was aware that Bob Dowling was on the ground holding what looked like a large ice cream cornet to his lips. The only sound I could hear was a garbled hysterical voice shouting some kind of instruction. His loose arm was waving to me in a gesture that I simply could not interpret. The sheer joy of touching down did send me into raptures to the extent that I stood upright and punched the air with delight. At least I was in one piece.

During our training we had been warned about 'ground rush'. This occurs at a height between 150 to 200 feet. At this point the parachutist must decide which position they are going to take up, landing left or right. In reality most first timers leave this decision far too late and can injure themselves in the process. Fortunately I made my decision early enough and went for the left option. I had landed on the grass runway and the little Cessna was about to come back in to land. Lying flat on my belly I certainly heard the roar of the engine as the plane went past but I was not in any danger. However, Bob, by now standing over me, was not about to congratulate me on a safe landing, but I did not expect the onslaught that followed.

'What the fuck were you trying to do when you landed? Punching the air is fine if you had just scored the winning bloody goal in a Cup Final.' That is not a true record of the conversation as more profanities were used putting Bob on an equal basis with Gordon Ramsay.

Spurs' second game of the 1978–1979 season against Chelsea brought with it another milestone, the first ever sponsored game at Spurs. Some weeks earlier, Mike, the odd job man at the club, pulled me to one side in the car park and asked me if I had ever visited the Trophy room. 'Mike all the trophies are either in the boardroom or the Blue Room (The inner sanctum)' was my reply.

'No, it's the room that was last used for Pat Jennings' testimonial. It's in the middle of the main West Stand.'

'Can you open it up and show me?'

With some difficulty due to its non use, the door opened and I stepped on to a parquet floor, which, although somewhat dirty, would certainly buff up a treat. To my left I saw a trophy cabinet measuring approximately 15 feet by 6 feet containing wonderful trophies collected by the club over the years. Most impressive of all was a huge shiny piece of coal stood on a wooden base. This was presented to the club after a visit to Gornik in the European Cup. On the opposite wall was the nameplate taken from a locomotive called Tottenham Hotspur. It now stands proudly in the reception area of the club in the 'new' West Stand. I wondered if this loco had ever steamed past Somerton Park

Newport. The room measuring 25 yards by 10 yards was perfect for a sponsors' room and I was getting excited about the prospect of using this 'jewel'. There was a problem however. I tell no lies when I say that I tried in vain to raise the matter of match sponsorship the following week at a board meeting only to find that Charles Cox, the commercial director (he of Oxo fame), was away on holiday. Chairman Sidney Wale had to dash off early, so the respective Chair and Vice were not there to hear my submission. Would the remaining members be brave enough to give me the nod?

My proposal was brief and I made great play out of the fact that this glorious room had been left idle and we should really be putting it to good use. Expecting to hear the immortal words suggesting that such a decision can only be made by the full board of directors, I was knocked off my feet when Jeffrey Richardson proposed that I should go ahead and use it to commercial advantage.

Smiths Crisps were the inaugural sponsors and it was all carried out in the best possible taste, as Kenny Everett would have said.

After several successful sponsorships, I decided to stretch my wings a little and test the water with regard to attracting celebrities to our games. Coincidentally, during November of 1978, I received a call from a guy called Harry Dawson. Perhaps he had heard through the football grapevine that Spurs were going to relax their rules a little with regard to famous visitors. Harry was a theatrical agent. He asked if the club would like to entertain stars if they were in town on the day or night of a home game. As I was desperate to see showbiz people at the club, I suggested to Harry the next time he had a 'star' in town to give me a ring.

Within a week Harry was back, this time giving me a schedule of stars and available dates. Fortunately this gave me some time to canvass the Chairman and Vice-Chairman. Mr Wale did not seem too happy with the proposal. He provided a compromise and said that as long as they are not seen to be wandering around the club and causing a stir he would approve a trial run.

Harry and I discussed the arrangements. They would be: No fee. Lunch in our restaurant before the game. Join the Sponsors at 2.30 pm then take their seats in the directors' box to watch the game.

'Brilliant Mike, look I've got James Garner in town this

weekend and Eartha Kitt in two weeks time, is that okay?'

Garner was hugely popular at the time because of his *Rockford Files* series. What a dream it was to be in his company. He was a gentleman who unfortunately was seeing the early onslaught of severe rheumatism, mainly affecting his hands.

Eartha Kitt's visit with Harry was bizarre. She enjoyed a superb meal with us and when the opportunity arose I thanked her for coming to the club and hoped that she would enjoy the game. My grave mistake was to call her 'Eartha' as she liked to be referred to as 'Miss Kitt'. Her reaction to my being over familiar was astounding. She gave me that look that would frighten the life out of the gorillas at the zoo and bellowed, 'And what do you do here?'

I noticed that she had consumed several brandies when she asked me just before kick off if she could use a telephone. I said that she could use my office. I ushered her in and asked if she wanted a drink as I had a drinks cabinet (by then I was using a more comfortable office). She made herself comfortable and then asked if I would stay with her while she called her daughter whose birthday it was that day. Now this seemed a strange request given we had got off to a bad start only half an hour earlier.

I tried not to listen to her side of the phone call but it's impossible isn't it? She swallowed the last of her drink and then broke down and cried, putting her head on my shoulder murmuring, 'I'm sorry, I'm sorry'. Apparently this was the first time that she had been away on her daughter's birthday. We ended up friends for the day.

It was not quite the case with Hilda Baker. Once again, Harry was the escort. The game was against Middlesboro. Harry had, in fairness, warned me that Hilda liked her whisky and she was not too clever after several glasses of the amber nectar. By 'clever' I imagined he meant not too steady on the old pins. If only that had been the case. Harry asked me to check on Hilda if he had to leave the table. Sod's law intervened during lunch. I was called over to another table to speak to a customer leaving Hilda and Harry alone. In my absence Harry had gone to the loo leaving Hilda alone for a few minutes. I rushed back as soon as I realised that she was the sole occupant of the table. It was too late. She had commandeered a waiter, knocked back a treble whisky and ordered the same again, thank you. By the time Harry returned Hilda was flying.

'Where's my record now Harry?' This referred to her hit with Arthur Mullard when they combined to make *You're the One that I Want* from the hit movie *Grease*.

Hilda continued, 'Someone came to the table and congratulated me for reaching number one in the charts. You told me it was 32nd, what's going on Harry?'

During the game that ranked as one of the most boring I had ever witnessed she shouted at Harry. 'Harry, I could have been opening that flower shop today not sat here watching this rubbish.' Unfortunately, my seat in the directors' box was immediately behind the Chairman's. He turned around and asked if the lady was with me and if so, could she be escorted from the box? Leave she did with Harry wagging his finger at her.

The following Monday morning Hilda rang me and asked if I would go to her home for dinner, as she wanted to apologise for her behaviour.

Some weeks after the door had opened on celebs coming to the club, Peter Cook came. I received a call from Fred who was Peter's minder. He was also a gentle adviser who told Peter when he could go out to play, or when he should stay at home, certainly in relation to his visits to White Hart Lane. Fred had arranged with me that he would call on a Saturday morning before a home game and let me know if Peter was 'up to it' for the afternoon, if you follow my drift. Peter's first game as a guest was Spurs versus Manchester United at White Hart Lane. Incidentally, he was one of dozens of Spurs season ticket holders who had made their name in the entertainment industry. The star supporters included Bruce Forsyth, Dickie Henderson, Henry Kelly, Frankie Vaughan, Chas and Dave, Jim Davidson, and would you believe, Warren Mitchell (old Alf Garnet himself). I asked Fred if Peter could come suitably attired. Shall we say that the request was not met in its entirety? Like a schoolboy before his headmaster, Peter on arrival at the ground came to my office, stood before me and asked if he was suitably dressed for the occasion. He looked magnificent in a very smart lightweight suit, cut away collared shirt and his general disposition was excellent. It was only when he turned to walk away that I noticed that he had on a pair of trainers! Still they were new. Off we went to the 'unofficial' sponsors' room for lunch. The room looked magnificent. The sponsors were delighted with the general ambience. They were even more delighted when they saw Peter Cook arrive. Now, as it happened, we had a glass-covered model of the new West Stand sat on a table surrounded with brochures explaining the cost and the facilities sponsors would receive in return for a hefty cheque. Peter asked if he could look at the model. There were five or six other people looking at it. One of them turned to me and said, 'Mike. How much are these executive boxes in the centre?'

Before I could answer Peter stepped in. 'None left. I've bought four, two on the top and two on the bottom.'

Hell! He can't be serious can he? No it was Peter's idea to stimulate interest and to have a little fun. The opposite effect was achieved. Off walked the real potential customer. He did eventually take a top tier box.

The game against United was a classic. It ended 1–1 and was watched by 36,665 spectators. The first half saw Spurs struggling to get any rhythm, to the extent that Peter, sitting next to me and directly behind the Chairman, decided to 'stoke up the fans' by standing up and shouting across to The Shelf (the area where the most fervent fans would stand). 'Come on, we can't fucking hear you, come on you Spurs.' Sidney Wale didn't budge. Fred whispered something in Peter's ear and we heard no more from him at the game.

By now, Spurs was *the* place to be if you were a celeb. One of my favourites was Warren Mitchell. I was asked to contact him because there was some bad blood from the past and he wanted to put his side of the dispute forward. It became apparent that the dispute was over the issue of what team he really supported. Some of the old directors felt, because of that wonderful series *Till Death Us Do Part* that Alf, sorry Warren, was a West Ham supporter. That wasn't the case as Warren had been a Spurs supporter and season ticket holder for many years. There was a fear that Spurs would be ridiculed by Alf in his show. Nothing was further from the truth. He agreed to visit our sponsorship suite. That day heralded for me a relationship with Warren that I greatly valued. Conscious of the need to ensure that he wasn't pestered all afternoon by sponsors' guests, I pointed out to the host that Warren was here for the football and whilst he was happy to sign autographs and chat to people, could the host ask his guests in his welcoming speech to be considerate and remember that Warren was here to enjoy the afternoon. Warren loved it.

On his third visit to the sponsorship suite he rang me and asked if he could have some fun with the Chairman of the sponsoring company that day. The suggestion was made purely in the interests of embellishing the afternoon a little. His only request was that I was not to let on to the sponsors that he was coming to the game.

Guests were assembled, food was ready to be served, the Chairman of the timber company was on his feet about to propose a toast to his guests and Tottenham Hotspur and we were all set for the off. I caught sight of Warren stood behind a large concrete pillar well out of sight of the Chairman and his guests. Just as mine host was about to speak, Warren, with his best Alf Garnett voice, bellowed, 'Sit down you old fart, they want to eat not listen to you. Sit down'.

The room erupted with laughter with one exception. Yes you've guessed, mine host.

Once again, Alf shouted out. This time it was, 'Look, look, you silly old bugger, we wouldn't allow this down the 'ammers it's the football they've come for not to listen to you'. By now Alf had popped out from behind the pillar to rapturous applause, joined the host, who by now was red in the face and managed just 30 seconds more of his welcoming speech.

It was Warren Mitchell that advised me 23 years ago that I should write a book. He kindly invited me to go to the theatre to watch him take the lead role of Willy Loman in Arthur Miller's *Death of a Salesman* at the National Theatre. He was absolutely brilliant. He asked if I could meet him after the performance so that we could go to his favourite Italian restaurant. I was delighted to accept this invitation.

It was a delightful few hours. I was desperate to hear his life story, but hesitant to spend the night putting him under any pressure to answer questions he must have heard a thousand times before. To my surprise he said, 'You know all about me, what about you?' We all love to be asked about our life and this was certainly no exception. I spilled out all the Newport County stories, the fun, the sorrow, the occasional excitement, and it was during these revelations that he stopped me, wiping his eyes with laughter. He said, 'Write it down, you've got to write it down'. I couldn't believe it. Warren Mitchell, the king of humour, laughing at my silly stories! Well Warren, I have scribbled away for years and after many rejection slips from publishers I found someone brave enough to let the thoughts of Mike Lewis be published.

Those of you on the other side of 50 will hopefully remember stars such as Chas McDevitt and Lonnie Donegan. Chas was far more a talent than his one hit with Nancy Whiskey suggested. *Freight Train* was a massive success, but he turned out some cracking performances on vinyl that never got the recognition they deserved. Chas came to see Spurs and joined us in the sponsors' room on several occasions.

Lonnie was a legend and produced great records with his skiffle band. It was a complete surprise when, on return from America, he brought a young lady to a game at Spurs. Thank God I hesitated before the introduction, as I was about to say what a beautiful daughter he had. Just before I opened my mouth, Lonnie introduced me to his wife! She must have been a teenager at the time and the partnership had caused massive problems in the USA. His death in 2002 did not come as a huge surprise as he had suffered with heart problems for several years. Whilst he could not realistically be labelled as the greatest of stars, he certainly brought a new dimension to the British pop scene and was the very best advocate of skiffle music.

It seemed that we had well and truly stolen the march on Chelsea for a while as White Hart Lane became a magnet for celebs. Any criticism aimed at me by board members was more likely to be in the form of a moan that occasionally I did not bring their favourites to the boardroom.

10

HIS KNEES WENT ALL TREMBLY

Rumours about a multi-million pound new stand were rife, but it was not until a subsequent board meeting that the plans were unveiled. Sworn to secrecy about the financial details surrounding this massive project, I was amazed that the model standing in the middle of the boardroom table only contained 36 executive boxes. When asked for comments my first question was, 'Why so few executive boxes?' This was changed to 72 boxes at a later date, albeit adding a further £1,000,000 to the costs as the roof needed lifting higher.

Civil engineers, Balfour Beatty, were appointed to construct the stand and the professional team of architects, designers and engineers assembled. Imagine my surprise when a few weeks later I was asked by the chairman to make daily visits to the site foreman's hut when the contractors started work to make sure that the budget was not being overrun. In essence, this meant that I was to instruct the site foreman and not to authorise any 'extras' without board approval.

What followed in the early months of construction was nothing short of a farce. Geoffrey Richardson, son of Arthur and heir apparent to the chair, came to see me to explain that he would also be around to keep an eye on matters. Dave, the site foreman employed by Balfour Beatty, was a formidable man. He was 6 feet 3 inches tall, weighing at least 20 stone and stereotypical of a 'long in the tooth' builder. Dave made no secret of his concern about the arrangement that allowed Geoff and me to visit the site on a regular basis. As Geoff could only make the occasional visit to the site it was me who strode into Dave's office every morning for an update.

Eventually we struck up an understanding and apart from Geoff Richardson insisting that they move a wall in the Bill

Nicholson suite because he felt that the lighting factor would improve, all went fairly well. Dave was obviously annoyed by the attendance of Geoff Richardson as he would come into my office after Geoff's visits to moan about new instructions issued to him.

Geoff Richardson meant well and he and I got on very well. I liked him enormously as he did represent the younger element on the board. I felt that it was his influence that helped to get me the job in the first place.

On 27th January 1982 we played Middlesbrough at home. This was the last game before the official opening of the West Stand. By now Dave and I had struck up an understanding that meant that when I wanted to take potential clients into the new stand, he would arrange for the appropriate headgear to be provided and I could show off the boxes and hospitality areas, even if this meant potential clients getting their Saville Row suits soiled. This arrangement was completely unofficial as public liability insurance did not cover members of the public climbing rickety old ladders. I asked Dave if I could show some visitors the boxes on the day of the Middlesbrough game. They were very impressed and bought boxes on the spot. To point out the proximity of their box to the central boxes, I opened the top centre box to find 12 Irishmen sat on beer crates and planks drinking lager from a stack of cases that would have graced the cellar of a good sized pub! They had also brought in their own central heating via a calor gas heater. Dave occupied the middle of the plank balanced between two beer crates. This Frank Carson look-a-like smiled, asked us if we wanted a beer and turned to continue watching the game.

The building of this magnificent stand for £3.4 million was a bold step for the board to take. The fact that the costs escalated to £4.5 million not leaving enough money to complete the build represented an open embarrassment to the club. It left three floors of empty shells, including the area where a fitted kitchen should have been. This highlighted the club's financial problems and created a desperate need for financial remedies. This was made very clear to me when Mr Arthur Richardson, the new chairman, came to my office to enquire how box sales were going. 'We need as much money as possible over the next month, Mike as the bank is getting nervous.'

'We've shifted 26 boxes in three months, chairman and we still have plenty of interest,' Was my reply.

If the original plan that included 36 boxes had been adhered to, then our target of filling all the boxes before the first game using the new stand was a distinct possibility. To some extent I had shot myself in the foot. However, the board had laid down the prices for boxes asking companies to part with £30,000 up front for a three-year tenure and this proved to be a difficult sell. I was not consulted on this important issue. Over time I was able to convince the board that a graduated system, whereby central boxes were sold at a premium with those boxes further away from the halfway line offered at a discount. As one of the old brigade, Arthur Richardson was not likely to over emphasise the need for cash as this matter was a matter for the board only, but I could tell from his face that he was worried. I didn't know if Richardson was a Christian or had some other devout belief, but what happened the next day was, I felt sure, fortuitous to say the least.

The visitor looked like a city gent. And that was exactly what he was. He walked straight into my office, brief case in hand and came straight to the point.

'These hospitality boxes Mr Lewis, do you have any left?'

'Yes, can I show you one?'

Dave the Foreman slapped yellow hats on our heads and we climbed up flimsy ladders to the executive box area. Safely escorted to the best box left, he took a cursory look inside and said that he would take it. On returning to my office the city gent in the pinstriped suit opened his briefcase. He pulled out a chequebook, looked up and asked if he could buy a box for £100,000 and if so, asked how many years that amount of money would buy. Perhaps it was the expression on my face that prompted him to explain why he was so anxious to do this massive deal.

'I need to shift money quickly and this is a good investment. It's unlikely that as a company we shall be using it too often, so please feel free to use it on the occasions we are not.'

Now alarm bells did ring and as soon as I could, I used my good friend Tony Jewitt, head of a company called ICC, to check out this gentleman's company. All was well thank goodness.

I hadn't been so stunned since a visitor from America popped into Somerton Park Newport back in 1977 asking me if his company, Force For Fitness, could take the whole of the perimeter wall at the infamous 'Railway End' and paint the company's logo on it for £3,000. I resisted the temptation to punch the air in delight. I remained as calm as I possibly could under the circumstances. I had a quick conversation with the club's accountant about discounted cash flows and we struck a deal for 12 years.

I waited for the cheque to clear before ringing the chairman. 'Chairman, I hope this will help. I've sold a box for £100,000 and the money has cleared the system.'

'Well done Mike.' That was all he said.

The next occasion I felt that the club was near to the brink was when the Vice-Chairman, Geoff Richardson, rang to ask me if I could do a deal on the catering side whereby the caterers put in the kitchens thus saving the club £300,000. A series of meetings with various catering companies took place. Some were not in a position to put money in for kitchens, others were skimming so much off the profit to cover their investment that there was little or nothing left for the club. After careful consideration I recommended Letherby and Christopher. This was agreed by the board. They allowed the club to make a good profit on private and ground catering to the extent that I viewed their investment in the kitchen equipment as a franchise right only. When the club changed hands and Irving Scholar became Chairman, he heavily criticised my decision to go with Letherby and Christopher saying that the long term contract given to them was something he would never have entered into. On reading this I was reminded of the old Chinese proverb: 'Walk a mile in my shoes before you judge me'. What was even more ironic was the fact that here was a man who subsequently cocked up the finances of the club to the extent that they were on the brink of going out of business. The deal with Letherby and Christopher saved our bacon and meant that we could start to provide hospitality in line with the high standards we had set ourselves.

Commercially the club was thrusting ahead but I was aware of some resentment felt by other members of staff due to the fact that the department was now employing more people than the rest of the non-playing staff. Fortunately I had the full support of the board and every new project that was put before them got the green light. This included the launch of a TV and radio advertising programme using Saatchi & Saatchi as our agents. Even now I can see the furrowed brow of the directors when I had completed my sales pitch with the immortal words 'We will, yet again gentlemen, be seen as innovators'. My reference embraced the signing of Ardiles and Villa. Once again I believed that it was due to the success of the commercial department that gave the board the confidence to go the extra mile with the Argentineans and would also win the day with our advertising campaign.

My contact at Saatchi was Alex Fynn. Soon after that board meeting we sat down and began to devise a storyline for TV advertising. We produced story boards and scheduled the campaign for the start of the 1983–1984 season. Our sole aim was to increase gates and we estimated that during the three months of heavy advertising that home gates improved by 8 percent. Equally as important was the fact that Spurs was spearheading an advertising campaign the likes of which soccer had not seen before. The eyes of the football world were upon us.

We were ridiculed by some chairmen and directors of fellow First Division clubs. However they got short shrift from me when I was questioned about the campaign. True to form the first question they asked was about the cost. No one asked me about the potential benefits.

The TV campaign featured the team running out of the tunnel at White Hart Lane followed by hundreds of fans. The tag line being, 'Join the throng of new supporters at Tottenham'. The procession of players and fans was headed by Mrs Ridlington and her family, closely followed by Peter Cook. Mrs Ridlington became a local hero and within a few weeks was not only being asked to open new shops in Haringey, but match sponsors demanded her attendance. The TV campaign was supported by bus back and radio promotion.

The commercials shown weeks before the first game of the season did the trick. Coventry City, not the most glamorous of visitors, opened our campaign at White Hart Lane and we expected a gate of 30,000. In total 35,500 turned up.

Out of the blue I was asked if the club could do anything about the pre-season tours that had become a farce because they were normally organised by an agent who also represented players. The board resented this fact. It was not a job I wanted to see end up on my desk. So many things can go wrong with pre-season tours. In an effort to retain the status quo, I wrote a report, somewhat tongue in cheek, explaining that the only way to conduct these tours properly was through a bona fide travel agent. I didn't stop there. I suggested that as the club had premises right outside the ground that had remained empty for years, that we could convert one of them and turn it into a travel shop.

Can you believe it? The report was accepted and I was told to get on with the refurbishment of the building, appoint staff and open Spurs Travel as soon as possible. This meant an application to join ABTA and IATA (the relevant bodies covering holidays, travel, and flights). The Chairman of ABTA was the owner of Tottenham Travel, a rival company one mile from the ground. Expecting some resistance, or at best a long delay in our application being considered and passed, it came as a complete surprise to me that our application seemed to be expressed to the extent that we got our ABTA within one month.

Back at the ranch, chaos reigned. Our allocation of FA Cup Final tickets had arrived. The team had successfully navigated their way to Wembley disposing of QPR, Hull City, Coventry City, Exeter City and Wolves en route. Spurs played the semi final against Wolves at Hillsborough on 11th April 1981. It was a nerve tingling affair. Wolves were up for it, as they say, and had managed a draw in the earlier league meeting between the clubs. But then Spurs, 2–1 up and looking confidently towards another Wembley visit were rocked by an awful refereeing decision by a Welshman! Ex-World Cup referee, Clive Thomas, pointed to the penalty spot after Glenn Hoddle had brought down Kenny Hibbitt a good two yards outside the box. Thomas, waving protests aside and strutting around the penalty area with indignation etched all over his face, did not even consult the linesman. The linesman was in a far better position to see what had really happed as he was in line with play, not 10 yards behind.

Glenn Hoddle was an intelligent player and, despite criticism from his manager Keith Burkinshaw that he was not aggressive enough, had raced 40 yards back to tackle Hibbitt. Well I say tackle him, in reality it was more of a tap on the heel. The Wolves player fell and rolled over in true Italian style. They converted the penalty and both sides had to meet at Highbury for a replay.

Two years later Thomas visited me at Tottenham touting for business for his cleaning company. I was not sure that I wanted to meet him as I was not a fan of his petulant style of refereeing and would find it difficult to keep my thoughts to myself, certainly in respect of his mistake at Hillsborough. We met, as after all, business is business as they say. I didn't waste the opportunity, however, to pop the question. Did he make a mistake that day? All he would say was that if he could do it all again he would have consulted his linesman first.

We thrashed Wolves 3–0 in the replay with Ricky Villa scoring another wonder goal. Perhaps Clive The Whistle had done us a favour after all!

I met Kenny Hibbitt at Cardiff City some years later. I asked him if he felt that Thomas had made a mistake by awarding the penalty when the tackle was two yards outside the box. Kenny laughed and said, 'Four yards, I dived the rest.'

Clive Thomas became infamous on the World Cup scene when he blew his whistle for the end of play just as Brazil had taken a corner. The subsequent cross was converted into a goal. Doesn't that tell all about Mr Thomas' refereeing abilities? I know that it is a very difficult job and one that I must admit would be beyond me, but the game is about players and not the man in the middle. This is a fact sometimes lost on these prima donnas who are capable of ruining a good game by their spotlight mentality. This is not meant to be an attack on referees because the vast majority understand the game.

The last league match of the 1980–1981 campaign was against West Bromwich Albion at the Hawthorns. The drama that followed that 4–2 defeat nearly split the players from the board on a permanent basis.

I had negotiated a deal with Tesco's worth £50,000. It included the facility for Tesco to cover the open topped bus with their advertising. The bus would drive through Tottenham if and when we had won the cup. Players, as they always manage to do, heard about the deal and refused to play in the final unless they had a share of the sponsorship monies. In the boardroom at West Brom after the last league match before the final, the chairman asked me what could be done to prevent any embarrassment. My view was that the players *would* play and that they were using the importance of the occasion to blackmail the club. I arranged for a schoolroom across the road from the Hawthorns to be used for a meeting with Ossie Ardiles and Steve Perryman, representing the players, together with the Chairman and myself. The players were adamant and there was little doubt that they were being fired up by an agent, a recent breed of pariah at the time that saw football as an easy touch. The players wanted all the 'bus' money on the basis that they got us to the final. The club took the view that the commercial department had raised it so the club had a right to keep it. Stalemate ensued. The players left the table without any progress being made. The Chairman was beside himself.

I called a meeting with the players' representative for the following Monday. Their representative turned out to be 'Monster, Monster agent' Eric Hall. He walked into my office sporting a huge cigar and a cheery smile. We sized each other up then went into battle. I threatened to get Tesco to divert their sponsorship into another area, Eric claiming that the players could not go to Wembley in the right frame of mind if this matter was not resolved. Well that was a move in the right direction. At least they were going to play! He took a big puff on his stogie, accompanied by a huge grin, and then said the words, 'We'll have to see what we can do Mike,' before he disappeared through the blue haze of his finest Cuban cigar.

Coincidentally the club was being asked to approve the sales of the record *Ossie's Going to Wembley* in the club shop. The record was zooming up the charts having been released just five days earlier but as yet had not been put in the club shop. Eric was conscious of this and knew that it represented an Achilles heel for the players. The club agreed to put the record in the shop in return for keeping the commercial proceeds from the Tesco adverts on the victory bus.

Another crisis loomed on the horizon. This one was on a Richter scale of 10 compared to the Tesco fiasco. The ticket office was preparing for the distribution of Cup Final tickets. There were no computers in those days so it was a matter of all hands to the wheel. My one and only visit to the ticket office during this hectic period filled me with horror. There was cash and cheques on the floor, some hanging out of drawers and every nook and cranny seemed to occupy a cheque with a hand written note and ticket requirements scribbled on it. The ticket office had lost control. Season ticket holders would receive preference of course for Cup Final tickets. The remainder of the 25,000 were to be sold on application to supporters.

Mick Pouncett, the ticket office Manager, was a serious man and it was a challenge for me to break him out of what can only be described as a permanent depressive mood that seemed to envelop him when ticketing became a problem. Remember this was a time when Spurs would regularly get crowds of 40,000. With all the tickets being manually processed it was no surprise that mistakes occurred with Mick suffering as a consequence. But I was not prepared for what happened two days after they started to allocate tickets to season ticket holders.

Mick's office was next to mine. On this particular morning he came into my office, shut the door behind him, and with tears in his eyes he asked me if he could have a drink. Now Mick was not a drinker so the request was a bolt out of the blue. I poured him a double whisky and placed it on the edge of the desk. At this point he put his head in his hands and broke down and cried. The poor lad had duplicated the sale of a whole block of seats and in doing so had oversold to season ticket holders to the tune of 600 tickets. I was the first person he was breaking the news to and that in itself was a surprise as we were never close in our working relationship. Perhaps he thought that as I was the current Golden Bollocks that he could rely on me to talk to the directors on his behalf and get them to understand the invidious position that both he and the club were in.

I was extremely worried about Mick. He was in no fit state to carry on. I took it upon myself to arrange for him to be taken home. I consoled him just a little by telling him that I would speak to the chairman.

Diving into action, we managed to retrieve 60 percent of the doubles and reduce the number left for allocation to supporters in order to rectify the situation. Many regular punters were up in arms, but our options were severely limited. We didn't see Mick again.

11

RICKY PROVES THE ART OF DRIBBLING IS FAR FROM DEAD

It was Saturday 9th May 1981; the venue was Wembley; the occasion was the FA Cup Final, Spurs versus Manchester City. With a 1-1 final score, the highlights of the game included Tommy Hutchison, the City player scoring for both teams putting city ahead with a diving header and then deflecting a Hoddle free kick into his own net. The other highlight was when Ricardo Villa was substituted and trudged forlornly off the pitch and down the tunnel. His head was bowed and he fought back the tears. The replay was the following Thursday.

Desperately wanting Spurs to win the first game, I was not completely disappointed at the draw because that gave me an opportunity to actually *enjoy* the replay. It is hard to believe when I say that I cannot remember too much of the first game. I remember that Neil Kinnock sat in front of me as he had a rather heated discussion with a gentlemen sat one row in front. The man allowed his young son to utter a generous sprinkling of profanities much to the annoyance of Kinnock who threatened to knock the man's block off!

We successfully managed to wine and dine 100 executives before the game and safely deposited them in their seats. The rest of the day was a complete mish-mash in terms of what I can and cannot remember. Perhaps it was too much for this greenhorn from Wales to take in? I'd gone from Newport County to Tottenham and then on to Wembley for a Cup Final!

The replay was far more memorable. Incidentally it was the first ever replay to be played at Wembley. The result was 3–2 to the Lilywhites with *that* goal from Ricky Villa going down in the annals of football as one of the best goals ever seen at Wembley. Let me take you back to the Monday of that week. I received a frantic call from Keith Birkenshaw, 'Mike, get down here quickly, can you?'

On entering Keith's office I found Ricky sat in a chair with his legs sprawled out in front of him, head bowed.

'Mike, Ricky's upset because I took him off at Wembley. He wants me to tear up his contract as he is going back to Argentina to farm his cattle. Is there anything you can do?'

'What do you want Ricky?' I asked

'I want to go home, Keith not play me again.'

'Look you big fucker, I'm putting you in the team for the replay,' was the manager's response. Keith's promise was not entirely met with the enthusiasm he expected.

'Maybe Keith, but my head is not okay. I let people of Argentina down.'

'Well what are you going to do about it Ricky? Because I'm running out of patience.'

Villa looked across at me. 'Mike, any chance of me having Jaguar like Ossie?'

'Yes Ricky. I'll get it here before Thursday.' Bloody hell! What have I said now? One Jaguar for Ossie was hard work; another for Ricky was going to be more difficult.

'Okay Keith, I play Wembley.'

That was not the end of the story. The following day Dr Brian Curtin the club doctor came into my office for his usual chat. He was a terrific guy, in his late 50s at the time and enjoyed life to the full. He also spoke his mind openly and frankly even if it offended. That 'quality' nearly got him the sack. At a rugby club dinner where he was guest speaker he 'let the cat out of the bag' by suggesting that Spurs were about to be taken over by Scholar and his friends and that Sidney Wale was selling his shares to Scholar. This was at a time when no formal moves to obtain control had taken place.

We talked about the Cup Final and I told him how upset Ricky Villa was. The doc admitted that Ricky had been to see him and asked for some help before the replay. I was under no disillusion about the type of help he was referring too. Brian said that he would sort him out before the game.

'Mike, they are going to be placebos, he won't know any different.'

As Ricky rounded the last defender at Wembley and slotted the ball into the back of the net for that 'miracle' goal, I immediately wondered if those tablets had done the trick. We will never know. In my opinion it was Ricky's natural ability that led to that amazing feat, not any perceived outside interference. The result was 3–2 to Spurs. The FA Cup was ours and it was time to celebrate.

By winning the FA cup in 1981 we qualified to enter the European Cup Winners Cup the following season. There was no better time, I thought on reflection, to be opening Spurs Travel. The day after our memorable FA Cup Final replay success against Manchester City, I had to interview prospective travel shop managers. The interviews were to take place in my office and I was feeling like shit as I hadn't gone to bed until 4.00 am. This was understandable after the celebrations. The problem was that I didn't have any sleep at all despite being pretty well tanked up after attending the cup winning celebrations in the club restaurant. The surfeit of wine should have seen me sleeping like a top. A remarkable event took place the previous evening that led to me having to take the FA Cup home to Hertford. As the restaurant was being cleared of players (the directors left it to us at 1.00 am), Albert Thorn, the restaurant manager, turned to me as he was switching off the lights and asked me who was going to take care of the trophy still sat in the middle of the top table.

'Well, you lock it away Albert.'

'Not bloody likely Mike,' was his very quick response.

'Look Albert, I can't get back into the club as I haven't got the keys to the gates. Anyway, I have a taxi waiting outside to take me home to Hertford.'

Albert's blank stare suggested that this little conversation had come to an end. He certainly was not going to be held responsible for looking after this valuable trinket. So we put the cup back in its wooden box, locked it up and carried it to my taxi. The taxi driver opened the cab door and I stepped in, placing the wooden box and its valuable contents on the back seat. As we set off he quickly turned his head around and in a laughing manner asked me if the box contained the FA Cup. What could I say? No, it's a coffin for a midget. On the basis that black cab drivers are generally speaking an honest bunch, I decided to own up and confirm that, yes it was.

'If I can touch the cup sir, you can travel free to Hertford.'

He touched the cup and I caressed it all the way home, bid the driver goodnight and walked up the path to my house. My wife was fast asleep in bed. The cup had to stay with me at all times.

It did. As I climbed into bed with the FA Cup out of its box and resting alongside the bed, my wife started to mumble almost incoherent words that women do when awoken and in a half state of consciousness.

'What's the time? You've been drinking. I hope you didn't drive home like that, etc, etc.'

I was once told that the best remedy to get the girls straight back to sleep in the early hours was to utter the words, 'Bloody hell. I feel sexy'. But all I could manage was a pitiful reference to what it was I had next to me.

'You should see what my hand is resting on darling.' That innocently did the trick.

The next day at White Hart Lane I had to conduct the travel shop manager interviews. Having taken possession of the most coveted trophy in the world, I had to keep it close to my side at all times. This included putting it in my office during the interviews. The first interview was at 9.30 am. I placed the cup on the corner of my desk in all its glory. I could hardly contain my excitement at having the best known trophy in the world sat resplendent on my desk. The first candidate was a lad called Greg Mould (he got the job by the way). His eyes popped out of their sockets as he looked admiringly at the trophy. He was a Spurs season ticket holder and seemed totally hypnotised by the sight of this magnificent artefact.

'Can I touch it?' Here we go again, I thought.

We gave the job of keeping the trophy safe to a Welshman called Gary who was also the club's caretaker. He kept a book that recorded the days the cup was taken out on show and he was always accompanied by a security guard. Without going into too much detail, Gary got his marching orders after a national newspaper reported that he had taken the cup to a working men's club in the Tottenham area one evening. Matters got out of hand to the extent that someone shit in the FA Cup. It was a bloody sacrilege. I was ashamed to be Welsh with plonkers like him embarrassing the club.

I used the FA Cup very sparingly. On one occasion I took it along to a sponsorship convention at the Royal Lancaster Hotel in London. I was asked to deliver a talk on the methods that football was using to increase its support and to encourage corporate sponsorship. My problem was that 80 percent of the audience was Japanese. They understood English, but would they appreciate the glory of the cup that I had originally planned to put on a blue velvet covered table to the right of the platform? I decided to try something entirely different.

The cup *was* placed on the blue velvet covered table. Then, with the help of a new security guard, I covered it with a black bin liner. At the appropriate time I planned to lift the bin liner off carefully and simultaneously utter these words, 'And gentlemen, this [pointing to the cup] is the most famous trophy in the world of sport.' I did this and there was a three-second silence, during which time I became convinced that I had made a bloody fool of myself on the basis that these guys had no idea what the hell this piece of silverware meant. Then suddenly, dozens of Japanese businessmen leapt forward onto the platform producing miniature cameras from their inside pockets and I spent the next 30 minutes waiting for them to finish their photo shoot.

The summer before the new season was frantic. Spurs Travel opened for business. I hired planes and buses ready for our re-entry into Europe via the Cup Winners Cup. Our opponents in the first round were Ajax and we were drawn away in the first leg. We expected 5,000 fans to travel. The reality of organising supporters' trips abroad certainly hit home when I enquired about chartering planes to take us to Amsterdam. At the same time I had to book a plane for the players and staff. As we were going to use a 120-seat plane there was room on the team plane for executives to travel. We had no problem filling the plane and it worked like a dream, apart from a little trauma, which I will come to a little later.

Buses were no problem. We hired 60 buses each of them carrying 43 passengers. The aircraft cost £8,000 each. I chartered two plus the team plane. What I did not realise was that the hirers were responsible for relaying everything about the flight whilst on board. There were no lovely legs stewardesses to do that for us. So I put on my best BBC voice and informed the passengers on the executive plane that we were travelling at 530 miles per hour at an altitude of 28,000 feet and we were expected to land at Schiphol in 35 minutes. I am sure that there was no real necessity for me to go that far but what the hell.

I managed to get a supporter called John Harris safely to Amsterdam. That was an achievement in itself. John had not flown for 30 years having had a bad experience in the air. Weeks before we travelled, John asked me if I would join him for breakfast at the Savoy and travel to Luton with him for the 1.30

pm flight on the day of departure. This was hardly convenient, but as John was 'off the top shelf' as a supporter to the extent that his spare room at home had become a shrine to Spurs, I took the view that this was a little sacrifice on my part so we met.

After breakfast we went to his car. As he opened the boot all I could see was an array of pill bottles. John took doses from each in preparation for his flight. I warned the captain before take off that we had an extremely nervous passenger on board. I sat next to John on the plane and took the view that if I kept talking to him through take off then we stood a chance of him not freaking out. There was no problem. The 40-minute flight was uneventful. This is more than I can say for the return journey. On board the plane on the return journey there was laughter and singing as we had disposed of Ajax with an emphatic 3–1 win. John seemed quite happy and settled as we took off. The fact that we had taken off late because of fog didn't seem to bother him.

Shortly after take off I was called to the deck to visit the captain. He asked me to explain over the public address system to my passengers, who included the team and backroom staff, that because of fog we were going to be diverted to East Midlands rather than Luton. On returning to my seat next to John, I was aware that he had pulled of his tie and was busily undoing the top buttons of his shirt. Within a minute he was undoing his seat belt, slumped to the floor and started writhing about in a fit. A stewardess tried to restrain him. I went on the PA system again and asked for the club doctor to come forward. Leaning over John the doc shouted, 'Get a large brandy!' Off rushed the stewardess and she quickly returned with a brandy bowl full of Courvoisier. 'Shall I give it to him doctor?' she enquired.

'Bloody hell no, it's for me not him,' cried the doc.

Dundalk was our next opponent in the Cup Winners Cup and after a draw in Ireland we beat them 1–0 in London to move on to the next round. It was at this time that I appointed an assistant commercial manager. The workload was immense and cracks were beginning to appear in the department. The board fully supported my proposition that I seek a number two. Mike Rollo was not necessarily the best applicant, but he was the most enthusiastic. He's still there after 23 years after taking over from me in 1984.

The next round of the Cup Winners Cup matched us with Eintracht Frankfurt. I sat down with Rollo and we discussed the sponsorship of the match against Eintracht that was due to be played at White Hart Lane on 3rd March 1982. I gave Mike an exercise that was pretty boring but it brought a result that was to impact the club for the next 10 years. I asked Mike to identify the German companies that had an office in London. He scurried away and came back with a list that contained the names of BMW, Volkswagen, Thyssen, and any company that had German connections. Mike beavered away. I could hear the sighs and groans emanating from the office next door as he hit disappointment after disappointment. On his way home that evening Mike popped into the pub that graced the corner of the ground on Tottenham High Road. His reward for sealing off a not too successful day was just one beer. He asked for a Holsten Pils. As he stared forlornly at his glass, he noticed that the bottle that had been left half emptied alongside had a London address on the label. He asked the pub manager if Holsten was a German Company. The manager said that they were and that they had a distribution office in the city. Mike made the call next morning.

Excitedly Mike came rushing into my office the next day. 'They want to see us Mike!'

'When?'

'This afternoon.'

We trotted off to the city to meet their managing director.

Alan Bridgett, Holstens' managing director was a delightful man who wasted no time telling us that as a company they were looking at their sponsorship opportunities for the medium term future as they felt that sponsorship of horse racing was having a limited appeal. They had poured £4,000,000 into that sport and were not entirely sure that continuing sponsorship would give them the full value they were seeking. He agreed to sponsor the Eintracht match.

The evening of the game saw the stadium packed with 38,172 spectators who saw the Lilywhites win 2–0. In the sponsors' room there was great delight and celebrating. The Holsten party were having a great time and when the players came up to join the celebs after the game the evening was rounded off perfectly.

It was during my trip home after that game that a 'near death' incident shook me to the core. It was a cold night, but I never imagined for one moment that the A10 road to Hertford from Tottenham would harbour a sinister component – black ice. I was not travelling particularly fast on the dual carriageway stretch north of Cheshunt when suddenly, without any warning, the Audi

I was driving took on a mind of its own and started to weave all over the road. There was a light sprinkling of snow on the embankment where the car decided to end the journey. I sat in horror as the car started to slide back down the embankment coming to rest in the gulley at the side of the road. Flashing yellow lights could be seen in my rear view mirror. A breakdown lorry pulled up behind me. The driver came to the window and asked if I was okay. Although I was in a state of shock, I was able to explain what had happened. He took a look at the car and was able to report no visible damage.

Just before I slowly drove off he said, 'You are bloody lucky mate. We have just been at an accident one mile back where the driver was taken to hospital after his car did the same of yours but hit a bridge parapet. I don't think he is going to make it'.

On the back of the huge success with Holsten at the Eintracht game I decided to go for the jugular a few days later. Exactly one month after that great win against the Germans, we were due to play Manchester United at Old Trafford. One of my main tasks at the time was to secure a shirt sponsor, the first ever for the club. Some of the first division clubs had sponsors and we didn't want to be last out of the blocks so I approached Holsten with the following proposition. If they gave us £25,000 for the privilege of putting their name on our shirts for the Manchester United game as a one-off (which was going out live on TV) then perhaps they would consider doing a deal for three seasons. Once again Holsten agreed.

We had three weeks to prepare the shirts to carry the Holsten name for the TV game. I gave Mike Rollo sole responsibility for overseeing the production of the shirts and their safe keeping until worn by the players at Old Trafford. As it was a midweek game, the players travelled up on the day. I passed the new kit as satisfactory the previous evening and we left the training ground on the team coach followed by Mr Rollo who, as directed, was keeping a close eye on the kit. He was instructed to follow the coach, walk alongside the kit man and the coach driver as they off loaded at the ground in Manchester and actually go into the dressing room and observe the kit being hung up. At the same time I stressed to him the importance of keeping a low profile as the playing side staff were not really interested in the success or not of this exciting new commercial venture. To them a shirt was a shirt.

Meanwhile I was entertaining Alan Bridgett and his top

executives from Holsten at the Piccadilly Hotel in Manchester. In my briefcase I carried the draft contract for shirt sponsorship for the next three seasons. Surely nothing could go wrong.

On arrival at the ground we were ushered up to the Executive Club where the Holsten directors, Spur's secretary Peter Day and I were left chatting away whilst holding glasses of Holsten lager. I am not a beer drinker, but on that night I could have merrily got pissed on the German brew. Suddenly from nowhere up popped Mike Rollo.

'Have a drink Mike,' I said.

'No, not yet Mike,' said Rollo

'Are you okay Mike? Because you look very pale.'

'Can we talk privately because there's a problem with the shirts,' whispered Rollo.

'Christ Mike, what's happened?'

'I've stayed with the shirts all day, honest Mike, I even helped Johnny Wallis (the kit man) put them up on the pegs in the dressing room. But the number 8 shirt hasn't got Holsten on it.'

'That's Ossie's shirt Mike. You told me that you had checked every single shirt that left London.'

'I did.' By now Rollo's face was a patchwork quilt of colours. On the edge of tears he exclaimed, 'Will I lose my job?'

'Lose your bloody job? You will be close to losing your bloody life it this isn't sorted out!'

'I'll check again,' he said before rushing of to the dressing room.

He came back after five minutes to inform me that he had found a solution to the problem. With the help of Mike Varney, the club's physiotherapist, they proceeded to write HOLSTEN on the shirt with a black felt pen. Ardiles was stretched out on the treatment table with Rollo's hands holding his shirt taut while Varney, black felt tip in hand, began to copy the word Holsten onto the pure white fabric of the number 8 shirt.

'Mike,' I said, 'it won't work it's fucking raining out there, get your arse in gear son.'

I offered to go down to the dressing rooms with him to find another solution to the problem. My own problem was that the Holsten crew were beginning to suspect there was something amiss. I stayed with them. I explained that because the two sets of shirts, one old without a sponsor, and one with the sponsor's name on it were brought up, that mistakenly one of the old shirts had been put out. It was a load of rubbish but I was playing for time. A handsome sponsorship package of £750,000 was at stake.

At this very point Peter Day, a close friend of Birkenshaw, let me in on the scam. He delivered the news with some relish. 'Mike, they're winding Rollo up. They have the proper shirt in the kit bag. Do you know what they are doing now? They're pinning a piece of cardboard to Ossie's shirt and writing Holsten on it with a black felt pen. Rollo's going spare. Keith [the manager] has just told him to fuck off from the dressing room as he wants to do his team talk. Ossie's going ape shit and everyone in the dressing room is screaming at Rollo to get out.'

Rollo returned to the room. 'You'll have my resignation in the morning Mike.'

'Look, stop feeling sorry for yourself. Get down there in the tunnel and watch the teams come out. Check that the temporary logo is well and truly fixed on Ossie's shirt before the kick off even it means that you warm up with him.' Wicked I know, but we are all 'baptised' in one way or another in a new job.

I returned to the Holsten group, explained the situation to them and although feeling some sympathy for Mike Rollo, the breaking of the good news caused everyone to crease up with laughter. We took our places in the directors' box in time to see the teams come out. Mike Rollo looked very anxious as he stood alongside the players' tunnel. Ossie trotted out. Rollo realised that all was well and turned to the directors' box, fist in the air with a smile as wide as the pitch itself. After he had regained his self control he looked up to the directors' box and I am sure he mouthed the words, 'You bastards.'

We lost the game 2–0 but won the sponsorship for three years.

Barcelona knocked us out of the Cup Winners Cup which was hardly surprising taking into account the fact that we had already booked another place in the domestic Cup Final having beaten Leicester City in the semis two weeks earlier. It was during this time that I met a man called John Marshall. Marshall had been introduced to me by Steve Perryman the Spurs captain some weeks earlier. They both had a mutual admiration for each other. John, because he saw Steve as the epitome of a true pro, and Steve as he was most impressed with the fact that John had produced the film *The Greatest* in which Cassius Clay had portrayed himself in a bio telling the story of his incredible life.

John had a dream. The dream was to introduce American Football to the UK big time. He outlined his plans, which included a visit to America with me to meet Pete Roselle the commissioner for the NFL, probably the most influential man in American Football at that time. I was cautious because the project, if viable, would take a huge chunk of my staff's time and effort to make it happen.

As a matter of courtesy to John and Steve, I took the project to the board. Once again, quite amazingly, the project was rubber-stamped. Although the board was not exactly over the moon about the proposal, nevertheless it wanted to examine the possibility of once again leading the way.

The Cup Final paired us with second division Queens Park Rangers. I was fairly confident that on this occasion a replay four days after the original game would not be necessary. So with that in mind, I scheduled the trip to the States for the Tuesday following the Cup Final date of Saturday 22nd May. The QPR game ended in a draw. It was sod's law I suppose.

Marshall was bordering on neurotic during the flight across the pond. He was jumpy, nervy, arrogant and generally not good company. I wondered if he was on drugs. On arrival at Kennedy Airport he immediately called up a limo and had a protracted conversation with the driver culminating with the passing over of a roll up fag. The driver, having taken his first puff, uttered, 'That's good shit man'. I was a small town lad from the valleys. My only experience of the after-effects of a drag was fighting off sickness after Peachy's Turf cigarette back in 1951.

The ride from Kennedy Airport to our hotel in the city was fairly quiet. At Brooklyn Bridge Marshall bought four bunches of flowers off the guy straddling the road markings. Marshall got the taxi to the hotel at a discounted rate due to the good shit he had handed the driver. We spent a quiet first night in preparation for our meeting at NFL headquarters the next morning.

Next morning over breakfast, slowly but very surely John passed on details of what he was planning to achieve at this meeting.

'We've got eight franchise holders attending together with our consultant.'

'Consultant. What consultant John?'

'Oh! He's well known over here and if anyone can pull off a deal it's the Juice.'

On the short walk to the NFL offices my mind was a mixture of excitement and anxiety. I thought Consultant? What the hell's he on about?

At the NFL I was stunned to be introduced to the owners of Miami Dolphins, Washington Redskins, Houston Texans, Green Bay Packers, Chicago Bears, New York Giants, San Francisco 49ers, and the Pittsburgh Steelers. My first thought was 'I wonder how much this lot are worth?' This little boy from Newport really felt out of his depth. Pete Roselle opened the meeting and was very complimentary about Tottenham Hotspurs (Hotspurs? Bill Nicholson would have slaughtered him if he had been there). Pete explained to the franchisees that Spurs was a very old Soccer club back in the UK and had more history than all of their clubs put together. Then the door to the boardroom opened, all the owners stood up at once and started greeting the new arrival with calls of, 'Hi OJ!' and 'How ya doing Juice?' Marshall, seeing the quizzical look on my face, rushed over to introduce me to this tall, handsome black guy. 'Mike, this is OJ Simpson the finest running back the game has ever known.' I was still curious about the reference to 'Juice'. Later that day John explained why. 'It's quite simple Mike, OJ – orange juice, got it?'

I shook OJ by the hand and stared at him for a few seconds as I knew that this guy's face was familiar. Then the penny dropped. It wasn't his exploits on the grid that had left an impact. It was his appearances in the *Naked Gun* films that I remembered.

After two hours, with the Juice being prominent in discussions, it was decided that the Redskins and the Dolphins would be invited to play in London before the start of their new season. John, OJ and I went for a coffee a few blocks away. On route I witnessed something that was completely new to me. It was hero-worship on a bigger scale than I had ever seen before. OJ literally stopped the traffic! Yellow cab drivers pulled to a halt and ran across the busy road simply to touch him. I witnessed office workers leaning precariously out of eighth floor windows yelling out, 'We love you OJ'. I remember Bobby Moore being hero-worshipped but it was nothing like this.

Before returning to my hotel I went to the nearest book shop to buy any book mentioning OJ Simpson. I was lucky enough to find a pocket edition of NFL football that told me all I wanted to know about the Juice. OJ had invited John and me to his favourite restaurant. This meant that at some time we would presumably start talking American Football. I felt that I should go armed with at least a little information about the man. OJ played with the Buffalo Bills from 1969–1977 and was, without question, the greatest player to wear their colours. He set records galore including one the most career rushing yards (11,236) and highest career rushing average (4.7 yards per carry). He was named the NFL's Most Valuable Player three times in 1972, 1973, and 1975. He also appeared in many films including the successful *Naked Gun* movies.

I ditched the idea of reciting statistics that I had hastily learned after witnessing so called football experts trying to convince others that they were aficionados of the game only to be found wanting when questioned. On entering the chintzy restaurant at 7.00 pm with John Marshall and the Juice, we were ambushed by the maître d'. He asked OJ if he was happy to meet any admirers who happened to be in the restaurant at the time. OJ said he was happy to say hello to a few people but only after 9.00 pm. John did most of the talking. At one point OJ turned to me and asked me to explain the rudimentary rules of soccer. I was only too delighted to oblige on the condition that he would explain American Football rules. Surprisingly, he picked up the offside rule straight away. This is a rule that is not easy to explain. The use of a table napkin that John had placed out before me was a very useful aide for the purpose of explaining where the last man in defence would be positioned. OJ turned the napkin over, drew a grid and explained the basics of *his game*. I asked him where he used to play and he drew a figure of a running back. Then he drew a series of lines that crossed the diagram in many different directions. Time marched on and folk came to the table, fondly introducing themselves. I pushed the napkin in my pocket.

Later that night I received a phone call from Steve Perryman the Spurs captain. He was in the middle of celebrating the club's victory in the cup final replay and took time out to ring me.

Unfortunately OJ's napkin got lost between house moves long before OJ was arrested on 17th June 1994 on suspicion of the double murder of ex-wife Nicole Brown Simpson and her friend Ronald Goldman. I found it very hard to believe that this gentle giant was capable of treading on a fly, never mind double murder. He came across as a true gentleman, displayed humility and a great sense of humour. His trial in 1995 when charged with first degree murder on two counts was probably the trial of that century. We worked together for two weeks organising jumbo jets and making transatlantic calls to Wembley Stadium when it became apparent that White Hart Lane at Tottenham did not have sufficient 'run off' space behind the posts to accommodate

American Football. We visited a famous nightclub where Marshall openly smoked cannabis and did the rounds of his old flames. Included in one of the parties of old acquaintances was Diana Ross. Words stuck in my throat as I tried to say hello on introduction. She was beautiful.

On returning to London I reported details of the trip to the board and the general feeling was that we should see how the first match went at Wembley, try not to make a loss, but tie up the contract with Marshall in such a way that Spurs would not be disenfranchised.

The first game between the Dolphins and the Redskins attracted 40,000 people to Wembley and the event 'washed its face'.

John Marshall rang me from his hospital bed on Christmas Eve 1984. He was seriously ill. Before I could get to the hospital he died. We never entertained American Football again.

OJ continues to attract media interest. In July 2005 almost to the 10th anniversary of his trial he was involved in a skirmish with his 'on/off' girlfriend Christie Prody who slapped and scratched Simpson to the extent that the police were called. No charges were brought. Then on 16th September 2007 Simpson was arrested on two counts of robbery with a deadly weapon and two counts of assault with a deadly weapon which could lead to Simpson facing up to 30 years in a state prison. It's at times like that that I start to question my ability to successfully pigeonhole people.

12

WIND OF CHANGE BLOWS DOWN THE LANE

The 1983–1984 season was to be my last at Spurs. It started off quietly with the team winning only one game in the first six. In early September we received notification from the Football League that our scheduled game against Nottingham Forest on Sunday 1st October 1983 was to be switched to the following day to allow live televising of the game. Once again it seemed that Spurs had been given some priority. This was the first live TV game to be shown and the BBC had the honour of staging the event.

The possibility of live televising of games was causing uproar in boardrooms up and down the country. There was a fear that gates would suffer drastically. The Spurs board was genuinely concerned that the advent of live TV games would bring with it untold damage to the club's budgets. At a board meeting three weeks before the televised game, I was asked if I had any ideas of how to minimise the loss of spectators which was expected to represent as much as 20 percent of our average attendance. I came up with a plan. I suggested that we provide an extravaganza of entertainment starting at 1.00 pm and leading up to the kick off at 3.00 pm.

'How much would that cost Michael?' asked the Chairman.

'I reckon we could do it for £7,000.' This was the equivalent of 700 paying spectators at the time.

'Sounds a fair proposition to me,' was the response of the Chairman. This was rapidly supported by the rest of the board who had been subjected to alarmist views. The views suggested a gate as low as 12,000 for the televised game.

After much wheeling and dealing, the line up for the day included Chas and Dave, Warren Mitchell, the world's tallest man, fire eaters, an escapologist, and a world record attempt by

Brian Jacks the judo king to break 100 house bricks with his hand within 30 seconds. Our average gate for the previous three home games that season had been 30,000 so anything within 3,000 of that figure was acceptable.

The crowd that day was 30,596. The weather was fine and the entertainment superb, even if Alf Garnett paraded his West Ham scarf from the 20 feet by 30 feet stage built into the terracing. He gave us everything he had, he was brilliant. I particularly remember him having a go at our most fervent supporters nestled on The Shelf. I am not too sure that Forest manager Brian Clough was too impressed with what he saw as he entered the stadium pre-match. His reaction to a young fan who only wanted his autograph was one of complete disdain. Perhaps the sight of Chas and Dave performing *Rabbit, Rabbit, Rabbit* was a bit too close to home for him. Warren, in his very best 'Alf mode' hit them with 'Look, look, you might have won that bloody FA Cup a few times, but what 'appened four weeks ago, yeah, four weeks ago, here on this bloody dung heap of a ground? Let me tell you in case you've forgotten. We slaughtered you 2–0, bloody 2–0. We don't 'av bloody foreigners in our team, all white, white as the driven snow. Martin Peters only came here because he was bloody bored at West 'Am, yes bloody bored with winning. They don't call the 'ammers the academy of football for nuffing you know'. Warren had walked the fine line and stepped off the end in one piece. The Shelf loved it. Surely this was the only time that anyone had gone out and purposely tried to offend a football crowd only to find that they laughed and clapped in response, rather than turned into a violent mob. They were great and responded with their own version of *I'm forever blowing bubbles* as Alf left the stage.

At a post match press conference, the media were anxious to know if the club felt that spending a significant amount of money to bring entertainment to the ground was worth the effort. The Chairman who was hosting the conference asked me to answer that question. My reply was a simple one. 'How will we ever know? The attendance figures suggest that the money was very well spent, but if nothing else didn't the crowd have fun?'

Then Jeff Powell from the *Daily Mail* piped up with, 'It should be all about football not Chas and Dave, Alf Garnet and Houdini's'.

I got the feeling that he wanted to see the exercise fail. That would have made better copy than having to write that the project was a success. In the event he decided to ditch the story. At times these scribes reach sewer level. As Jeff is still a prominent writer I wonder if his attitudes have changed somewhat and he has accepted that the game *has* now become an event rather than just a game of football?

Spurs was in turmoil. The 'old board' were facing a Herculean task to hang on to the club. Irving Scholar, with the assistance of Paul Bobroff, was mounting a take-over bid. Bobroff had been a good supporter of the club. We benefited from his generosity on many occasions. His company, Markheath, always sponsored the Arsenal home games and they promised to take an executive box. He warned me of the consequences if the board snubbed him.

'Mike, we will win. We have enough shares now to move in.'

As a person Paul was not the easiest to relate to. He seemed a stranger to humour and never let his hair down but I liked him because he was always straight with me and supportive. This was proven when he told me that he wanted to meet the board in order to propose that he inject a considerable amount of money into the club in return for a seat on the board. I asked him to contact the chairman direct, but he was uneasy with this suggestion, as he feared there was still an anti-Jewish policy on the board. Paul asked me to approach the board and see if it was prepared to meet him.

At the next meeting I raised the subject. The facial expression on Chairman Arthur Richardson's face when I asked the question was enough to explain why Bobroff was right to feel nervous about the approach. I wanted to tell them what might happen if they refused to see him. I hesitated because I was not sure whether Bobroff and Scholar really had the shares. Rumour had it that with the help of new board member Douglas Alexiou, who was married to the Ex-Chairman's daughter, that Sidney Wale had done a deal with them. The rumours were spot on.

Bobroff invited me out for dinner the day after the board meeting. He didn't mess about and cut straight to the chase.

'What did they say Mike?'

'They're not interested Paul.'

'I'm not surprised, Mike. Look, you need to know that in anticipation of this response, we will take control of the club within two weeks.'

They were as good as their word. Spurs was due for another radical re-shaping. I sensed that the change upstairs was not going to suit me. Yes, Bobroff had said that they valued my contributions and wanted me to stay whilst others would be shown the door, but within four months I departed. The club had become insular and sterile. The turnover of staff was reaching an all time peak. The second generation of this great club had come to an end and it was facing a new era. Perhaps the change was needed, but the resulting failure of Scholar and his board to 'steady the ship' was, in a way, a testimony to the 'old masters' who had kept a disciplined crew for many years until it was time to take 'SS Tottenham Hotspur' to the breakers yard. It was past its best. Much as I liked Scholar I was becoming wary of him. On the day of the launch of the Holsten deal, I became even more wary. The deal I set up with Holsten for the major sponsorship of the club worth a healthy £250,000 per season was due to be publicly announced. The Bill Nicholson suite was crowded with journalists, radio and television reporters plus a large contingent of Holsten executives, all awaiting the breaking of the news. I sat in my office in the new West Stand collecting my papers in readiness to support the announcement that was to be made by Paul Bobroff on Scholars behalf. Suddenly Paul burst into my office and proceeded to tell me that Irving wanted us to hold back the announcement as he had found an Italian Company prepared to give the club £300,000 per year.

'No way Paul. My bloody reputation's on the line here, anyhow why hasn't Irving told us about this before?'

'I don't know Mike. Look, I'll get him on the phone.'

I only heard Bobroff's responses to the points put by Scholar who was sitting at his home in Monaco.

'Mike, he really wants to hold back the deal.'

'Okay Paul, I'm off, that's it for me. *You* go and tell the Board of Holsten the deal's off.'

'Wait a minute Mike, don't do anything silly.'

'Hey Paul, it's not me being silly. Holsten is a fine company and I believe that we will be partners for a long time. [The deal with Holsten lasted nine years, the second longest sponsorship deal in football.] It's Irving that's being silly, but if that is the way he wants to do business so be it, he's the gaffer. I just cannot work like that. He knew that I had closed the deal three weeks ago so why didn't he say anything before?'

Bobroff asked me to leave the room for a minute. I imagined that he was straight back on the phone to Irving. He came out a few minutes later and told me to carry on and sign the Holsten deal.

What a preparation for a press conference! I felt that we were taking a huge step forward with an excellent partner. Scholar had put my reputation on the line and at the same time lacked any sensitivity towards the good name of the club. His actions were very surprising as this was a man who once said that he would die for the club and would never do anything harmful. It came as no surprise therefore, to learn that team manager Keith Burkinshaw subsequently left the club after complaining about Scholar's interference with team selection. I took the view that it was natural for a supporter who made it to the top of his club and had salivated at the sight of Hoddle and company turning on the Spurs magic to want some input into team matters. He planned to take Tottenham into the stock market by circumventing FA rule 34, a rule that was introduced to safeguard football from being used as a means to make vast profits and to asset strip clubs. Rule 34 limited a director's income, safeguarded club grounds and preserved clubs as sporting institutions. Scholar won the day and rule 34 was scrapped leading the way for an even shadier bunch of characters than some of the butcher, baker and the candlestick makers who previously had sat at the head of boardroom tables. The poor man's ballet was dying. Punters were asked to pay opera seat prices for a cramped plastic bucket seat that could leave them permanently disabled. There was little concern for the historic fan as the TV monies began to mount.

After Burkinshaw, there followed a host of managers including George Graham. Oh to have been a fly on the wall when that decision was made! Imagine the scene:

Yuppy Chairman to fellow directors: *'Well gentlemen, you know my penchant for details. After a short study I have come to the conclusion that we have not had too much success with recent managers. Christian [Christian Gross Manager 1997–1998] only managed 10 wins in 29 games. Gerry [Gerry Francis 1994–1997] only managed 56 wins out of 146 games, little Ossie managed 20 wins out of 65, Peter Shreeve managed 23 wins out of 60 and Terry [Terry Venables 1987–1991] managed 67 wins out of 165! Perhaps we need to grasp the nettle and go for someone completely different. Someone the fans can immediately take to. Someone they can see taking us back to our former glory. Now let's see, any ideas chaps?'*

At this point, the five legged chair that was provided to stop any of the city brigade running the club falling asleep after a heavy lunch with their stockbroker, rocked into action with the occupier making his recommendation. *'Chairman, that Graham George feller, he's out of work isn't he?'*

'Worked in the game before according to my little nephew. He used to work somewhere in North London apparently, so he should know his way around'

The Chairman with a surprised look on his face follows up with: *'Any other suggestions guys? Look I've got a meeting in the next half an hour with the planning officer to see if we can re-locate to Hackney Marshes, so if there are no further suggestions then I'll make an approach for this Graham George chappie. I'll leave it to the secretary to inform the media. Now to the last item of the agenda, the removal of The Shelf on the East Stand and the re-building of the East Stand'.*

Most of the new board were too young or ignorant to the fact that back in 1974 the club appointed ex-Gooner Terry Neill. The fans reaction to that appointment still reverberated around White Hart Lane when I joined in 1978. Was it any surprise that Mr Graham's appointment caused a huge furore?

Looking back through the managerial records of the club, it comes as a great surprise to me that one of the more successful periods in the history of the club was between 1908 and 1913 when *the directors* picked the team. Over that period the club won 99 games out of 231 comparing favourably with the best of the latter day managers.

Some criticism was meted in my direction by Irving in his biography *Behind Closed Doors*. He suggested that the three week tour of America and Canada conducted by Irving, Peter Day and myself looking at their sports marketing produced nothing in terms of new ideas. We visited Florida and talked to Gordon Jago who was spearheading five-a-side football in that region. We took in a game of baseball at the NY Mets. We looked at new stadia in Vancouver, San Diego and Toronto. We held endless meetings with marketing people. We even looked at the golf scene staying at the Saddlebrooke Club in Tampa. Yes we did take in a game of golf. Peter decided to leave the course at the 14th when he was chased by a baby alligator that had come out of the lake nearby for a spot of sunbathing. In his book Scholar suggests that Peter and I learned very little on that excursion. The day before departure back to the UK, we met Irving for dinner in Tampa for a round up. He asked us both to produce a report overnight indicating what changes we would like to see at Spurs. After Irving had been whisked off at 9.00 pm for a 'meeting' Peter and I discussed what we should put in our report. After a couple of hours Peter announced that he wasn't going to bother as whatever he said would be consigned to the waste paper basket. I thought that this was slightly cynical and told Peter that I was going to attempt to put my thoughts down on paper. I handed Irving my report the next morning. He asked me what, if anything, was the most important element of my report. Putting the marketing aspects to one side I stated that the single most important action he could take was to reduce the board of directors to two. Whether that was him and Paul Bobroff or him and Frank Sinclair or Douglas Alexiou wasn't important.

Peter Day had called it right. Irving gave my report short shrift.

Whatever Peter and I learned on the American trip was 100 percent more than Irving as he linked up with us on just three occasions during the three weeks we were there! I will not go into detail of what it was that denied us the privilege of having more of Irving's company, suffice to say that it was far more enjoyable than the city hopping conducted by Peter and myself!

I approached Alan Sugar at Amstrad in 1981. Amstrad were operating out of a warehouse in Tottenham and looked an ideal choice as a shirt sponsor for a number of reasons. The first reason was their location, the second reason was their emerging prominence in a new market and the third reason was that their logo had only seven letters on it that would look very neat on a shirt.

Alan Sugar was not available when I went for my appointment. I was introduced to his marketing director. I wish I could say that the meeting was fruitful. The only offer I could extract was a deal that produced a cash sum of £50,000 per year plus 10 percent of the selling price of all products sold to Spurs season ticket holders or any Spurs contacts. At the time Amstrad was finding its feet and the offer was speculative to say the least. On reflection perhaps I should have taken the gamble.

The listing of Spurs on the Stock Exchange and the creation of Tottenham Hotspur PLC was a first for the club and was engineered by Irving. He managed to gain a significant interest in the club, despite the apparent impossibility of purchasing shares without the approval of directors. The issuing of shares in Spurs was based on the assumption that on the first day of trading, the shares would open above £1. Some 'experts' suggested that on opening, the value on the shares could be in excess of £1.30 making a healthy profit for those who were 'stagging', a system whereupon investors enter the market with their investment and sell immediately after the opening bell at the stock exchange. The share price should have risen steeply before settling down. That is the theory anyway!

The shares opened at 93 pence and tumbled during the day. Apparently, part of the reason for the shortfall on opening was because so many Spurs staff had gone for the quick profit using their preferential pink forms. It took many years for the share price to recover to its launch target.

It was not too long before Irving's star fell gently from the sky. In the mid 1980s, just after I had left White Hart Lane, Spurs 'diversified' with disastrous results, partly due to the losses incurred by the Hummel range of sportswear. Spurs linked up with a Danish company with a view to jointly capturing European markets. This venture came as no surprise. Irving had suggested several years earlier that we should negotiate with the owner of the small engineering works adjacent to the club's main car park next to the West Stand, to purchase his company. He thought that we should replace lathes with sewing machines and produce our own label of replica shirts, tracksuits and other sportswear apparel. There was nothing wrong with the principle as the cost of replica shirts could be slashed by cutting out the middle men, but the cost of purchase of the engineering company meant that the payback period would be at least five years. Spurs needed finance urgently. However, I believed that it was far better to franchise than to diversify our interests and move into areas that necessitated a learning curve before the particular business could be regarded as profitable. That was the reason I sought a good kit sponsorship deal with Le Coq Sportif in 1981. The deal, one of the first such tie ups in the country, proved to be highly successful. Le Coq paid us £75,000 per year for the franchise and bonuses on top if sales exceeded a certain level, which they inevitably did.

I did the deal with Robbie Brightwell, their managing director. Robbie was of Olympic fame as he was one of the four men running the 4 x 400 metres in the Tokyo games in 1964. He won a silver medal in the process. He was just the man to represent his company. He was always ready with a witty comment and very patient. He would need all these attributes to deal with the new born Spurs. His wife, Ann Packer, 'The White

Rose of Tokyo' had won a gold medal in the 800 metres. Their son Ian became a professional footballer, enjoying many years at Manchester City. Their other son David also started his football career at Manchester City before moving on to several lower division clubs.

Eventually, when Irving Scholar had nowhere else to turn he handed over the reins to Alan Sugar. Irving went into hiding for a few years only to resurface at Nottingham Forest. They too hit major cash problems during Irving's stewardship and I felt, albeit looking in from the outside, that Irving had lost the plot and it was time for him to 'hang up his boots'. I have empathy with him. His judgement started to fail, the domino factor kicked in, and then he had to face difficulties on the field. It was an impossible task. Irving is a football man. I use the word 'is' as in my humble opinion he should still be involved in the sport. In his book he finishes by saying that he was born a Spurs supporter, will die a Spurs supporter and there cannot be any other club. Why he stepped into Nottingham Forest is a mystery to me given that premise.

There is no doubting Sir Alan Sugar's financial aptitude. If only he had the persona to accompany it. On the day the deal was done to install him as owner and chairman he looked into the TV cameras and came out with these immortal words. 'I will do all I can to return this club to former glory, but it is not going to done overnight. Tottenham *Hotspurs* is a great club.'

Tottenham *Hotspurs? Hotspurs?* Surely it would have been better for him to be completely honest and admit that his knowledge of the club was negligible. He was caught out again when asked by a journalist about the famous double years. Once again he showed his ignorance by asking, 'What double?'

As the late Bill Nicholson said to me on my first day at the club when I made the same cardinal mistake as Mr Sugar by putting an 's' on the end of Hotspur, 'Mr Lewis, we are Tottenham Hotspur, Hotspurs are something to do with cowboys, just remember that'.

What Bill would have made out of Sugar's 'double' faux pas one can only guess.

Football is packed with ironies. In the early 1990s when the Holsten deal came to an end, I received a call from Mr Sugar's office asking me if I could rake up another major sponsor to replace Holsten. Surely with his many contacts in the city Sugar was capable of finding his own sponsor. I was completely taken aback by his approach and came to question my earlier opinions of the man as he was obviously not too proud to seek help from outside his organisation. I gave him 10 out of 10 for that. I was rather surprised and disappointed to hear that the association with the brewers had come to an end. Perhaps Holsten had drunk the barrel dry in terms of what more they could extract from the sponsorship.

As I was working freelance at the time, I readily agreed to take on Sugar's invitation. I wish I could say that doing business with Mr Sugar and his son Daniel (who was working alongside his dad at the time) was enjoyable. I was left with the impression that they wanted my contacts and would have been quite happy to push me to one side once I had opened the door. My fee of £25,000 for securing a £4,000,000 sponsorship was peanuts, yet Daniel Sugar made it quite clear that he thought that it was a lot of money for an introduction. Introduction! I had worked my balls off convincing the managing director of Hewlett Packard (a QPR season ticket holder) that Spurs was the club for them. They were at the time heavily into Formula 1 and I was told quite clearly that any money for the Spurs deal would have to come out of the marketing budgets allocated to the four main distributors in the UK. Ultimately it would the distributors decision whether or not to invest in Spurs.

Because I had met John Golding (Hewlett Packard's managing director) many times before, we held our meetings to discuss the Spurs project in a friendly environment. It was at our first meeting that he told me what the formula for Hewlett Packard raising £4,000,000 for the sponsorship would entail. As we were sipping our coffees and I was listening to John's remorse at the failure of his club QPR to make any headway, we were interrupted by a senior colleague asking John if he had uttered the word 'Spurs' a few moments ago. As the office was open plan it was quite possible for staff walking past the managing director's section to overhear parts of conversation. The gentleman concerned happened to be the marketing director and, would you believe, a season ticket holder at Spurs.

'Are we going to sponsor Spurs, John?' he asked.

John's response was simply to re-iterate the point made to me earlier that the money would have to come out of the promotional budgets for the distributors.

'That's no problem. Leave it to me John. The only bugger who is going to be difficult is Joe, he's Ken Bates' friend and an avid

Chelsea supporter,' said the marketing man.

I conjured up a reason to make a quick exit from the managing director's office as I had a question for the marketing director who was hot footing it back to his own desk. I formally introduced myself and popped this question to him.

'The Joe you were referring to, was he the Joe Hermani of Westcoast?' (Westcoast was based in Reading where I lived at the time and Joe was a golfing buddy of mine.)

'Yes Mike. The other three distributors will follow my lead on this proposition and I can vouch for them, but Joe is a completely different kettle of fish as he is our main distributor for the UK.'

'Would you mind if I spoke to Joe?' I believed that etiquette was important at this stage of the proceedings.

'Mike, if you think it will help, by all means.'

I rushed out of their head quarters back to Reading. I went straight to Joe's office hoping that he would be in. As luck would have it, Joe was in his office. I Navigated my way around receptionists and secretaries and found myself sat in front of Joe. Looking at him behind his huge desk I was drawn to the battered silver cup flattened to a slither hanging on the wall behind his desk. Some years earlier Joe had won the inaugural TITS golfing competition. Together with another business friend in Reading we set up the Titanic International Trading Society (TITS) golf competition. Only failed businessmen could join. That was not too onerous a qualifier in the early 1980s as most businesses were having a hard time. Joe's company however was riding on a crest of a wave so we had to give him special dispensation for membership. The society turned every constitutional golfing rule on its head. The first event included just nine holes of golf and a left handed putting competition before lunch. Medals and cups were lined up for presentation at the top table when dinner was served. Joe, whose golf skills were a joke at the time, won the longest drive competition because he had the biggest house with the longest drive! Unfortunately he put the large cup that he had won on *that* drive before putting his car in the garage. He dropped back a few feet before moving forward and flattened the cup, which, to this day adorns his office wall. Gingerly I approached the subject of Tottenham Hotspur with Joe. His response was amazing.

'Will it help you Mike if I say yes?'

Within four days we had all four distributors in agreement. At this point I invited Mike Rollo to join in and put the deal into a format that would be acceptable to both parties. Mike, with his embracing personality, was welcomed by the directors of Hewlett Packard. However, when Mike was told by the hierarchy back at Spurs that financial guru, Claude Litner, was going to attend the next meeting at Hewlett Packard to sign contracts, Mike became very nervy and indicated to me that Litner's attendance was not a good idea.

I had the full support of Hewlett Packard. They took to Mike Rollo and were very pleased that the day to day servicing of the sponsorship would be in Mike's hands. Together with Rollo, Litner, Steve Bradley the sponsorship director, the marketing director and Hewlett Packard's legal representative, we met in an office at Hewlett Packard's headquarters to put the deal to bed. But Litner opened up with this barnstormer, 'It's only fair to tell you gentlemen that we have had another offer from an international company that exceeds the money you are offering'. Memories came flooding back of Scholar's last ditch attempt to scupper the Holsten deal. What the hell was the man trying to achieve? I looked at Rollo whose mouth had dropped a mile.

Hewlett Packard's marketing director stood up and simply said that he was disappointed and felt that Spurs were acting in an unprofessional way and that Hewlett Packard was not a company who enter an auction for anything. He then collected his papers and walked out of the room.

I turned to Rollo and told him that the manner in which this meeting was conducted was a disgrace and I left the room. Rollo picked up the unsigned contract and he asked if he and I could have a private chat. Litner left without saying a word.

Rollo and I sat in the reception area of the company completely deflated. I truly felt that he, Rollo, had let me down, as the surprise visit of Litner should never have occurred. If there was another interested party then he, Rollo, should have surely been aware of their interest. He denied any knowledge of another party coming to the table and informed me that he was going straight back to London to, 'Sort things out with Litner and Sugar'.

Rollo, on his return from London, explained that he had gone straight to Alan Sugar's office and voiced his disgust at the manner in which Litner had effectively torpedoed the deal. Apparently, Sugar knew nothing of his financial director's attendance at the meeting and was equally as shocked as Rollo. He instructed Rollo to return to Berkshire and resurrect the deal.

Fortunately, managing director John Golding, the marketing director and Steve Bradley were hosting a dinner that evening for some American visitors. As luck would have it the dinner was going to take place in the Copped Beach Hotel immediately next door to Hewlett Packard's office. Mike Rollo and I sat in the lounge of the hotel from 7.00 pm until 9.00 pm in the vain hope that the deal could be rescued and that the Hewlett Packard executives, having enjoyed a good dinner, would be accommodating. At 9.00 pm, Steve Bradley came dashing out to us, thrust the back page of the contract in front of Rollo and asked him to quickly sign. John Golding had already signed on the dotted line.

As Mike Rollo, who I appointed as my assistant back in 1982, was still at the club, I thought it rather strange that as he was holding the commercial reins that I should be asked to find a major sponsor. I soon realised after speaking to him that there was some doubt in Sugar's mind about Mike's ability to find a top corporate sponsor. He had proved to be an admirable number two during the two years we worked together. His personality and enthusiasm shone through. Whether he had the confidence to sit down with the decision makers at international companies and cut a deal, was I suppose, debatable.

When I watch Sir Alan Sugar star in the TV programme *The Apprentice* I am impressed with his ability to get to the core of the many issues that arise in this captivating programme. However, on the basis that we Brits hold a secret desire to see great men fall from grace occasionally, couldn't the producers arrange for Sir Alan to sell Christmas Club schemes to the populous?

13

BISCUITS AND ROYALS

It was during the Ipswich home game on 14th January 1984 that I bumped into Roger Smee. He was a vice president of Reading Football Club at the time and a man making his mark in property development at a rapid rate of knots. He was a guest in an executive box and at the end of the game, when eyes were turned to the television for the rest of the football results, Roger was knocked off his feet by a flash announcement that Robert Maxwell was about to combine two football clubs. He was going to combine the one he owned and the other where he was a major shareholder. They were Oxford United and Reading respectively and Maxwell was going to rename the two clubs Thames Valley Royals.

Roger turned white. He asked me if I knew where he could borrow a phone. I gave him my office, as it was quiet. On returning to the executive box, all he said was that he was going to take Maxwell on and prevent him from making this unholy alliance. Little did I know at that time that I would be joining Roger in his fight to keep Reading away from the clutches of Maxwell. As the Spurs legend Jimmy Greaves said, 'It's a funny old game'.

Reading, once referred to as the hernia of the Midlands, was never credited with having a either a very good football team or fanatical support. Because the town was a little too close to London it meant that there was always the temptation for die-hard soccer fans to turn their attention to Chelsea, Arsenal or Spurs rather than pop along to Elm Park and watch a lower level of football. Smee was a very ambitious man and had tasted the delight of playing for the mighty Chelsea, so he was well aware of the huge mountain Reading would have to climb to even put the club at first base camp. His knowledge of the game, coupled with his business expertise, meant that he was better qualified than most other Football League Chairmen to make the right decisions and put round pegs into round holes.

It was in the early spring of 1984 that I was appointed as managing director of the Thames Valley Club. At the time Maurice Evans was the manager with Ian Branfoot as his assistant. The club was in a very good position in Division Three at the time and looked capable of gaining promotion. However, cosy laid back Reading FC was in for a shock. When Roger Smee took over as Chairman he had ambitious ideas for the club. These did not include retaining anything that represented mediocrity. Only the best would do.

My appointment was confirmed at Smee's farmhouse just outside Reading. After Roger moved to Henley, the new occupants of the farmhouse were to be Lennie Henry and Dawn French. The sound of a champagne cork exploding out of its bottle signalled the end of contract discussions and the signing of a two-year service agreement. His co-directors were there to witness the occasion. Roger was well known for his 'Champagne Charlie' lifestyle, but I wondered if this was the right moment in time to celebrate. The job at Reading was going to be very tough. The club was technically trading whilst insolvent and the bank was threatening foreclosure.

'Lewis,' bellowed Smee, 'I have just got rid of the worst job in football, drink up.'

Roger and I discussed the immediate future of the club. It was obvious to me that he was not prepared to leave matters as they were and wanted swift action. Swift action is what he got.

'Mike, I want you to remove Roy Bentley as secretary and Maurice Evans as manager. Promote Branfoot to manager and give the secretary's job to Pat Byrne [Bentley's secretary]'.

'Over what period Roger?' I asked.

'In 24 hours,' was his reply.

Now bear in mind that Roy Bentley, ex-Chelsea and England legend, was still highly regarded by everyone in football and that Maurice Evans was the perfect gentleman (and I emphasise the word 'gentle'). Also Pat Byrne was very close to Roy and they worked together well as a team, I was beginning to think that Roger had set me up. However, I had to face these unsuspecting troops on Monday morning and dish out the bad news. I was not comfortable. Maurice, as dignified as ever, quietly walked away but I could see the hurt in his eyes. Smee had decided on the change of management purely on the basis that he regarded Branfoot as the ideal manager who seemed to possess the qualities that his new Chairman valued. He was young enough to learn but old enough and experienced enough at second tier level to mould a bunch of average players into a side capable of getting out of the old Division Four. Some critics pointed the finger at Smee and asked why he should remove Evans when the team was in a promotion winning position in the league. Maurice steered the club to promotion from the Division Four in 1978–1979 in his second season as manager. What's more he presided over a team that set a Football League record by not conceding a goal in 1,074 minutes. Steve Death was the goalkeeper for the whole of that time. But who could argue with Smee's judgement for at the end of the 1983–1984 season, Branfoot guided his troops to promotion into Division Three.

One employee, who escaped the axe due to his loyalty to the club over many years as a player and latterly as groundsman, was Gordon 'Fred' Neate. Fred, an uncompromising full back having made 106 appearances for the Royals between 1958 and 1965, drifted into pitch care. Whilst he was from the old school regarding matters of agronomy seeing little difference between front garden lawns and Wembley playing surfaces, he nevertheless put in endless hours of care and attention into his own 102 x 68 metre garden that adorned Elm Park.

Ian Branfoot made it known that he was a fan of the Graham Taylor school of football. This meant that the pitch was hardly ever used as the ball spent most of its time during a game flying through the air after being hoofed! I seriously thought of inviting British Airways to sponsor the club, not just because Elm Park was under the flight path of dozens of jets a day winging their way across 'the pond'. It was more because our Minerva footballs threatened to join the jet set on match days often being hoisted 40 feet in the air! Fred, like many other groundsmen, hated the pitch being used for playing football so Branfoot's tactics suited him down to the ground. Why destroy a hard week's work by allowing 22 men plus a ref to run around ripping up his precious turf? During a period of a big freeze when a ball was not kicked in anger for three weeks, Fred was in his element. Desperately needing income from any home game, I contacted the local council to ask if they were prepared to help us stage a four times postponed game against Leyton Orient. The pitch was rutted and hard from the frost. The referee making the last inspection of the pitch before calling the game off said that if the pitch had been flat he would have allowed the game to be played. On the basis that a wink is as good as a nod, I approached the council and they kindly offered to loan us a steamroller for a day. Fred was shown how to drive the machine and he spent the whole day careering up and down the pitch until it was flat. At one point I had to ask him to take the vibrator off the machine as he passed down the touchline nearest the main stand underneath which the offices were located. Walls and ceilings were shaking every time he made a pass and office lights were flicking on and off. We managed to get the game played in front of 1,567 spectators.

Returning from holiday on a Friday in July 1985, I made the classic mistake of ringing the club to check that nothing had gone amiss in my absence. Before I could be put through to Ian Branfoot's office, the telephonist asked if I could go down to the club urgently. She was not prepared to tell me why. Racing down the three miles from my home to Elm Park, my mind was swilling with all kinds of possibilities. Had someone died? Had the ground caught fire? Were the players in revolt? On arrival I was ushered through the offices by the delightful receptionist Jane into the vice president's lounge where she whispered to me that Fred was out on the ground in tears. Climbing the short series of steps that led from the dressing room and office area out onto the arena, I was blinded by the late afternoon sun peeping over the roof of the South Stand. As I looked to my right I could see Fred, head in hands, sitting on the low perimeter wall that divided the running track from the front row of seats. As I approached him he wiped tears from his eyes and started to tell me his tale of woe. Earlier that week he had taken a new drum of weed killer and covered the pitch with it in straight up and down lines. By the Wednesday of the week he had become concerned that the grass covering the pitch seemed to be dying. Sure enough not only was it dying but it was turning into a straw colour at the same time. As I looked out onto the playing area I could see that what was left of the grass was now presenting a very good imitation of a freshly harvested straw field. Fred confessed. He had put undiluted weed killer on the pitch. With eight days to go before the first home game of the new season against Millwall we had a huge problem.

By now the media were aware of the problem and although we placed Elm Park out of bounds to prying cameras, some of the more adventurous photographers were to be seen perched on top of 15 feet perimeter walls pointing their cameras at the playing area that now resembled a patchwork quilt of colours. There were some green patches where Fred had missed with his weed killer but mostly the grass was straw coloured.

I contacted the Football League and they told me to contact Millwall and ask for them to send a delegation to Elm Park to decide whether or not they were prepared to play on this surface. John Docherty was the Millwall manager at the time. He attended together with the club secretary. John stated that his team was ready for the new season and on balance they would want to play, after all the pitch was flat and not at all dangerous. The game was staged even if it was secondary in interest to that of the straw pitch.

Slowly but surely the pitch improved. At the very end of the season it looked like a snooker table. In successive seasons rave reviews were a regular feature of visiting team's comments on the pitch. Gordon Neate was constantly asked how he managed to produce such a lush carpet. If I happened to be near when these compliments were being paid I had to walk away in embarrassment.

During the 1983–1984 season, Trevor Senior and Dean Horrix struck up a lethal partnership for the Royals providing 50 goals and paving the way for promotion. The latter became a firm favourite of mine as I saw in him the type of player I would have loved to become. During that promotion season I witnessed a skill that I would place alongside the Ricky Villa goal at Wembley, the Beckham free kick against Greece or Gordon Banks' save against Pelé. Taking up a wide right position Horrix signalled to Gary Westwood, the Reading keeper, to send the ball in his direction. The ball sailed through the air and because of the close proximity of the directors' box at Elm Park, it really did seem that its final destination would be somewhere between the first and second row of the padded seats. A gust of wind kept the ball in play and enabled it to drop on the end of Horrix's right foot as he was standing facing the keeper on the half way line. In one movement, not allowing the ball to touch the ground, he swept the ball through the legs of a close marking defender, chased it down the line, cut inside and blasted it with his left foot past the startled opposition keeper.

The goal he scored against Bristol City in April 1984 came a close second to this one. A 50 yard cross by Deano almost broke the net behind John Shaw (the bald headed city keeper). It might have been a fluke but it was poetic justice for a player who spent most of his time providing goals for others. Deano was loved by the fans. His awkward style, his big heart and his unselfish assists, which gave Senior most of his goals, often provoked the crowd into chanting, 'Deano, Deano'. Dean was sold to Millwall by Ian Branfoot in March 1988. The sale caused consternation with the Elm Park crowd. Although Dean had not featured in many games prior to his sale, the £250,000 lashed out on Steve Moran from Leicester meant that Moran had to be given preference if for no other reason than to justify what was then a huge expenditure for Reading. In addition the £75,000 received from Millwall for Dean went someway to bridging the gap.

I did the Moran deal with the Leicester Chairman at the time and must admit to being curious as to why they should be offloading a player who, only six years earlier, had been the Professional Footballers Association Young Player of the Year. Moran was a failure at Reading although I put some blame for his poor form down to the fact that the team was struggling as a whole.

Dean could not command a regular place in the successful Millwall team, being kept out of contention by the likes of Tony Cascarino and Teddy Sherringham. So it came as no surprise that he moved to Bristol City for £50,000. His stay at Ashton Gate proved to be tragically short. On a return journey home to Tadley Hampshire on 10th March 1990 he was killed in a car crash.

The season 1984–1985 was one of consolidation, although the club's away form reached an all time peak with a total of 11 away wins. The highlight was the magnificent 5–2 away win over Bradford City. On our arrival at Valley Parade, the home directors were in a celebratory mood. In great anticipation of a home victory that would secure them the third division championship, I was shown a huge refrigerator by their Chairman, Stafford Heginbotham that contained at least 50 bottles of bubbly. Well matters took a turn for the worse for the Bantams as the Royals romped home with goals from David Crown, Dean Horrix (2), Mark White and Martin Hicks. During the first half I sat next to Jim Brooks the Reading Club President. Jim, a heavy smoker, not only smoked through the whole of the game, but lit up a fresh one every time we scored, even if the smouldering ember stuck between his lips was still a long way from being consigned to the floor of the stand. I made a comment to Jim as we left the directors' box at half time. Looking down at the wooden floor boards where Jim had discarded his ends I said, 'Bloody hell Jim, you've got through a packet in the first half!' This was no surprise really as Jim would chain smoke his way through a game at Elm Park until Mrs Brooks put a stop to it when Jim was later diagnosed with a serious chest infection. I still cherish and value the Crombie overcoat that Jim left to me in his will.

Just a week after that fantastic win, Valley Parade was the scene of one of the worst disasters in the history of the game. Some 52 people died and hundreds spent months in hospital recovering from burns after fire engulfed the main stand at the stadium. Their game against Lincoln City was never completed. The bubbly was presumably lost in the fire.

The following season was sensational. The 1985–1986 season saw the club promoted to the second division after an absence of 55 years. The Royals set a Football League record by winning their first 12 games. A remarkable personal coincidence occurred in achieving that record. The record was achieved at my old club Newport County and snatched from Tottenham Hotspur where I had spent six very happy years. The occasion was such that it drew civic recognition. The Mayor of Newport at the time was Councillor Trevor Warren. He was someone I often clashed with in the civic chamber when he occupied a seat on the Conservative benches and I sat opposite on the Labour benches. Our heated debates never allowed our mutual respect for each other to be compromised. Trevor kindly invited me to spend the night of the historic game in the Mansion House where he was giving a party. I was to be the guest of honour. A good night was to be had by all with the proviso that we climbed into our beds before midnight as the next day the Mayor was entertaining Princess Margaret.

Some 5,000 Reading fans made the trip to Wales to witness this historic game. The M4 was a flurry of blue and white scarves and banners flying out of car and van windows. Reading, famous for its beer, biscuits and Suttons Seeds, was the repository for a mixed bag of exiles from Wales, the Midlands and London coupled with an increasing population of ethnics. It lacked a heart and was desperately in need of a fillip. The rugby club had a limited appeal; the speedway team attracted fewer than 2,000 spectators to its meetings. The town held an annual pop concert at the end of August each year giving the town some national recognition. The Royals, having spent most of their time since their formation in 1871 in the lower leagues, did little to improve the profile of Reading. The trip to Newport however, brought the community together. Interest outside the travelling thousands was at a high level attracting huge media interest. BBC TV commentator Barry Davies met me straight off the team coach at Somerton Park and fielded the following question: 'Was it a good idea for you to be quoted in this morning's *Western Mail* stating that the decline of Welsh Football was self inflicted and that the game in the principality would take years to recover from mismanagement at club and international level?'

I told Davies that those were my beliefs. Little did I know that the quote had been pinned up in the County's dressing room as an incentive for the home team players to prove me wrong.

The packed little ground watched an exciting game. Newport was no pushover. Reading's remorseless style supported by oodles of confidence brought on by the success of the previous 11 games saw them go ahead after 19 minutes. Ex-Spurs likely lad Stuart Beavon fired home a low drive past the Newport keeper. Striker Kevin Bremner came on for the injured Dean Horrix and headed a superb second goal after 65 minutes. Ian Branfoot's team, assembled for £150,000 had won its twelfth consecutive game from the start of the season and smashed the record held by Spurs for a quarter of a century.

I did make a quick sentimental journey to that same spot on the terraces where I had stood for many years. Now it was cracked concrete rather than a railway sleeper. The small boardroom at Newport where I had spent some considerable time in the mid 1970s placing my plans before the board, was not exactly the place for me to show too much emotion after the Reading victory. I was aware that whilst the match was historically important to the Royals, it was as equally important to the County as they desperately needed the points. Nevertheless, it was extremely disappointing for me to hear Archie Menzies, one of the old directors on the board at the time of my stay at the club, turn to me and comment that Reading had put another nail in the coffin of Newport. He added that he hoped that I felt satisfied. If I had any doubts before the game that my split loyalties might just give me a problem on the day then these were quickly wiped away on the back of Menzies' comments. He should have realised that my undying loyalty to his club was just as deep as his.

Included in the Royals' record breaking team on that infamous day, was a player called Colin Bailie. The signing of Colin from Swindon Town provided another little cameo that even to this day can bring a smile to my face as I remember the never to be forgotten details. Ian Branfoot wanted a regular right back in order to release Jerry Williams into a more adventurous midfield role. Bailie was his choice and he left it to me to organise the transfer.

We knew that Swindon Town was desperate to obtain the services of Lawrie Sanchez who was out of favour with Branfoot. A straight swap was on the cards. Sanchez was only too pleased to move to Swindon as he could not see a future at Reading. The Chairman of Swindon at the time was Brian Hillier who was later found guilty for his part in a betting scandal when he placed bets on his team losing at Newcastle United in the FA Cup. Hillier and Bailie came to the club and I asked them to wait in the boardroom while I took an urgent call. The call was from the secretary of Wimbledon who said that his Chairman had instructed him to make a £20,000 bid for Sanchez! In the knowledge that Swindon valued Bailie at £20,000 I attempted to make the club a few bob by pushing up the price Wimbledon had put on Sanchez's head. I managed to get to £25,000. Fine, but what about Bailie and his Chairman, to say nothing of Lawrie Sanchez who was anticipating a short move down the M4 to Swindon? Hurriedly I got Lawrie into my office and explained the situation to him. In order to get him to accept a move to South London I had to offer a sweetener and this came in the form of a better pay off than the one offered to him for a move to Swindon. I felt for Lawrie as he was, in my humble opinion, playing well, but I was not the manager and Branfoot thought that his game lacked aggression. This was why he needed to replace him. With tears filling his eyes and a heartfelt outburst of how he felt about being ousted from Reading, Lawrie finally agreed to the move. His huge success as the manager of Northern Ireland followed by his permanent appointment as manager of Fulham on the back of him being a member of the FA Cup winning Wimbledon team (Sanchez scoring the winning goal) is a testimony to his professionalism.

I didn't have time to feel too much sympathy for Lawrie as I had unfinished business with Hillier and Bailie who were getting increasingly impatient pacing up and down in the upstairs

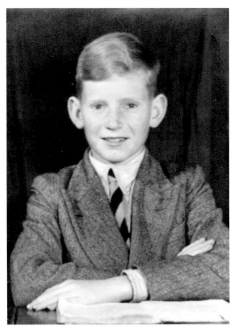

Pictured at my desk in secondary school.
(I wonder why they called me Dumbo?)

Molly and Albert at my wedding day in 1970.

The 'crowd' drift in at Somerton Park before a home game.

Glenn Hoddle my idol being substituted at a home game at White Hart Lane. Manager Keith Burkinshaw claimed that Hoddle did not do enough defending. Can a ballet dancer kick box?

With my PA entertaining James Garner at White Hart Lane.

Henry the cockatoo pictured seconds before he escaped and inflicted hand injuries on a famous boxer in the Sponsors Lounge at Spurs.

Boxing legend Henry Cooper visits Spurs for the game against Aston Villa on 5th September 1981.

*Ricky Villa scores **that** goal at Wembley in the Cup Final replay against Manchester City in 1981. The goal was given the title of Wembley Goal of the Century in 2001.*   © PA Photos

The wonderful Harrodian Cavaliers pictured before their epic match against Setubal in Portugal. Martin Peters on the far left in the back row looking younger than ever, well he was 10 years ahead of his time anyway!

From left to right; myself, Bobby Keetch, Martin Peters and Paul Kirby pictured after our less than successful match against Setubal in Portugal.

Here I am pictured with Gordon Banks and George Best, two of football's greatest at Wembley Stadium in November 1986 on the occasion of England beating Yugoslavia.

The back row includes Trevor Brooking, David Platt and Bobby Moore, who it seems is once again trying to take the shirt off my back!

The ref is on hand to spot this late challenge in a charity game at Elm Park Reading.

Reading Chairman John Madejski presents me with my 'going away' present surrounded by my staff at the club. Current Motherwell boss Mark McGhee is seen on the far right.

Mohamed Al Fayed at a pre-match presentation at Craven Cottage.

Fulham fans pay their tributes to Diana and Dodi.

Cyril the Swan goes 'head to head' with Millwall mascot Zampa the Lion before drop kicking Zampa's head into the crowd! © PA Photos

Whacko Jacko with Uri Geller and David Blaine at St James' Park, Exeter on 14th June 2002. © PA Photos

One of the last pictures taken of my mate Ernie before he tragically died in 2006. My partner Glenys is sat alongside.

Leaving Bristol Crown Court on 30th May 2007 after being sentenced to 200 hours community service.   © *PA Photos*

To the left of the signal was Somerton Park where my beloved Newport County played. The trains don't stop there anymore.

boardroom. I climbed the stairs and entered the oak panelled room full of trepidation deciding to be perfectly honest telling them the stark facts. The player and his Chairman left the boardroom in a very disgruntled manner.

Some months later Bailie came to Reading for £20,000. Bailie was a nice lad with a broad Northern Irish accent. He fancied himself as a barrack room lawyer though and on one occasion came in on a Monday morning to complain that the crowd at the home game two days earlier was far in excess of the disclosed figure. He felt that the club had purposely under declared the gate in order to reduce their payments to the players (who had a gate bonus attached to their contracts). I was not enjoying that particular Monday morning as I knew that I had to sack two members of staff later. I certainly did not want to listen to a whinging player. I looked up at Bailie from my desk and simply said, 'Well, Colin I am not going to argue with you. If you say there were 2,000 more in the ground than the published figure then so be it, because the way you played you had time to count everyone in the ground!'

He smiled, walked away and the matter was never discussed again.

The Royals record breaking start to the season was extended in the next match with Trevor Senior scoring with an overhead kick at Lincoln City but the run came to a halt the following Wednesday when the Royals played host to Wolves. The game ended in a 2–2 draw in front of a lock-out 13,245 spectators (well that was the figure released). In fact many more attended the game as the police allowed hundreds more to enter the ground instead of having to police them outside Elm Park.

The Royals lasted just two seasons in Division Two. During the 1985–1986 season the club signed Terry Hurlock from Brentford. This particular transfer provided me with an experience that I shall never forget. The deal was for Terry to come to us for £75,000. Roger Smee gave me the authority to do the deal with Martin Lange, the Chairman of Brentford. Martin wanted £85,000 but Smee wouldn't budge from £75,000. I knew that the arrival of 'wildman' Hurlock would not only go down well with the fans, but that he would bring substance to the midfield that was sadly lacking steel. Together with manager Ian Branfoot we put pressure on Smee to secure the player's signing. The stalemate between the clubs lasted for 24 hours. I made yet another call to Martin Lange to see if he had softened overnight. Smee had told me to go to £80,000 if pushed. Lange puffed and blowed and finally lost patience exclaiming, 'Tell Smee to send me a box of his finest Havana cigars and we will do the deal at £82,500'. Smee agreed. The deal was done and Hurlock was on his way to Elm Park.

He arrived the next morning, boots in hand. His appearance explained why he was tagged 'the wildman'. He had abundant, shoulder length hair and a swarthy gait which gave credence to his other title of 'gypsy'. I sat in my office with a desk covered in paperwork ranging from four sets of blue contract forms through to club rules, medical forms and insurance forms; I could see he looked ill at ease. I asked him to look at the contract details and confirm that they were as agreed. He said that he trusted me and was sure that everything was in order and there was no need for him to examine the paperwork. In fact he was more interested in using my telephone to call home. Home was a terraced house opposite the ground at Brentford FC. Legend had it that he used to turn up for training wearing his carpet slippers!

I suggested that I leave him alone to make this call but he insisted that I stayed in the room. His call to his wife was quite short. He told her that he had signed for Reading and that Reading was quote, 'Just down the M4'. He turned to me and asked how far it was.

'Yeah darling we can stay where we are; it's only 40 miles away.'

I took to Terry straight away. Normally I would not go in search of sponsored cars for players as it could lead to disharmony in the dressing room. When Terry asked if I could get a sponsored car I felt that an exception could be made. Brian Vanderwolf owned a Ford franchise in Alton near Reading and was a vice-president of the club. He was always immaculately dressed, complete with a carnation in his lapel. Brian was always approachable and just loved being involved. I called Brian and arranged that he meet Terry at the next home game. They met up in the vice-president's lounge after a game in which Terry excelled. Perhaps it was the absolute opposite of styles that Brian found fascinating as Terry stood before him completely bedraggled with his club tie undone and hanging over his trouser top. Terry, showing total respect for the man, handed Brian a duty free carrier bag that contained litre bottles of whisky, gin and brandy. Vanderwolf's face was a picture. How could he resist? A deal was done and Terry got his car.

Some three months later Brian gingerly approached me and asked if Terry was doing a lot of miles scouting on behalf of the club. As this was a curious question to ask I enquired as to the reason for the question.

'Well Mike, I have just had a look at the milometer and he has run up 14,000 in three months!'

'Leave it to me Mike, he's such a great bloke that I don't want to upset him but I need to know when I will have to change the car.'

Brian never found out the real reason for the high mileage. Reportedly Terry's dad used the car as a mini cab when Terry got back from training.

His first game for the Royals was at Swansea on 22nd February 1986 and his appearance would normally have been the main point of discussion. However a bizarre incident after eight minutes provided the drama of the afternoon. Royals' winger Andy Rogers in attempting to head the ball in front of a Swans defender fell heavily on the bone hard pitch. He swallowed his tongue and stopped breathing. The Swansea doctor and the Royals' physiotherapist Glenn Hunter rushed to the player lying prostrate on the ground. It was Hunter who hooked the player's tongue from the back of his throat and got him breathing again by inserting an airway tube into his windpipe. It was a full 12 minutes before Andy could be lifted onto a stretcher. I got down to the players tunnel just as he was being carried into the dressing room. An ambulance was waiting outside to take him to the nearest hospital at Singleton Swansea. I travelled with him and he regained full consciousness on the trip to the hospital. His main concern was for his wife and I promised him that the moment we reached the hospital I would call her. This was many years before the advent of the mobile phone and whilst there are many occasions when I curse the very existence of these social infiltrators, on this occasion the use of a mobile could have saved Mrs Rogers from serious heartache as she had heard, via the radio, the news of Andy's misfortune before we reached the hospital. Andy's home number could not be obtained until he regained consciousness so my call from the hospital was met with a sobbing Mrs Rogers who feared the worst as reports were suggesting that he had died on the pitch. I was able to comfort her and reassure her that Andy was okay and that he would speak to her the moment the medics had fully revived him.

The Royals won the game 3–2, a victory that equalled the record of 11 away wins that was set the season before. Andy made a full recovery and was playing again within three weeks.

Another shock awaited me in connection with Terry Hurlock. It came in the form of 'unofficial' appearances made by Terry. Reading visited Derby County for a league fixture and the Harrodian Cavaliers football team decided that they would organise a trip to Derby and watch the game. Although 43 years of age, I still had a desire to pull on my football boots so I had become a member of the Cavaliers who were a mixture of players with loose connections to the famous Harrods store. I was to meet up with the Cavaliers after the Derby game to play against a local village side. Together with my co-directors, I climbed aboard the Reading team bus that left Elm Park at 8.00 am. We arrived for our pre-match meal at a Post House Hotel in the Midlands at 11.30 am. Imagine my surprise when I was asked by a member of the hotel staff if I could go to the foyer to meet someone who knew me. As I walked into the foyer I was greeted by the whole of the Harrods team who, coincidentally, had arranged for a stop off drink at the same hotel. Keith Cooke, the Harrods centre forward, asked me if Terry Hurlock had travelled with us. On linking the two together I was curious as to how they knew each other. Later that day (well in fact in the early hours of the following morning) with a belly full of curry and beer, I asked Keith Cooke how he knew Terry.

'Well Mike, he plays in the London Business League with me on a Wednesday afternoon.'

'What?'

'It's okay Mike, he plays under another name.'

How the hell could Terry Hurlock play under another name? What a guy. He gave heart and soul to Reading and it was no surprise to me that after his transfer to Millwall for £95,000 in February 1987, he went on to be transferred to Glasgow Rangers for £375,000 in August 1990 gaining an England B International cap during the same period.

Reading reached Wembley for the first time in their history in 1988 beating four first division sides on their way to the Simod Cup Final. Their victory over Coventry City at Elm Park heralded another Football League record. With the sides level after extra time, the game entered into penalties with the Royals finally winning the shoot out at 10.40 pm. This was the latest time any football match had finished.

Their 4–1 defeat of Luton Town in front of 61,470 at Wembley, whilst not placing itself alongside personal memories of the great Spurs Cup Final victories over Manchester City and QPR, still ranked as a huge landmark in my career.

On hearing the final whistle blow, Roger Smee turned to me and barked out, 'Go and get the champagne Lewis!'

His instruction provided me with a problem as I had not organised for champagne to be on hand (we were on a tight budget after all). Smee, on learning of my oversight hollered, 'Call yourself a fucking managing director? Go and get some bloody bubbly'.

A hasty visit to the nearest off licence by our kit man saved the day.

Our success in winning the Simod Cup couldn't have anything to do with an African village chief sending us a good luck charm could it? Before the start of the 1987–1988 season the club had sent, via an aid worker, some old kit and 20 training balls to a village in Nigeria. The chief of the village sent me a thank you letter to which he had appended what looked like human hair. In fact, as he explained in his letter, the hair had belonged to an elephant and had been removed from the area surrounding the animal's testes. I placed it in front of Ron Grant, the kit man, who showed little enthusiasm for its possible magical affect on the team's performance to say nothing of his unwillingness to handle the same wiry hair. It wasn't until the celebratory dinner back in Reading after the infamous victory over Luton that Ron declared that the elephant hair had travelled with the team on every away trip, having been accommodated in an empty tape cassette box and strapped to the lid of the aluminium kit container.

14

CAVALIER STYLE

'Come and play for the wonderful Harrodian Cavaliers Mike,' was the invitation extended to me by Paul Kirby when I first met him. Paul, a man of mystery, had been known to me since joining Spurs in 1976. At the time I was player/manager of Cheshunt Park FC a side that struggled in the Herts & Bucks Fifth Division (Sunday Section).

Most of my players were Spurs fanatics. I promised them if we could steer clear of relegation in season 1978–1979 then I would arrange for them to play at White Hart Lane. With the groundman's approval, the game would be played the Monday after the last home fixture of the season, just before he took the posts down. My lads responded as if they had been offered a world cruise. We avoided relegation by two points to stay in the division.

As my playing days, even at fifth division level were coming to an end, and a game with the wonderful Harrodian Cavaliers was on the cards, it seemed sensible to invite *them* to play against us as they contained players of celebrity status. I turned out for the Cheshunt team and we lost 2–1.

The second season saw us play the second match, again at White Hart Lane. This time the result was a draw.

The Cavaliers played a Tottenham select team in the third season as Cheshunt Park had effectively folded. The Spurs team included club secretary Peter Day, ticket office manager Peter Barnes, Colin White the groundsman, Ray Rayland the kit man, myself plus a few 'outsiders'. Harrodians, who incidentally started some years earlier as a team made up of Harrods' management, included Martin Peters, Bobby Keetch and Roger Smee. They were joined by Paul Kirby, Steve the meat manager from the store, the head of tailoring services, Robert a *Daily Mirror* sports reporter, Bobby Hall a carpenter, and an amalgam of others who, if asked, would swear some allegiance to Harrods even if that meant that they spent a day there on a plumbing job! Kirby played in his usual left back position. This place was reserved for him as he did, in fairness, conduct all the arrangements. In true Harrodian fashion, he insisted on a 'nothing but the best' approach which meant that the sound of champagne corks popping in the away dressing room *before the game* came as no surprise.

The match was videoed for posterity with Jim Rosenthal conducting the match commentary. A section of the Royal Marines Band played us out onto the field.

I asked Bill Nicholson if he would sit in the dugout and give the Spurs team some advice. At half time at 2–0 down I asked Bill how were we doing. His response is not printable.

The second half saw a slight improvement from the Spurs side including a 40 yard cross ball on the half way line from me that had every mark of a Hoddle special. It was done right in front of Mr Nicholson too! I turned quickly and gave the thumbs up to Bill who, had either ignored my signal of joy or had missed the moment entirely. Instead he screamed at me, 'Move your arse and get down the bloody pitch.'

That pass, treasured on video, has been shown to every member of my family, friends and even animals if they cared to watch. I might add that before making this wonderful pass I had 'turned' Paul Kirby on a sixpence much to his chagrin.

The referee that night was Peter Leaver QC, then a director of Spurs and latterly chief executive of the Premiership. He handled the game with composure and, as expected from a legal man, was totally fair. He also understood that the game had to flow even if some of the tackles flying in from the over 50s were a little late.

Peter was a jolly chap who dodged the political issues at the club and always voiced the words of a wise man. But in his role as the CEO of the Premiership, I wondered if he was strong enough to take on the Premiership heavyweights.

Peter was invited to become a member of The Football Task Force in 1997. Fellow members included Graham Kelly (former Chief Executive of the FA), David Sheepshanks (Football League/Chairman of Ipswich Town) and Gordon Taylor (Professional Footballers Association).

The Sports Minister at the time was the late Tony Banks. Upon launching the Task Force he declared that the tasks in front of them included '...*encouraging ticketing and pricing policies that are geared to reflect the needs of all on an equitable basis and to develop the opportunities for players to act as good role models in terms of behaviour and sportsmanship'.* I would suggest that on both counts the Task Force failed miserably. I suppose the appointment of a 'Johnny come-lately' in the form of David Mellor as Chairman was really not a very clever move. His radio programme devoted to football was so bloody patronising to the real fans that any hope of fundamental change was going to be impossible. Add to that the revelations about his bedtime antics whilst wearing a Chelsea shirt meant that he was never going to be taken seriously.

Football saw the introduction of the task force as the pre-curser to the arrival of a government watchdog on football with far wider terms of reference. Football, being the incestuous animal it is, managed to push aside that threat. The Football Association set up their own Financial Advisory Department as a half-baked attempt to appease the government. Their initial effectiveness was mind blowingly devoid of any real constructive headway with clubs being made. At a meeting of Third Division Chairmen held in a London hotel during late summer 2002, I asked Barry Hearn, the Chairman that day, how many clubs had been visited by the new FA unit. Before answers were forthcoming from the floor, Barry Hearn uttered the immortal words, 'If they want to come and see you, tell them to sod off. They are nothing but nosey sods. When they asked to come to my club (Leyton Orient) I told them to piss off. I will decide when to have board meetings and not be told by "jobsworths" that I should have regular meetings. The only reason they have been set up is to prevent the Government doing the job for them'.

What has happened to the Task Force? And what are their achievements? If anyone knows, then please tell me.

As for Peter Leaver QC, Let us hope that his flirtation with football on the inside looking out did not poison him against the world's greatest game.

The match at White Hart Lane ended 4–1 in favour of the Harrodian Cavaliers. It was followed by a dinner when all and sundry had their own story to tell. When Bill Nicholson was asked for his views, all he could say was that it was unlike any other football match he had ever seen and that he was not anxious to take on the job on a permanent basis.

It was the occasion of Bill Nicholson's 64th birthday that prompted Kirby to ring me the day before and ask me if I could gently mention to Bill that Paul wanted to treat him to lunch to celebrate. Bill, never one to rush into a decision, said that it was nice of Paul, who he knew quite well, to invite him for lunch but he had work to do and really could not find time to accept Paul's invitation. I persevered. 'Come on Bill, you are so much respected by all age groups at the club and this would give them the opportunity to say thank you for all the good times you have brought to White Hart Lane.' He reluctantly agreed.

I drove Bill to the Royal Chase Hotel in Enfield that was to be the venue for lunch. On arrival at 12.30 pm the only other company we had in the lounge bar of the hotel was the barman. I handed Bill a large gin and tonic and we chatted for a while until he showed signs of agitation as the clock moved on toward 1.00 pm. At this time he leapt up and asked me to take him back to the club. Suddenly, through the double doors leading out to the back of the hotel strode Kirby with two others. Behind them came a waiter carrying a silver tray laden with champagne.

'What's going on?' asked Bill.

'Have a glass of bubbly Bill then we'll go for lunch,' said Paul.

'I thought we were having lunch here,' Bill responded.

After a few minutes during which Paul made small talk, he got up and asked Bill to follow him. Out through the same doors they had entered and into the area at the back of the hotel marched Bill, myself, Paul and one other. On seeing a helicopter standing on the pad Bill said, 'Somebody's got money'. Paul explained to Bill that the whirly bird was there to take him for lunch.

'I'm not getting into that!'

'Sit in the front Bill. See what it feels like.'

By now the effects of that large gin and tonic were starting to have an effect. 'Where are we going Paul?' asked Bill as he clambered aboard.

'Relax Bill, we'll be there soon,' was Paul's reply.

The helicopter took off to the sound of Bill shouting over the noise of the rotors, 'Bloody hell, this is marvellous.'

Over the years I had come to accept that Paul has to have his fun. This meant not annoying him with silly questions such as 'Where are we going?', and, 'How long will it take?' Sweeping over the English countryside it was not too long before the pilot started to descend. I recognised the scenery below. We were passing over Reading and the Thames. The landing just off the 18th green at Goring and Streatley Golf Club created great interest from those golfers making their way down the 18th or teeing off from the 1st. The club had issued a warning to players that they were not to approach the 18th green until the helicopter had set down, but this didn't prevent those curious members from getting as close as they safely could. Bill stepped out with his hair being blown in all directions by the down draft of the blades and made his way to the pathway leading to the clubhouse.

'Mike, what are you doing to me?' was his only comment before Paul grabbed his arm, marched him upstairs and escorted Bill and myself to the top table. The room was full of Harrodian Cavaliers, Spurs fanatics and friends of Paul. Bill was given a standing ovation and as he sat down eight members of the Royal Marines Band entered the room playing, *Glory, Glory, Hallelujah*. I turned to see the expression on Bill's face. This hard, uncompromising Yorkshire man had tears in his eyes. It was a moment to savour.

Lunch was served and then Paul read a dedication to Bill that covered his momentous years at Spurs. Bill's response was also short as he was totally knocked off his feet by the reception he received.

I cannot remember the precise time of our departure. I can remember Bill uttering on a few occasions as lunch was being consumed, 'What will Darky say? I said I would be home by 3.00 pm'. Darky was Bill's good lady who was always the first to be considered by the great man. The return journey was uneventful until the pilot took a short detour and landed at Elstree airstrip where another little reception party was waiting. By now Bill was in excellent form and kept repeating to those close to him, 'I never thought I would ever go up in one of those bloody things!'

Bill returned home at 8.00 pm concerned that Darky would not be at all happy. The next morning I popped into Bill's office and asked him if he was okay. Almost as if the previous day had not happened, Bill commented to me that he was going to see Scarborough play that evening as he was interested in one of their players.

'Mike, I've never seen a player like him before. He's all over the pitch. He takes all the free kicks, corners and if the referee would let him he would take his whistle as well!' There was no mention of helicopter rides.

At the next midweek home game, Bill asked me if I could take him up to see Paul Kirby in the Centenary Club Lounge. They met and I can remember Bill and Paul hugging each other as if they had both stepped on to the summit of Everest together.

Bill was a wonderful man, sadly gone. Should there be a soccer team in heaven then you can bet your last penny that Bill Nicholson will be the manager.

Thanks to my friendship with Paul Kirby, my life took on a new meaning. Weekends were never dull. For instance my first game as a Cavalier was in March 1987. I was managing director at Reading at the time and living with my wife, Angela, and daughter, Karen.

Lying in bed on a dull overcast Sunday morning, wondering if it was time to get up and pop down the newsagents for a paper, I was startled by the sound of the phone ringing. Mr Kirby was on the end of the line.

'Michael, Michael, Michael [this was always his opener] we need you to play today for the WHC.' (WHC stood for Wonderful Harrodian Cavaliers).

'Paul it's 8.00 am.'

'Yes I know but we are playing at Gatwick against the baggage handling guys. Can you make it? Bring Angela with you.'

The meeting place was the Hilton Hotel at Gatwick at 11.00 am. On arriving at the Hilton I was surprised to see that Kirby was passing champagne amongst the players willy nilly. I met the lads for the first time and Angela and I joined the pre-match hospitality. I didn't take a glass of champers because it is one of a few drinks that I cannot stomach. Kirby asked what my favourite drink was and returned within seconds with the largest glass of Bells and a small bottle of American. I was well aware that the team did not train or take too kindly to pre match preparations, but this was ridiculous.

I asked the player next to me where we were going to play.

'Somewhere on the outskirts of Amsterdam,' was his reply.

'Amsterdam ... Amsterdam?' I cried. 'I can't go to Amsterdam I haven't brought my passport.'

'Don't worry Mike, you know Paul. He can fix anything,' said the player who I now knew as Lennie. Lennie was as round as he was tall and not surprisingly played up front in a rather static role.

I approached Paul and asked him what was happening.

'Relax, relax, relax, Michael,' was his response.

Suddenly at 11.45 am, Paul stood up and asked us all to get on the bus that would take us to the terminal. By now Angela, on the wrong side of several glasses of champagne, was quite relaxed about the situation and would go along with anything. We all descended upon the airport with Paul waving his hands in the air like a travel courier insisting that we all stay together. I was ushered into the middle of the squad as we approached passport control. What happened next was surreal. Together with Angela I was waved through by a passport control officer who seemed completely disinterested in the group.

We boarded the plane where more beverages were dispensed in generous quantities and went straight through passport control at the other end. From there we stepped on a bus that took us to a little stadium some six miles from Amsterdam.

The club house was full of people on its ground floor with another 100 or so upstairs where they could move out to a balcony to watch the game. That's where I deposited Angela who by now had a circle of lady friends all looking the worse for wear. The team made its way to a dressing room that was one of six, all fully utilised. I recognised the German, Dutch, French and Spanish accents coming from down the corridors.

Torrential rain had started to fall as we made our way to the pitch ready for kick off. I asked Paul who we were playing as we lined up. I was playing left sided centre back and Paul was in his usual left back position six yards away.

'It's only the Ajax veterans Mike. We'll take them apart.'

They didn't look in good shape, but our team was well on its way to being pissed except for the immaculate Martin Peters who, as expected, treated every game as if it was the 1966 world cup final all over again. Looks can deceive. The overweight strikers facing me soon proved to be decent players.

Just as the referee blew his whistle to start the game, rain started to fall and within minutes the pitch resembled a paddy field. As the early pattern of play was more akin to Sunday morning football with the ball being booted rather than caressed, it seemed that the victors would probably turn out to be the strongest team. What most of the other team members were not prepared for was another 'Kirby' surprise. I was aware that there was activity to my left. However, what met my eyes was awesome. Running the full length of both touch lines were waiters in their working gear (white shirt, black waistcoat and trousers) carrying litres of beer on silver trays. They were trying to follow the pattern of play so that when the ball went out of play they were never more than 10 yards away from providing refreshment. The moment the ball went dead, players rushed over and grabbed a swig of beer. This continued throughout the match. The game ended 2–2 after playing only 30 minutes each half.

We went off to the dressing room and just as we were all rushing to get into the warm showers, Kirby arrived still in his playing gear to say that we had another game to play! This time it was a team of German players representing Eintracht Frankfurt. Once again the team was a veteran side, but they appeared to be very fit and anxious to get on with it. Fortunately the rain had subsided a little and the pitch was no worse than when we had left it. Waiters appeared yet again and Lenny Barker, our joint front man together with Colin Brown, Antonio Taperelli our 67 year old full back, Don O'Keefe from the Harrods men's department, John Bulfin and Phil Lowe weighing in jointly at 34 stone, all finished off a full litre of beer before the referee had tossed his coin. I managed a good half a litre, and that, coupled with the three litres consumed in the first game, made me shrug off any conservatism I had about crossing the half way line. This was manifested in me going up for corners, taking free kicks (much to the annoyance of Mr Peters) and as Bobby Hall our keeper was feeling the strain, taking goal kicks as well. By half time I was knackered.

'Can you put a sub on for me Paul?' I asked hopefully.

'They're in a worst state than you Mike. They've been drinking throughout the first game. You'll have to stay on.'

Oh! How I loved the wonderful Harrodian Cavaliers.

We finished the second game 0–0. As the Germans had beaten the Dutch in the final game of the afternoon, they won the trophy presented that evening by the chairman of the local council in the council chamber.

We went into Amsterdam for a meal before catching a flight home (hopefully, anyway!) We were enjoying a Chinese buffet swilled down with even more beer, although this time it seemed to be served in a bucket rather than a litre glass, when someone innocently asked Paul what time the plane was leaving.

He had a quick look at his watch and with hardly a movement of a facial muscle he replied, 'In 35 minutes'.

Now Kirby does not get ruffled. His attitude towards social events is quite simply that the world will wait for him. And that included planes parked and ready for departure. Suddenly taxis appeared and the whole team, their wives and girlfriends were on their way to the airport. On route to the airport Kirby picked up huge bunches of tulips. The first bunch was presented to the irritated check-in girl who explained that the pilot was about to close the flight.

Our party consisted of 28 people; I imagine that the pilot took the view that it would be unreasonable to leave that number of passengers behind, so we clambered aboard with Kirby and all the players handing out bunches of tulips to passengers and crew alike. The jeering that accompanied our entry into the passenger cabin quickly dissipated as the passengers received their gifts with a cheery smile.

With the exception of two or three UK and European tours, the Harrodian Cavaliers only played home games. These were played at the Harrods sports ground at Barnes near the River Thames. Our pitch was immaculate, the dressing rooms comfortable, albeit aged. There were wooden huts, wooden floors and ancient shower rooms, all kept in good condition. The clubhouse was large and always full on a Sunday morning. We played a range of friendly fixtures against teams that were 'safe'. Should any visitors start to rough it up a bit then they would be instantly withdrawn from an invitation the following season.

I remember marking a retired consultant surgeon who was guesting for the St Thomas's hospital team. He made me look foolish. His quick feet and speed of turn made me look like a statue in comparison and my frustration was not appeased at half time when Kirby, with great relish, informed me that my opponent was 72 years of age!

One of the most embarrassing moments of my life occurred on that pitch. I used to travel up from Reading on a Sunday morning full of anticipation and eagerness arriving with at least a half hour to spare before kick off. Even at 43 years of age I still got a kick out of being with the lads and talking a good game. Then we'd go out onto the pitch, trying banana shots that more often than not went straighter than an arrow from a bow. I took corner kicks with the sole intention of putting the ball straight into the onion bag. I lashed half volleys against the cross bar. I leapt above Lennie, Phil and David as the ball came in from a cross to head the ball past a bewildered Bobby Hall only to hear him mumble, 'It's a pity you can't do that during the game'. This particular Sunday morning in March 1982 I had to watch my speed on the M4 travelling up to Barnes as the roads had been icy the night before. I arrived 30 minutes late. I rushed into the dressing room and there on my peg hung my green and gold shirt, green and gold shorts and socks. As I pulled the shirt down, horror struck me. This wasn't my number six shirt but a number five shirt! Like a spoilt child I started to sulk as I pulled on a shirt that was foreign to me. Hurriedly I raced out onto the pitch just as the ref was calling the captains together for the toss up. I could see the number six shirt being worn by a stranger.

'Excuse me, I think you've got my shirt,' I declared, And then the words stuck in my throat as I was face to face with none other than Bobby Moore.

'Sorry mate, but Paul told me I had to wear number six. Look I'll swap with you.'

'No, no, please wear it uh; um, um, yes please keep it.' How I wished that the ground would swallow me up.

'Where do you want me to play?' asked Bobby.

'Anywhere Bobby, yes, anywhere.'

'Are you Mike from Spurs?'

'Yes'

'Look, if you're a centre back I will play just in front of you and you can take the high balls because I was never very good at heading the ball.'

'I'm dreaming, I've passed on, this cannot be happening to me.' I thought. My hero, the man I tried to style my own game on, was standing discussing with me about where he should play. I was to play in his natural position. I cannot for a moment explain how exhilarated I felt every time Bobby called out, 'It's yours Mike,' when the muddy, plastic coated sphere came dropping out of the sky in the direction of Bobby's head. He would then move forward and leave it to me.

'Good 'ed, Mike.'

Bloody hell, Bobby Moore has just paid me a compliment.

I attended an England International at Wembley some years later and had the privilege of sitting on the same table as Bobby and his wife Stephanie. Bobby was giving a pre and post match analysis. He looked awful. His skin was yellow and his voice was very weak. Looking into the eyes of Stephanie, I could see the sadness that engulfed her. Bobby was dying. Only a few weeks later he passed on. That night, considering his health, he made what must have been for him a painful effort to come around the table tap me on the shoulder and say hello. What really knocked me off my feet was his question to me relating to 'that business'. He wanted reassurance that it had been sorted out.

'That business' was a project that Paul Kirby had been involved with. The common denominator was the New Zealand Football Association. Paul was the Football Association's representative on the Oceanic Group and with special responsibility for the New Zealand Football Association. His position meant that he could plan and arrange for visits of the New Zealand International Soccer team to Europe.

As managing director of Reading FC at the time I was delighted to welcome New Zealand to Elm Park in 1985. This was arranged by Paul. The match was a great success as we had George Best and Martin Peters guesting for us. A crowd of 7,000 turned up and for 20 minutes, George put on the magic. He performed nutmegs, flicks, and whilst any burst of speed was outside his capability, he did enough with the ball to delight the crowd.

Paul suggested another game with New Zealand two years later. Preparations were in hand and once again famous guest players were lined up to supplement the Royals team. One week before the game, I received a call from Kirby to say that the match could not go ahead as New Zealand had now agreed to play Newcastle United on the same day as the scheduled game against Reading. I was gutted and asked how could this possibly happen. He told me that the promotions company responsible for the trip had decided to take the Newcastle game as the gate would be far in excess of what we might expect at Reading. The promotions company was headed by John Mitchell, the ex-Fulham hero, with support from Bobby Moore as an associate director. I claimed compensation for the loss of the fixture and expenses already incurred. Payment was never received, even after I had sent a serious debt collector (ex-chief of police for the Thames Valley) to visit Mr Mitchell. My answer to Bobby's question about 'that business' being sorted had to be in the affirmative. How could I possibly place more woe on his head in his darkest hour?

Bobby Moore's world cup colleague, Martin Peters, played several times for the Cavaliers. On one occasion when we played at home on a bright winter's morning we had words, or should I say he had words with me. In a high scoring match that saw Martin claim a hat-trick before half time, their keeper launched a drop kick from inside his box. I didn't want to head this missile dropping out of the sky as the previous night had been a bit hairy and my skull was not up to receiving what would have felt like an Exocet shot through it. I moved back a few yards and as the ball dropped in front of me, I drove the ball forward on the half volley. Unfortunately Mr Peters faced me some five yards away and the ball hit him in the bollocks. As he fell to the ground he screamed, 'Are you fucking incapable of hitting the ball short?'

'I just did Martin.'

Remember, my upbringing meant that the short mamby, pamby, intricate passing that came as second nature to Peters was an anathema to me. Newport County didn't mess about playing in triangles. They just got it down the field fast as they could let the front men deal with it. Playing the game the Brazilian style was never a mode this very ordinary player could identify with.

Certainly the Hertfordshire Sunday League Division Five was far away from the boys on the Copacabana Beach! I was quite incapable of playing the short passing game as I was too slow and by the time I had decided who to play it to I was robbed of the ball.

I found myself on the opposite side to Martin a few months later when I brought a Reading directors XI to play the Cavaliers. This was the fifth game between the two teams who were competing on a home and away basis for the Pol Roger Cup (Pol derived from Paul Kirby and Roger meaning Roger Smee the Reading Chairman as the two of them were close friends). The first game was played at Elm Park on 13th May 1984 and ended in a 6–6 draw when Mr Kirby hired half the Royal Marines Band and led the teams out before 85 people, two dogs and a worried groundsman. The return leg played at Barnes on 23rd September 1984 was won 3–2 by the directors' team who thus became the first holders of the trophy. In 1985 the first game played at Elm Park was a 3–3 draw. The return leg saw a 7–3 victory for the Reading side, goals coming from Ian Branfoot, Bobby Williams (2) Roger Smee (2) Mark Mundell (1) and an own goal from me. I was playing for the Cavaliers in this game.

In the third season of the competition, the Directors XI began with an excellent 5–4 away win. I turned out for the Reading team in this particular season. After 10 minutes of play 'Bertie' Bassett, the Reading Youth team keeper and the son of our commercial manager Annie Bassett, fell awkwardly and a tennis ball size lump came up on his elbow. The problem now was who should go in goal? The lame excuses made by the rest of the team when asked if they could play in goal included:

'My eyes are not good enough.' (Ian Branfoot, Manager.)

'I'm too short.' (Stuart Henderson, Youth Team Coach.)

'Can't catch the ball.' (David Downes, Club Historian.)

'I'm the only one capable of scoring bloody goals.' (Roger Smee, Club Chairman.)

'I'm the only one with any height at the back' (Mike Kearney, Social Club Steward)

'My back is still hurting from mowing the pitch.' (Gordon Neate, Reading FC groundsman.)

'It's more than my jobs worth, what if I break a finger?' (Dr Williams, Reading FC club doc.)

'If I break a finger the club accounts will not get done.' (Dick Winter, club accountant.)

'Okay, okay give me the shirt,' I said in exasperation. In reality I was probably the worst player in the team. I had put on considerable weight over the previous 12 months. My mobility was at question so a spell of a little activity was welcomed.

For the next 35 minutes I kept a clean sheet making only a couple of mediocre saves near the post. My biggest problem was not always being in the right position. Scraping my left boot down the middle of the penalty box helped but was no use at all after a melee in the box when I became totally disorientated. As the second half was about to end, there was a magic moment. I should mention that by then I had let in four simple goals yet we were still 5–4 up. One of their goals was scored with the ball hardly crossing the line after my futile attempt to stop a feeble shot from Colin Brown, the Cavaliers' centre forward. It rolled under my bulging stomach and just inches over the goal line. Then came the moment of truth. With the referee looking at his watch for the third time I caught sight of a lean, mean player coming over the half way line twisting, turning and dropping his shoulder to drift past an outstretched leg or body check. Yes, Peters was at his best. He held no fear for me. I positioned myself slightly forward and off the line making made myself look big in the process. Peters looked around for support. He was on his own as his colleagues were some 20 yards behind sucking in oxygen. At 30 yards out he looked up, cocked his left foot and sent the ball through the air like a rocket. I was up to it though. I anticipated that the ball was going to my left as Martin was approaching from the left side of the field, and I took off. The ball hit the third finger of my left hand, dislocating it in the process, shot up and hit the cross bar rebounding and coming to rest in my arms. I turned to see the reaction from Martin. He stood with hands on his hips and shook his head in dismay. To this day my fourth finger on my left hand sticks out at an angle, incapable of resting alongside my middle finger.

I haven't exactly dined out on the story, but in the event that I am asked about my 'funny' finger, it gives me great pleasure in relaying the story, even if it is dramatised a little.

The return leg saw the Directors XI hold the Pol Roger cup for the third successive season with another narrow 3–2 victory against the Harrods team that included Bobby Moore. It was during the latter part of the 1986–1987 football season that the now re-named *International* Harrodian Cavaliers went on another European tour. This time the tour was to Portugal on a trip that would last three days.

Unfortunately for me, I could not travel out with the squad as Reading had a home game on Saturday. Kirby had other ideas about me flying out on Sunday and wanted me there on Saturday. He arranged for a VIP car to take me from Elm Park on the final whistle and speed me to Heathrow. From there I caught the 7.00 pm flight to Lisbon Faro. At Lisbon Faro, another driver and VIP car met me at the airport and then travelled way up in the mountains. Adding on an extra hour meant it was 10.30 pm before I met up with the Cavaliers committee at a very nice restaurant where I stood over a tank of fish and chose my meal. Anything from baby shark to lobster was on the menu.

The committee consisted of Paul, his partner Sue, Martin Peters and wife Cath, Bobby Keetch and his partner and a Portuguese gentleman who was unknown to me. They were all half way through their meal so I hurriedly ordered mine which from memory consisted of a large pink fish and accompanying rice. I was rather curious when my food was placed before me and all eyes seemed to be looking in my direction. I soon found out why. Under a wicked instruction from Kathy Peters, the waiter was told to include crushed chilli peppers discreetly tucked under my rice. Bloody hell! I have never experienced anything like the feeling that engulfed me shortly after taking the first spoonful. My mouth was on fire and as best as I could I called for water. Two jugs appeared. One was used to put out the fire dispensing with the need to pour it into a glass. The second unfortunately found its way to Mrs Peters who poured the contents over my head.

'Martin, can you control that bloody woman?' I shouted.

'Mike, you know her well enough by now. Control? You must be joking!'

'Yes Martin, where is my bloody dishwasher you promised me. Mike tells me they are really cheap now.' (What this outburst from Kathy had to do with my tongue being on fire I cannot imagine.)

The conversation she was referring to took place months before when the Cavaliers played one of their few away games on a Sunday in Manchester. During the after match lunch I remember getting into a conversation with her about dishwashers.

'Martin's so bloody mean Mike, I really should have all these luxuries shouldn't I? Go on tell him.'

To get matters into context I should add that both of us were well through a bottle of red, with side drinks of gin and tonic and whisky. Kathy had found a friend and we thoroughly enjoyed each other's company. My relationship with Martin was not really

147

cemented as I had only known him for a short while, so there was no way I was going to ask him to buy his wife a bloody dishwasher. Somehow, from the back of her mind as we were perched on top of a mountain in Portugal trying to enjoy a 'quiet' meal, she snapped into action. Perhaps the sight of seeing the water from the jug slide down my head in a cascade reminded her of water pouring over bowls and dishes, I don't know.

Paul described the first game held that afternoon when the International Harrodian Cavaliers had played a village team comprised mainly of waiters from the local restaurants and bistros. The Cavs won 9–0.

The squad and their partners or girlfriends were accommodated at Ernie Clay's hotel some 40 miles from Lisbon. Ernie became the Chairman of Fulham Football Club in 1977. His infamous quote at the time that, 'We've got a long-term plan for this club and, apart from the results it's going well,' was committed to the annals of football sayings. On selling the club for £7,000,000, giving himself an enormous profit, Clay joined the ranks of smash and grab merchants in a similar way to his predecessor Eric Miller, Robert Maxwell and an ever growing list of opportunists who see a football club as a potential cash cow. Nevertheless, it was a joy to meet and talk to Ernie as he was always ready for the funny quip, even if some of his tales were embellished a little.

Our second match the next day was, according to Paul, to be against another village team who were in a different league to Saturday's opponents. An executive coach arrived at the hotel to take us to the game. As we approached Lisbon I became curious. 'Paul, where's this village?'

'Michael, Michael, Michael, relax save your energy for the game.'

As we took the circular road around Lisbon, the players were getting restless. Even laid back Martin Peters was starting to complain.

'Where are we going Paul, Spain?'

Half an hour later we took the road to Setubal and parked up in the city centre. Cool, calculating Paul was starting to panic a little. Looking at his watch he ushered us off the coach and said that we had one hour to take lunch. Guiding the party into a fashionable restaurant in the heart of the city famous for its muscatel wine and sardines, Paul immediately took his place at what appeared to be a top table with half a dozen seats facing half a dozen round tables seating four people. The lads, dehydrated and hungry, got stuck into some Portuguese beer and nibbles. Hardly anyone noticed that the top table had filled up until Kirby banged an ashtray on the table and introduced his special guest.

'Lads, in case you don't recognise this gentleman sat to my left, can I introduce you to Malcolm Allison.'

I was sitting with Lenny Barker, Colin Brown and Barry Harrington. It was Barry who opened up with, 'What the hell is he doing here?'

I had always been an admirer of Allison as he was a personality and could be guaranteed to stir up the football authorities. He was a man with style too, symbolised by the wearing of a fedora and his penchant for a Havana cigar.

Malcolm was the current manager of Vitória Setubal. We listened to some of his funny stories under the illusion that he was going to join us and watch our performance against this village side. Oh no! He started to do a bio on *his* players. Not the first team but the veterans. The team was made up of three ex-Brazilian internationals, two former Dutch internationals and the remainder were ex-Portuguese professionals. Lenny Barker at 17 stone and 5 feet 6 inches, capable of turning into a sweaty jelly on a cold English Sunday morning was by now taking on the appearance of a giant raindrop. 'Mike, I'm going on the bench.'

It was 82 degrees with humidity to match at 2.00 pm in Setubal. This was no place for an overweight Sunday morning footballer to practice his skills.

I had sympathy for Lenny. His apprehension about taking part led me to take a swift head count of those fit enough to play. There were just 14 players with two carrying injuries from the previous day. Within 15 minutes of finishing lunch we entered the stadium carrying a bellyful of beer (most of us were past worrying about appearance and fitness). Our limited ability as a team of ageing, overweight and the unfit, was supplemented by Martin Peters, Colin Brown (ex-Palace trialist) and Keith Cooke (ex-Arsenal trialist).

As with most Southern European stadiums, the dressing rooms were underground where there was some degree of coolness. We waited for Paul to announce the team.

'Right lads, this is how we will start.'

He listed the team as follows: Gary Grant in goal, Tony Tapperelli, Mike Lewis, Bazza Harrington and Paul Kirby across the back; David Gray, Martin Peters, John Bulfin and Lenny Barker in midfield with Colin Brown and Bobby Keetch up front. On the bench was Don O'Keefe.

As we looked at the Setubal vets during the kick-in, a certain swell of confidence enveloped the Cavaliers. Our opponents were all sizes and ages. The game attracted hundreds of spectators. Little did they know that this was going to be the slowest ever game of football, with perhaps the only incident of note being the collapse through heat exhaustion of most of the Harrodian players!

It turned out that Malcolm, using his best PR technique, had convinced the local press that his vets were playing the England vets. What a shock the fans were in for. Then unbelievably before we had even kicked off, the late Bobby Keetch pulled a hamstring. This brought our only sub off the bench. Immaculate Don O'Keefe never got his kit dirty even if the pitch resembled a paddy field! There was no way he was going to pick up a grass stain on this lush turf.

The opening 10 minutes saw the sides weighing each other up with the Harrodians looking quite capable of springing a surprise. Suddenly the Setubal players stepped up their game. The ex-Brazilian International that Martin Peters told me to mark out of the game started to perform. He was as round as he was tall but that didn't stop him displaying the typical Brazilian magic of close ball control and awesome passing. His move towards me held no fear because he wasn't necessarily quick but with a drop of one shoulder, a drag back of the ball then a sprint to my left he was bloody well gone!

Peters howled at me, 'Get hold of him Mike!' then chased the Michelin man into the box himself. As the Brazilian was about to shoot, Martin clipped his heels and down he went. Penalty!

If that wasn't bad enough he returned after placing the ball on the penalty spot and chuckled. Swine!

They were one up and started to tear us apart. Kathy Peters was our bucket and sponge lady who was soon in action as the heat took its toll.

Allison had half a dozen subs on his bench plus a huge container of water and a physio carrying a medical bag so large that he could have climbed inside it himself.

By half time we were 4–0 down. There should have been a half time team talk but, apart from Martin Peters, we were too short of oxygen to manage a sentence never mind a talk.

We got a good reception from the Setubal fans on returning to the field of play for the second half. This reception was mostly out of sympathy, I suspect. Martin, together with Paul, decided that re-shuffling the pack meant that we would play a 4–5–1 formation, leaving Colin Brown up front on his own. The enlarged midfield was designed to cut out the incisive runs made by their three strikers including roly, poly man.

All went well for two minutes. Then two of our players pulled up with cramp at the same time. Both Lenny Barker and Bazza Harrington were in the course of chasing a speedy winger when they both crashed to the ground. Kathy Peters declined to come on to treat the fallen heroes as both men were clasping the tops of their thighs. The Setubal Physio, displaying an act of pure chivalry, signalled to Kathy that he would take care of the problem.

I wondered what was going through Martin Peters' mind at the time. Some 18 years earlier he had helped England to win the World Cup. Now here he was playing alongside a bunch of has-beens, never-beens, and never-will-bes. What a professional. He never complained, always had a smile and was always on hand to give advice. He gave me some advice half way through the second half. 'Mike, don't let that fat bastard get the ball down. You get forward 10 yards and take him out.'

'Okay Mart. Leave it to me.'

For some reason, the first thought that entered my head after the advice given by Mr Peters was to remember the bully Tommy Young from my school days. Now, he didn't have an ounce of the skill that this little feller had but he was intimidating nevertheless. The first opportunity to take him out presented itself soon after. I was standing about two yards from the half way line as unbelievably we were actually on the attack.

Their keeper picked up the ball and launched it 50 yards down the pitch. Michelin man had his back to me and from the flight of the ball I could see that he was in a position to bring it down, turn and run. 'No way chum,' I thought. Before the ball had dropped to a height where he could bring it on to his chest I was in. Leather smacked against my sunburned forehead. I placed a perfect header into their penalty box and in the process flattened the boy from Brazil who stayed on the ground for what seemed an eternity.

The ref blew his whistle to stop play. I was surrounded by Setubal players making all sorts of noises and waving their arms in the air. The ref, unable to speak English, gave me that look that suggested that he was considering taking some kind of action against me. To be honest I would have welcomed a return to the dressing room! Then Blobby got to his feet to be helped off the field. On his way to the touch line he wrenched himself free of the physio to come over to me. Christ, what's he going to do? To my surprise he offered me an outstretched hand accompanied by a huge smile.

Later in the hospitality lounge we did our best to make ourselves understood. I made a lot of hand movements and he used a smattering of English. He managed to explain as best he could that he was also knackered at the time of my clumsy challenge and was happy to be going off.

Setubal went on to score three more goals and we replied with a penalty. The game ended 7–1.

After the game Mr Peters came over and asked me if I had ever earned money from playing the football. I thought it a curious question but I told him no, never. Then he said, 'Well, there's some justice in the world.' This was followed by, 'When I said "Take fatty out", I didn't mean "Put him in hospital".'

It was time to strike back. 'Look Martin, a team is made up of all different sorts of players. You pussy foot around the arena like a bloody prima donna leaving it to the less talented players to sort out any problems. We complement each other.'

With a look of bewilderment and a shrug of his shoulders he walked away to take his shower.

Paul Kirby was, and probably still is an unusual character. If ever a rumour circulated that he was a spy for MI5 then not too many people would raise an eyebrow. His love of seeing others enjoy themselves (at his expense more often than not) was a sight to cherish. His huge brown eyes, youthful looks and a slightly protruding chin made him different from the rest. His globetrotting was legendary.

'Paul's in Florida with Jack Nicklaus.'

'Paul decided to fly off to see the Super Bowl.'

'Paul jumped on a plane this morning to see the World Cup Final in Spain.'

'Paul's at Wimbledon for the final.'

All these were responses to the question, 'Can I speak to Paul please?' made by his partner Sue.

One sunny afternoon sitting in my office at Spurs I received a call from him. 'Michael, Michael, Michael get down to Harrods' Sports Ground by 5.30.'

'Why Paul?'

'Michael, you have to learn to relax, just get down here and bring your tennis gear.'

On the dot of 5.30 pm, I entered the changing rooms at

Harrods Sports Ground. Someone I had never met before sat in the corner putting on his cricket pads. He looked and asked if I was Mike.

'Ah, Mike. Paul said to go straight to the tennis courts.'

I could see three players out on the grass court. There was Paul, plus a male partner and an old gentleman on his own the other side of the net. 'Michael, Michael, Michael, meet Larry. He's your partner tonight.'

I spun around and there was a little old man with such a familiar face that it didn't take me more that a couple of seconds to recognise him as Larry Adler the world famous harmonica player.

'Pleased to meet you Mike. Is it okay if I play the base line as my legs are not what they used to be?'

'Of course Mr Adler.' (I never forgot what my mum told me years before. If you don't know someone you are meeting for the first time always call them by their surname.)

'Larry it is Mike, call me Larry.'

I was not a good net player. This soon became obvious when the first set went to Kirby and partner 6–0.

It was the second set and by now Larry and I had a little bit of an understanding. Larry would come forward to any ball going down the right side of the court, so if I was to take up a position slightly left of centre we could maybe stop the rot. Well, we did up to a point. The second set went 6–1 to Kirby and partner.

In the clubhouse after the game Larry regaled us with showbiz stories. He also told me that he was a composer of music too. I didn't know this.

Paul somehow missed my 42nd birthday much to my relief as it meant that I stood a fair chance of celebrating at home with the family of my first wife Maureen, Karen and Tiger the dog without the terrifying thought of Kirby having organised some bash that would leave me prostrate for days after. Usually he would turn up unexpectedly and cart us all off in his Roller to some fantastic lunch or dinner. Four days after my birthday we played a home match against West Ham United. After thanking the match sponsors then taking two of their party to the boardroom to meet the chairman, I returned to the Bill Nicholson suite to enjoy a post match drink with my colleagues from the commercial department. Suddenly the double doors to the room burst open. In strode Kirby holding up a Parrot cage in one hand and a huge cigar in the other. The cage contained a cockatoo. It was a beautiful bird with white plumage and a red plume. He passed the cage over to me and asked if I would stand still whilst a photo was taken. As the amateur photographer struggled to get his camera into gear I had to put the cage on the floor and wait until he was ready. Now the next bit of this story should really have been videoed for posterity and shown on *You've Been Framed*. Finally 'David Bailey' was ready and signalled for me to pick up the cage. I lifted the cage only to find that the bottom stayed where it was and the bird took flight. Fortunately no windows were open. Of the few guests left in the room that afternoon were two aspiring middleweight boxers. The boxers were Mark Kaylor and Roy Gumbs. Together with their agents, they were keen to promote the fight in London 11 days later. We were happy to let the boxers go down on the pitch at half time and be introduced to the crowd of 32,000. I cannot remember which one of the two it was who decided to chase the bird around room in an effort to catch it. He succeeded in cornering the bird under a table and against the inside of a door. 'I've got it,' he shouted shortly followed by expletives that were regarded as funny by virtue of the number times he managed to get the word 'fuck' into 20 seconds. The bird bit him between his thumb and index finger in the fleshy part. Blood oozed out of the wound. My lasting memory of the incident was the way the promoter then blew his top and managed to cram more 'fucks' into 20 seconds than his boy had done earlier. He howled 'The fight is in danger now. Your opponent has seen you get injured you brainless sod'. All I could think of were two things: 'Where is that bloody bird?' and 'Who is going to take this exponent of the Queensbury Rules to hospital to get a tetanus jab?' Kirby meanwhile wore a sheepish grin and asked everyone to calm down and be quiet. Top of the cage in hand, he wandered to the far end of the room, crept up on the bird and slowly dropped the cage over him. All that was left to do was to fit the bottom of the cage to the top. This was easily achieved. Standing proud and holding the cage at shoulder height Paul announced, 'Michael, Michael, Michael, happy birthday'.

As I drove the 15 miles home to Hertford with the cockatoo on the back seat, I pictured the delight on my daughter's face when she saw what daddy had brought home. After all at 11 years of age she would be over the moon to have a beautiful bird as a pet. What I didn't appreciate as it was never a topic of conversation, was that my wife hated to see caged birds. She made this plainly clear to me as I stepped over the doorstep.

'Take that bloody thing back to where it came from.'

'But darling, it's a birthday present.'

Even with the support of my daughter who was close to tears and groaning, 'Oh Mum can't we keep it?' Maureen was not prepared to have the bird cross the doorstep. I made a quick call to Harry, the Security Manager at White Hart Lane, to ensure that he would still be at the club in the next hour so that I could deposit the bird in my office overnight and at least give me a little time to arrange permanent accommodation.

The capacity for women to change stances within a short period of time was never brought home to me so much as in the conversation that ensued upon my return home for the second time that day. Having successfully 'nested' the bird in my office I was hit with the opening salvo of, 'What have you done with it?'

'It's in my office.'

'What about food?'

'He's got a tray full in his cage.'

'What about water?'

'I filled the little basin full before I left.'

Then came the bombshell. 'You can't leave it there all night, go and get it back.'

'You must be joking!'

'No, get it back and we will put it in the kitchen for the night.'

Over her shoulder I could see Karen, hand over her mouth, stifling a chuckle. The bird was given the name 'Henry' by Karen for reasons to this day I fail to understand, but Henry it was. Henry is still alive and living with Karen's ex husband in Reading. He never talked during the time we had him. He was the most vicious animal I have ever met and obviously thoroughly enjoyed sinking his beak into anything that resembled a piece of human flesh.

As for Paul Kirby, well I haven't had a conversation with him for a few years. He had his own legal problems through his partnership with Terry Venables and I believe that the FA subsequently relieved him of his title of Representative of the Oceanic Group. But I would like to thank Paul for bringing a whole new dimension into my life. It was a real experience to know him. Many others will testify to the infectious personality that he had, even if at times this led many a good man down the wrong path taking him through a series of expensive divorces!

15

TIME FOR A CHANGE

It was shortly after the Royals won the Simod Cup that I decided to move on. During the 1987–1988 season, clubs were given a free weekend. Some clubs organised friendlies, others such as Reading took the opportunity to take the players on a mini break to foreign climes. I had good contacts in Southern Spain, so we booked a hotel at Miraflores near Marbella through my friend Terry Flores (a Spaniard educated in England and heavily involved in the property business along the Costa Del Sol). Flights were arranged on a budget airline.

I decided to accompany the team along with Ian Branfoot the manager and John Haselden the physio. For the first three days it rained cats and dogs. Fortunately we were provided with an all weather pitch near the hotel so at least the lads could keep fit. It was on one of these wet days that Terry Flores asked me to accompany him to look at a parcel of land some eight kilometres behind Valderamma Golf Club. The area was composed of 800 hectares of beautiful, undulating and partly forested land that nestled in a natural valley. Terry had options on the land that included an element of National Parkland. The reason for my invitation to accompany him on this viewing was to ask me what I thought the land could be used for. There was no hesitation, I cried out, 'Golf, Golf, Golf!' This was at a time when the coastline was saturated with half built property and not enough golf clubs to satisfy the burgeoning population.

A few weeks after my return home, I received a call from Terry. He said that he was coming over to the UK for a few days and asked if he could see me for a few hours. We met and he asked me if I would be interested in managing a golf project on his land. He told me that he would finance the setting up costs but would be looking to me to find an investment partner for his project.

Having just moved into a new house with a new baby, the offer could not have come at a worse time. Should I take yet another gamble? The four years at Reading FC had been eventful. I did feel that I was beginning to jump on the same carousel season after season and perhaps a change *was* needed. So after careful consideration I told Terry that I would take him up on his offer. There was one important proviso. I said that I would work in the UK for the first six months making the occasional visit to the site when necessary. I could start to formulate relationships in the golfing world far better working out of the UK than moving to Spain. I have to confess, however, that after four months of working in the UK, it was becoming impossible to move the project on without being 'on site'.

Taking the bold step to uproot and move to Spain I moved to a very comfortable Villa in Soto Grande that Terry had purchased in readiness for the development of the project. Seeing this magnificent property for the first time only endorsed my view that Terry meant business. Not only did this magnificent building have all the facilities necessary to entertain guests, it came with two housekeepers! Antonio and Marinesse, a young, recently married couple played host and looked after my every whim. Their English was as good as my Spanish, so we struggled at first with limited discussions. A succession of visitors to the villa brought the best out in the two and we enjoyed many an evening with good food and excellent wine provided in typical Andulucian style by the young couple.

The support of the local community for the project was vital. The land mass covered the parishes of five local mayors. They were wined and dined collectively at the villa. They had promised 100 percent support from their councils. The local mayor in Spain is God. I was not too happy about the passing of brown envelopes on several occasions when we met the elected representatives, but they promised us that the dosh was going into party funds. Who was I to argue?

Having become friendly with the general manager of the Valderrama Golf Club, I used every opportunity to pick his brain. It soon became evident that some of the world's best golf course designers and architects were American, so I arranged a trip to San Antonio in Texas to meet Bill Clover and Mike Reddy, both experienced golf course landscape designers. Our initial meeting was very productive. I liked their ideas and courtesy of a video recording I had made of the land they were able to make some exciting suggestions as to how we could blend in selective real estate development alongside golfing facilities. On the second day of my visit, Bill Clover was most apologetic about the fact that he had to split off from my meeting for a short while to talk to a German visitor who had flown in from Düsseldorf. He suggested that I go off with Michael Reddy and visit one of their developments near San Antonio and that we meet up later that afternoon. Bill suggested that we Europeans should join him for dinner that evening, so the German and I were entertained at one of San Antonio's swishiest restaurants. Klaus Dorr and I got on like a house on fire. From our first meeting it was obvious that we shared the same passion for football, good whisky and a love of the south coast of Spain. Klaus had come to America to seek out golf course architects who could point them to locations on a world map that were ideal for golf course development. He worked for the giant German Thyssen Steel Company. Klaus was their new project director.

The suggestion that we all dine together was made on the back of Clover's embarrassment about the relatively short time he could spend with me that day. Had he known the outcome of my introduction to Dorr, then perhaps he would have played his cards differently. After several liberal measures of Johnny Walker Black Label, Klaus dropped his guard and suggested that with or without Bill Clover we could strap together a deal depending on what he found when he visited the land. We arranged dates when he could visit Spain and examine the possibility of a joint partnership. He suggested that we both carry on using Bill Clover to enable us to quickly learn more about golf course development. Everyone was happy.

Clover took us on a tour of several other developments in Texas and whilst in Dallas he entertained us for lunch in the Dallas Oil Club. This was at the time of the oil crisis of the late 1980s. On the back of soaring oil prices in the early 1980s the bottom dropped out of the market eight years later. Here I was in the infamous Dallas Oil Club at a time when some banks in Dallas went out of business. Bill Clover suggested that we sat nearest the huge centre table that accommodated a dozen oilmen. 'Mike, you will overhear some interesting comments.'

Most of them were wearing their trademark Stetsons and Texan ties. Bill suggested that we sat quietly for a few minutes whilst scanning the menu and tune into what was being said on the next table. What followed was like something out of a Dallas episode.

'Hey Mack, is that your new Continental parked out there?'

'Yeah Frank, I've decided to downgrade a little. What are you driving?'

'It's the new Buick Riviera pal. Lorna [presumably his wife] just loved the colour so there it is. To hell with the expense.'

The next 10 minutes consisted of one-upmanship with Mack regretting his admission of downgrading. Clover quietly whispered to us that between them, they didn't have two dollars to rub together.

Within two months Klaus had visited me in Spain. The bond between us sealed to the extent that a partnership agreement was drafted. He loved southern Spain, loved the land and he loved the attention he was given courtesy of Antonio and Marinesse. I hate to think how many bottles of that wonderful Johnny Walker Black Label we ploughed through. The deal was actually done in the kitchen of the villa. Klaus perched himself on the working surface on one side of the kitchen and I was balanced precariously somewhere between the sink and the fridge on the opposite side. We had just returned from a late night in Puerto Banus. His very words to me were, 'Mike, next week I want to bring my financial director and marketing director down here to confirm and sign the arrangement'.

The relationship with Thyssen Steel meant that the forward financing of the project was secure. They were after all one of the biggest companies in Europe. As our German partners were sending various officials from their company down to Soto Grande, I was given the responsibility for not only entertaining them during the day, but looking after them at night as many of the regular monthly visits lasted for a few days. Klaus was always present, so a regular event was a late evening meal at the villa with his colleagues then off to Banus until the early hours. I was 'forced' to accompany the group. God it was hard work! It took a little while for our German partners to accept that nocturnal pleasures in Puerto Banus were best after midnight.

Six months into the partnership agreement, Thyssen sent a bevy of their top directors to visit us. Klaus was particularly nervous about this visit as he was the man who had spearheaded this giant company into taking the softer option to enter the leisure market and his reputation was at stake. Thyssen are famous for building warships, huge steel plants and escalators, so involvement in the leisure industry seemed light years away from their former profile and to some extent a gamble. At a convention

12 months earlier attended by all their senior managers, the question had been asked, 'How do we soften the image of our company?' It was Klaus Dorr's group of managers that won the day by suggesting that leisure was the answer and golf in particular. Klaus had managed to persuade the board that projects in Curacao and southern Spain should be the forerunners of that new policy. The visit of the 'top knobs' meant that Klaus could show them first hand how the southern Spain project would develop. Contrary to the perceived view some people have about Germans, I found that all of these officials were absolute gentlemen, enjoyed a good joke even if it contained some 'war' humour and more to the point they never got down to the villa's pool at 6.00 am and laid out their bath towels!

Two years later, just as the project was gaining momentum, the Gulf war started. Our marketing plan that included a 30 percent income stream from the sale of properties on the course was under a grave threat. Brits were selling up rather than buying on the Costa del Sol. My apartment in Marbella valued at £125,000 in 1989 was now valued at £85,000. Fear that the war could escalate made many UK passport holders run for home. Our budget was destroyed.

To make matters worse, the Berlin Wall was demolished. This enabled the Thyssen Steel Company to re-enter Eastern Germany and attempt to locate many properties and landholdings historically owned.

The golf project was put on ice. I was asked to stay on and keep matters ticking over until the conditions were more conducive. At that precise time John Madejski rang me.

16

ROYAL RETURN

Reading spent several seasons back in Division Two (the old Division Three) until John Madejski arrived as Chairman in 1990. After rescuing the club from possible extinction he immediately put new ideas into place. One of his new ideas was to invite an old friend called Tony Kennedy to take over the reigns as managing director. Tony was an insurance salesman with the gift of the gab who could not resist the temptation. Madejski honestly thought that as long as someone had business nous they could easily run a football club.

Tony found out very early on that the game was incestuous and did not take kindly to outsiders attempting to get up to speed quickly by pretending they knew it all. The signing of midfielder Danny Bailey by Tony from Leyton Orient for £50,000 was an example of how easily it is to be fooled if seen as a 'Johnny come lately'. Kennedy was a great insurance salesman but a very poor football club managing director. A fake is quickly spotted and exploited. His obvious delight in capturing this star player and the subsequent praise that it brought upon him when John Madejski congratulated him on his purchase, was short lived. Bailey was not a bad player making 53 appearances, but his barrel chest and flowing locks gave the wrong impression. He was not a Terry Hurlock, a Norman Hunter or a Robbie Savage. In fact he was bit of a pussy cat. He was a great engine that was incapable of hitting a barn door from 10 yards out! Reading paid twice as much as he was worth. It was a matter of some irony that Bailey became a cult hero at Exeter City of all places. Kennedy's days were numbered.

Madejski tracked me down via my office in Marbella to my tennis club. I was out on court playing a doubles match with an aggressive German lady as my partner. It was a rare occasion for me as we were leading two sets to one and a box of new balls awaited the victors. The match was well on its way to being done and dusted with the Fräulein taking most of the points as she commandeered the net. This was to be one of the few occasions when I was to be on the winning side with a tennis racket in my hand! His call came just as we were serving for victory.

The tennis club manager said there was a call from the UK and it was urgent. John's opening comment was, 'Lewis, Mummy's little boy has done something very stupid'.

I asked who was calling as John was prone to adopting a Benny Hill voice when he was being silly and I could not be sure that it was him or one of my crazy mates. His follow up left me in no doubt however.

'You know I told you years ago that I would never buy Reading Football Club? Well I have. They were going out of business within 24 hours Mike, so I've saved them. Look, I'll get straight to the point. Will you come back and run this crock of shit for me? I tried to run it for a few weeks calling in favours from old friends but it hasn't worked out. The staff who are still here from your previous stint are suggesting that I get you back. As you know Mike, I don't easily succumb to pressure, but when Little C (Phil Chant the lottery manager) made representations on your behalf it made me give the idea serious thought.'

I should explain why Phil Chant, the diminutive lottery manager was called Little C by Madejski. If I tell you that I was called Big C (6 feet 1 inches tall and weighing in at 16 stone) and the Chairman insisted on being called King C (in charge of everything) then perhaps you can work the rest out for yourself.

The manager at the time of my return was Ian Porterfield. Branfoot had sadly been sacked. Porterfield occupied the office next door to mine and our relationship was quite good for the first few months.

Results were not that impressive so the pressure was on the manager. Whether that pressure caused him to take the action that brought his downfall is purely a matter for conjecture. On a coach trip back from an away fixture, Ian consumed a fair quantity of lager together with the players. This was compounded by his visit to a nightclub in Berkshire on his return. He was charged with drink driving on his way home. The call from the local newspaper on the morning following his misdemeanour came as a complete surprise to me. I was asked what the club was going to do about Mr Porterfield. I assumed that the question was related to the poor performance of the team, but no, the reporter went on to inform me that Porterfield had been charged with a drink driving offence.

I called the manager in and confronted him. He admitted to

me that he had been charged. Later I found out that this was not the first offence of this kind that he had committed. I wanted to know why he had failed to tell me about his problem earlier as he had been sat next door to me for three hours. His response only confirmed that he was not the man for the job.

'It's got nothing to do with the club, Mike,' was his curious statement. He then reminded me that I had been 'done' in 1987. I reminded him that by the time the case got to court, I had left the club to work in Spain. I called John Madejski and asked that we hold an emergency board meeting to deal with the matter. Porterfield was sacked and Eddie Niedzwiecki installed as a caretaker manager until a new appointment could be made.

Porterfield eventually went on to manage the Armenian national side and successfully managed his team to an historic draw against Euro Champions Portugal. Sadly, only a few weeks after the game Ian died from colon cancer on 11th September 2007 at the age of 61. He will be forever remembered for his winning goal for Sunderland against Leeds United in the 1973 Cup Final. A remarkable feat as Sunderland were a second division club facing the all conquering Leeds team managed by Don Revie.

In his excellent book *Biscuits and Royals*, David Downs (author and fellow team mate of the Reading Directors XI) describes the three years from 1984 to 1987 as the triumpherate of Branfoot, Lewis and Smee bringing the most exciting period in the club's 115 year history. David's enthusiasm at times spilled over and became embarrassing. For instance, after our historic Simod Cup victory over Luton at Wembley, David asked me if it was okay for him to approach our groundsman's wife as she was responsible for washing, drying and ironing the team's kit. I thought it was a rather curious request and my curiosity was compounded by the fact that David explained that all he wanted was to bottle the dirty water from the first wash. He also rescued some of the players' tie ups and now both the water and the tie ups take pride of place in his memorabilia cabinet at home.

On one occasion he crept into my office late one afternoon and asked me if I could spare five minutes. Imagine my surprise when he asked if I could go out on the pitch with him, pretend to be Michael Gilkes, the speedy winger, and he (David) would play the part of Jimmy Quinn. Together we would recreate a goal scored by Jimmy that helped the Royals on the way to Wembley to lift the Simod Cup. Ensuring that the stadium was empty of any personnel, I agreed to take part in this charade on the basis that

David was a true and dedicated fan. It took me four attempts to get an accurate cross into 'Jimmy' who proceeded to nod the ball home. The goal was greeted by David doing a jig and running across the pitch to congratulate me. Boys will be boys.

After Ian Porterfield's departure in April 1991, it was not necessary to rush into a new appointment. There were only a few weeks to go before the groundsman took the posts down for the summer break. Eddie Niedzwiecki and physio John Haselden between them had seen us through to the last game as caretaker managers.

I mentioned to Chairman John Madejski that he would receive phone calls, letters and even personal approaches from many managerial candidates and at this stage it was wise to ask anyone making any kind of approach to submit their CV to me at the club. There was one exception to this. On the occasion of Manchester United playing their home return semi final leg against Legia Warsaw in May 1991, having beaten the Polish team 3–1 in the first leg, I received a call from Alex Ferguson. I was in my office at the time of his call and Jayne, our lovely telephone receptionist, put the call through to me. Alex asked if the Chairman was available and as luck would have it he was sat opposite me. Handing the phone over to John I remarked that he should wish Mr Ferguson the very best for tonight. I pointed to the television screen in the corner of my office so the Chairman could see the fixture list displayed on the screen that highlighted the European Cup Winners fixture between Manchester United and Legia Warsaw.

After asking me who Alex Ferguson was, John opened up the conversation with him along the following lines. 'Hello *Alec*, John Madejski here.'

I was praying that *Alex* had either ignored this faux pas or not heard the mispronunciation of his name, but matters got worse. The purpose of his call was to highly recommend Mark McGhee for interview for the vacant manager's position. He had managed Mark as a player at Aberdeen. In fairness to the Chairman he asked *Alec* to speak to me about the strengths and weaknesses of McGhee's application as he was not familiar with personalities in football. Sitting back in my chair in complete amazement that Mr Ferguson had taken time out on the occasion of an important European match to support McGhee's application just supported my lifetime view that it is the busy people who take time out to go the 'extra' mile. My comfort zone was partially destroyed as Chairman John wound up his conversation with *Alec*, turning his head around to look again at the TV and end the discussion with 'Oh by the way *Alec*, all the best for tonight when you play Warsaw!'

Now I am being grossly unfair to expect a man who self admittedly put his hands up and declared on taking over the club that he was not a football man, but would endeavour to learn as quickly as he could. Nevertheless, his all embracing description of Warsaw was akin to him saying that Reading was playing Sheffield or Bristol on Saturday! Was Alex Ferguson thinking to himself as he returned his telephone to its cradle, 'There's another Chairman who knows nothing about the bloody game?' Manchester United went on to beat Barcelona 2–1 in the final. The excellent article on Madejski written by Alan Fraser of the *Daily Mail* in February 2007 unfortunately misrepresents this story by suggesting that there was a room full of people witnessing this little cameo. For John's sake I am glad that I was the only witness!

The shortlist was drawn up. It included Mark McGhee. We decided to hold the interviews away from the club. Instead the venue for the interviews was the delightful home of Graham Denton, our latest recruit to the board. We started interviewing just before lunch. With just three directors the process should have been easy. However, Graham Denton said that he could not attend all the interviews. That left John Madejski and me to interview the first four candidates before Graham could join us. Madejski, who was learning the rudiments of the game and its administration admitted to not knowing anything about any of the candidates in terms of their footballing prowess. He suggested that we had private code words to express our impatience with a particular candidate in order to cut the interview short. He would turn to me and say, 'Well Mike, would you like to amplify any of my remarks?' Sadly we had to use this technique on three occasions: once, when the candidate spent 15 minutes telling us how wonderful he was; again when a pretender to the hot seat said that he would not come to Reading for less than £50,000 a year; and a third time when a candidate suggested by virtue of some awful body language, that he was doing us all a favour by attending. I took the view that all the selected candidates should be given a fair opportunity to put their case, but even my quest for fairness was tested to the limits when a former West Ham star asked if his agent could sit in on the interview!

McGhee arrived hot foot from Heathrow airport having just returned from Scandinavia where he had spent some time coaching and playing. He showed total enthusiasm. Included in his opening statement was reference to the fact that he knew the club's coffers were empty, but that he had enough confidence in his own ability to far outweigh the disadvantage of having to work with what was already there. At that point I thought the Chairman was going to have an orgasm! We decided to offer McGhee the post there and then. A celebratory dinner at the French Horn on the banks of the Thames at Sonning rounded off the day.

Mark was introduced to the media the next morning. He came across very well. My view was that he had 'played' the interview the previous day with precision. He was still registered as a player and Mark installed himself in the team but, as with many others, the joint responsibilities of managing and playing took its toll. We worked well as a team. Mark wanted nothing to do with finance and that included the transfer of players in and out. That suited me as I had witnessed the devastation caused by managers who interfered with the system and tried to play at being businessmen. I made it clear to Mark that budgets were sacrosanct and were to be adhered to whatever.

We became particularly close during the early part of the 1991–1992 season when Mark was experiencing some problems at home. I became his confidant. Together we discussed the problem and I did what little I could to ease his worries. The Royals started to play football as it was intended. At times the fluency and efficiency of the team was mind blowing. We scored goals. Our defence was solid and our away games were a pleasure to attend. McGhee was revered and looked upon as the man who could take the Royals all the way. My concern, even allowing for the euphoric state of mind I was in, was that Mark was beginning to show signs of arrogance and petulance. He dismissed most suggestions made by directors even if they were sensible. At board meetings he laid down ultimatums and bullied his way through, often to the disgust of the Chairman. Of course it was easy for McGhee to stick his chest out while we were winning. He was allowed more freedom than he deserved. This manifested itself when he arrived at my office one morning and suggested that I ripped up my playing side budgets as he had been entertained by Madejski the evening before and managed to extract £100,000 from him to finance the move of Uwe Hartenburger from an unknown second division German club. I blamed the Chairman as much as Mark for this blatant disregard of my position. I was totally unhappy about this transaction on two counts. Firstly, there was not enough money left in the players' budget and secondly the player was overvalued.

Hartenburger turned out to be a hustling, bustling overweight striker who would have been more at home with a 'hoof it and chase it' team and certainly not the team that McGhee had put together, a team that could hold its own with the very best and match them for ability and style. The whole episode left me frustrated and concerned and I let Madejski know in no uncertain terms that if he wanted the club run like a business then he must not break the cardinal rule and let his heart rule his head. His only riposte was to say that it was his money and he could do what he liked with it. The discussion ended at that point.

McGhee brought in Colin Lee as his youth team coach. I could see through this move and it came as no surprise that within a few months the club had an assistant manager in the form of Colin Lee. I felt that I was losing control. There was no doubt that Lee brought some new elements to the training and tactical activities, but he was an annoying sod who made repeated requests for pay increases.

The presentation of the Division Two Championship Cup at Elm Park on the occasion of a friendly against Gerona was a fit and deserved ending to the 1993–1994 season. McGhee, Lee and the team had worked wonders in securing promotion and providing a scintillating brand of football but something died inside me that day. As the team were parading the trophy around Elm Park before the game against the Italians, I slipped away to my office, shut the door behind me and sat staring into thin air. My mind was a vacuum. This contemplative mood was totally disturbed by the sight of fellow director Graham Denton standing in the doorway to my office. He sat down opposite me and simply said, 'Mike, I'm going home. I feel empty and sick. I can't explain why'. I understood his feelings as I felt the same, almost as if someone had popped the last balloon at a party. I just knew that it was time to move on.

John Madejski had steered the club from stormy waters through to a comparatively safe harbour. Together we had managed to effectively balance the books. He no longer had to write out cheques every Friday to keep us out of the red, the team was joining the semi-elite of the second division (now the Championship) and we had a marketing and commercial team that could compete with the best. To an extent, my job was done. I certainly had no regrets about returning to my old job even though several close friends in the game told me that I should never go back. Leaving the Royals was a sad affair. After eight years I had enjoyed many happy moments. Working with John Madejski was an experience with a capital 'E'. Alongside total admiration for the man there was a feeling of great sadness. At times I did see 'Mummy's little boy' standing in front of me. Born within months of each other and unfortunately having shared the same miserable circumstance of being unwanted as children, a bond was created early on in our relationship. He is not easily understood. His complex mind is constantly at work. He certainly does not suffer fools gladly, although at times *he* has behaved as the king of fools causing embarrassment to those in his company. In the pecking order of leagues of drinkers and their ability to remain compos mentis, John unfortunately belongs in the Conference. Half a bottle of a good red wine and his personality can change, normally for the worse. Some observers see this weakness as the manifestation of what the man is really like. They label him as arrogant, self centred and at times a bully. I saw a completely different picture. Having captured everything that money can buy, he has been left with an empty void that, in my opinion, can never be 100 percent filled. His antics at times when he would verbally 'set about' innocent victims, belittling them in the process, was not borne out of evil desire to embarrass them, but out of his own insecurity. What he finds difficult to deal with is confrontation. I liked to think that I was one of a few who could question his motives and criticise his actions when he overstepped the mark. Whether he appreciated my honest criticism is hard to say. I rather think that he resented it really as he had spent many years building up his suit of armour to make himself impregnable and to attract patronising friends.

It is with regret that events in latter years meant that we grew apart. I understand his reluctance to make contact at a time when by sheer association he might just weaken his position and standing in the football community. Football has benefited greatly from this man. Every man, woman and dog in Berkshire should kiss his feet for what he has achieved. The club, having successfully navigated their way through their first season in the Premiership can now move forward. Whether that will be with John at the helm remains to be seen. He has (almost to the point of boring repetition) said that should the right man come along then he would willingly give up the Chairmanship.

Had I learned a little more about John's business acumen during my four years of working with him then perhaps subsequent events at Swansea City and Exeter City could have been so much different. His steady hand at the tiller proved successful in Everestian terms, though at times his troops might have had thoughts of a Captain Bligh HMS Bounty type mutiny because of his sheer bloody mindedness.

17

41.3 MILES OF HELL

After leaving the Royals for the second time I went off to take up a role as a football consultant. I plied my trade with Luton, Millwall, Spurs, Cardiff and Fulham. Having visited the studios of 2-TEN FM every Thursday morning for two years prior to leaving Reading, my little spot on Rob Jones' morning show had obviously made some sort of impact. I was invited by the station to be the summariser for all Reading's games under the Classic Gold banner. The station took a bold decision to cover all the games both home and away. They saw me as the man to present the programme with a phone in one hour before kick off and then to sit alongside the commentator and make clever comments as the game progressed.

After two years of presenting *The Royals Show* with Classic Gold, I was approached by the BBC and asked if I would host a Sunday morning show called *Sport with Big Mike* (It's so pretentious isn't it?) I was on air for an hour and I would invite a guest to join me in the studio, take calls and generally have great fun. When BBC Radio Berkshire combined with BBC Radio Oxford there was no place for the show and sadly I came off air. As well as presenting radio shows, I was writing a full page every Friday in the local *Evening Post*. The page contained a letters section which I believe was very popular. Subject matter was kept to Reading Football Club and like every club in the land there was always some controversial discussion point that would push some supporters into taking up the quill and ink.

My role with BBC Radio Berkshire gave me the opportunity to follow the Royals in their push for promotion to the Premier League in the 1994–1995 season. I worked alongside Steve Beddow, now of Sky Sports golf coverage fame. Steve, in a moment of complete madness midway through the season, stated on air that should the Royals get to Wembley for the play-offs he would walk from Reading to Wembley for the game. Now Steve was carrying 18 stone of unused muscle at the time so his was a very brave statement. I was called in by the station managing director who asked me if I would be prepared to walk with him! I responded by saying that if I could get John Madejski to come on the walk as well, then count me in.

Honestly believing that John would have far too many entries in his business and social diaries to even contemplate the idea, I felt safe in the belief that my portly frame would be saved from this punishment. What I had omitted to take into account was the fact that the walk was going to raise money for the BBC Children in Need charity. When I mentioned this to John he immediately agreed to take part and took the opportunity to remind me of our humble beginnings in life having been raised by adoptive parents. Now get out of that Lewis!

Master publicity seeker, Uri Geller, decided that he would 'throw his hat in the ring' and hooked himself and his wife into the line up.

Steve Beddow and I were being constantly teased by the listening public as it became more possible that Reading FC were going all the way. With a 3–1 aggregate victory over Tranmere Rovers in the play-off semi finals and an encounter with Bolton Wanderers in the final, our fate was sealed. Beddow went off in his car to plot the route which included a four mile stretch along a canal which, according to Steve, would reduce the distance by one mile. His walk report did not make easy reading for me. Whilst 47 miles does not sound too onerous a journey (not by car anyway), on foot this is a different story. Steve suggested training for the walk, but the words stuck in his throat as he realised the futility of this rather silly suggestion.

'It's only 47 miles Steve, for goodness sake. Come on. We'll stick together and help each other if we get into trouble.' Who was I fooling?

Steve was a keen golfer. He was as round as he was tall, but he did take regular exercise. As for me, I took part in the odd charity game of football that left me prostrate for a week after. Plus I also played the odd game of tennis with my sadistic friend Kieran who laughed every time he sent that ball of white fluff past me at 80 miles an hour. Geller and his wife walked eight miles a day for fun. Madejski had less fat on him than a jockey's whip. Had bookies taken bets they would have marked Beddow and me down as even money not to finish the distance! Thankfully we decided to break the walk into two. On the initial journey we had to make a hotel in Slough for a night's rest before making the final walk to a Wembley hotel next to the stadium. The plan was then to enter the stadium the following day as the fans were arriving for the game.

As we reached Maidenhead, I made an excuse to pop into a pub. It was not for a drink, but to slip into the loo and examine the tops of my legs that felt as if they had been rubbed down with sand paper. On dropping my track suit bottoms I was shocked to see that my underpants were covered in blood. I kept this secret to myself until we reached the hotel in Slough. There I told Steve of my problem and said that I was going to have a cool bath.

Within minutes of entering my room there was a knock on the door and my visitor was a paramedic complete with medicine bag. We were very fortunate in having the services of a Territorial Army paramedic team accompanying us on the walk. What was totally unexpected was the sight of this rather good looking young lady paramedic standing in the doorway of my hotel room. As 'my injury' was at the top of my legs in an area that is normally out of bounds to the fairer sex, apart from those with special permission, I made some lame excuse to the nurse that included a reference to my amazing healing powers. She would have none of it. Lying on top of the bed with a lovely lady rubbing her hands along erogenous zones would normally be very satisfying. Not on this occasion though. She was concerned that infection could render me incapable of continuing the walk and that she would keep a close eye on my situation.

Walking along the Grand Union Canal the next morning was agonising, even allowing for the more than liberal covering of Vaseline applied to my groin, but thanks to the close attention of Steve Beddow, I was encouraged to keep going. Geller and Madejski found the pace too slow and my lasting picture of them was their disappearance through a thin mist that hung on top of the quiet waters of the canal. They were superbly fit. Normally I would look on in admiration but on this occasion I felt that their egos had taken over and they wanted to be first to reach the stadium. As Steve and I sat on a grass bank contemplating a lonely final lap of 14 miles, we had a chuckle. Was it important to see who got there first? No, it was the taking part that mattered, well, that's what we convinced ourselves of anyway.

As dozens of supporters in their cars passed us en-route, a cacophony of noise was produced from horns and shouts. Some stopped to shake us by the hand and put money in the collection buckets. The Wembley authorities allowed us to walk into the stadium and do a circuit of the arena. What a great feeling that was.

My radio duties during the game included that of roaming the stadium and obtaining the views of fans as the action was taking place. A co-presenter that day was Felicity Barr. She is a charming young lady who deserves every success as a lead presenter with a Middle Eastern TV company.

Royals players Lee Nogan and Adrian Williams gave Reading a 2–0 lead. The fans could hardly contain their excitement as I popped the question, 'How do you feel now?' Reading was on its way to the Premiership. Bolton looked dead on its feet. To compound Bolton's problems, Reading was awarded a penalty. If converted, a 3–0 lead would surely be unassailable. Stuart (Archie) Lovell stepped up to take the kick. The Bolton keeper saved it. It was as if all energy and inspiration went out of the window with that missed spot kick.

As I wandered around the stadium gaining reaction from the Reading fans I sensed that they were afraid of seeing the lead slip away as Bolton got stronger. Unfortunately this is what happened with Bolton running out 4–3 winners after extra time in one of the most thrilling matches ever seen at the national stadium.

Mark McGhee and Lee departed the Berkshire club in December 1994 leaving Jimmy Quinn and Micky Gooding to see out the remainder of that season and claim the recognition of taking the Royals to Wembley for only the second time in their history (even if that meant feeling the disappointment of failure). McGhee managed Brighton for a couple of seasons before departing the south coast club during season 2005–2006. Perhaps in his attempt to climb to the top of the tree and grab the sweetest apple he has damaged too many branches leading to his downfall. I have never fully understood the reluctance of managers to accept advice from outsiders. I don't mean supporters, but colleagues at management level. In the early days of Ian Branfoot's reign at Reading, Jim Brooks, the club's vice chairman at the time, quietly whispered to Ian after a home game that a goalkeeper who had played in a friendly for the Danish team, Brøndby, at Elm Park six months earlier was worth looking at. Branfoot, who at the time belonged to the ranks of those who would not listen, dismissed Jim's suggestion out of hand with the words, 'Jim, leave the football to me, you look after the business'. The goalkeeper in question was Peter Schmeichel. Branfoot never followed up the lead.

The early days of working alongside Ian were not always comfortable as he was stubborn and, at times, hard to communicate with. The breakthrough in our relationship came in a little cameo at a time when the Royals were not enjoying too much success. I looked forward to Friday afternoons as this was the time when the staff left no later than 5.00 pm if there was a home game the next day and this allowed Ian and I to stretch our legs, share a bottle of red wine in the boardroom and discuss matters. Ian, in a simple gesture made me feel part of 'his team'. He handed me a piece of paper and asked me to pick my team for the game the following day. Now this was not the action of a man so devoid of ideas that he needed advice from me who had never earned a penny from playing the game. It was a gesture that had a hidden significance and from that moment on we became good friends.

As the team ran out the next afternoon, it came as no surprise to me that it only contained six of the players I had listed on *my* team sheet. It didn't matter. Ian was a good manager. Little did I know at that time that our paths would cross again nine years later at another club. This time it was Fulham, and Ian, then performing the role of general manager, needed help. He didn't need help on the field of play necessarily, but he did need help with wider issues. He was very disappointed with the support he was receiving from other departments in the club and to use his own words, 'It needs a bloody good shake up Mike'. He wanted to know if I was interested in giving the club two or three days a week in order to look at the areas that were worrying him and his board.

An everlasting memory of Fulham and Craven Cottage was cemented in 1990 when, on returning to my old job at Reading, I sat with new Chairman John Madejski in the directors' box to watch them take on Fulham. Only the day before I had flown in from Malaga having packed up my job in Spain to return to the crazy world of football. I knew John well enough to realise that an invitation to join him for lunch before the game in his favourite King's Road restaurant was fine on the surface, but the man's reputation for not being able to control himself after half a bottle of red wine always gave me some cause for concern. Close friends of mine had suggested that he was in good shape, was on a fitness kick and had really cut down on his wine consumption. He referred to this 'private' lunch as a welcome home 'get together' rather than anything official, as he certainly did not want smartarse Lewis, hot with ideas bombarding his brain over lunch.

I was surprised that he omitted to invite Graham Denton affectionately known as 'Mr Grumpy'. Graham was to join the board on my recommendation. John was going to make the invitation formal at this match. John wanted this little get-together to be *very* private. He did voice his immediate doubts about Grumpy coming on board saying that he was bloody miserable and spread gloom and doom everywhere he went. I explained that any successful team needed a combination of personalities. Graham did have qualities that would benefit the club. The lack of any response reflected John's lingering doubts about Graham's appointment.

Long gone were the days when I watched Madejski like a hawk to see for myself the amazing transformation that the vino produced. We had been friends for years, enjoying each other's company. Occasionally we ended up in an alcoholic frenzy so I always took equal share of the blame should we disgrace ourselves. When God handed out good looks I was at the end of the queue, but when he dished out metabolism, he more than made up for his earlier oversight. Whisky and dry was my poison, and God help anyone that laid down a challenge to match me drink for drink. My record of seeing them off was immaculate!

Red wine is not a favourite of mine. After four bottles had bitten the dust, I expected John to be moving into auto pilot mode when anything and everything can happen. Apart from a silly moment when he called the waiter over and asked him what it was he had placed on the table before him. The waiter stated, 'As the gentleman had ordered spaghetti bolognese that was exactly what I have served', he was in full control. His driver took us to the school car park that was the only parking available at Craven Cottage. We got out and walked the 100 yards to the ground where we were ushered into the boardroom.

Two years in Spain had weakened my memories of John's stunning ability to act quite dumb and ignorant when it came to matters football. He cleverly covered for his lack of knowledge by openly admitting that he knew nothing about the game and that was why he had football people around him. Never was this more obvious than when a few months later we took Jimmy Quinn from Bournemouth. Jimmy, boots in hand, came to see us with a view to signing. We needed a striker at the time and Chairman John had agreed the price of £65,000.

Jimmy, a softly spoken Irishman was a little embarrassed when it came to discussing personal terms. John asked me to put the package to Jimmy. With furrowed brow, Jimmy listened and remarked that he needed a little more over the two years of his contract. I asked how much more and he said £5,000 per year would do it. At this point John swiftly moved into action.

'Come on Jimmy, we are all making sacrifices here to put the club right. Look [putting his cheque book on the table and inviting Jimmy to go through the slips] I'm putting £14,000 a week into this crock of shit just to keep it going.'

'Chairman,' said Jimmy, 'this is probably going to be my last move. I have to protect my family's interest.'

I stepped in. 'Jimmy, give us a few minutes please.'

Jimmy stepped out into the vice-president's suite. 'Look John, let's try it another way. Let's offer him his extra £5,000 per season if he manages to score 20 goals or more, that way we both win.'

'Bloody love it Lewis, you're not just an ugly face are you? Get him back in.'

John now took control of events. 'Look Jimmy, how about this. You can have an extra £5,000 a year if you score 20 goals.'

'John, that's 20 goals per season.' I interjected.

'Yes Mike, Jimmy knows that.'

I looked at the player and saw a wry smile creep across his face that indicated to me that he knew that the Chairman had got it wrong. 'Yes, Chairman, I'll sign for that.'

As he left the room, John stood up and thrust his arms in the air accompanied by crowing, 'See Mike, the magic's still there, it's all about selling yourself first. He'll never see that extra £5,000, bloody great.'

'What do you mean John?'

'Defenders don't score many goals.'

'He's a bloody striker, John with 27 goals under his belt last season.'

A stony silence for 10 seconds then…'Get him back, go on, get him back.'

'You go and get him. I told you three days ago that he was a striker.'

'This wanker in the Indian restaurant told me last night that the player we were chasing was a defender,' was his pitiful response.

'Yes John, we were looking for a defender as well, but that deal is off.'

Jimmy went on to score 23 and 26 respectively over the two years.

Back at Craven Cottage we were handed a glass of wine in the Boardroom. John pulled me to one side and asked me which one was Jimmy Hill. (I know, I know.) I introduced him to Jimmy and the two got on quite well. I was beginning to think that an all time first had been established that day by virtue of the fact that John was behaving 'normally' after so much wine. All that came to a crushing end when Mr Grumpy joined us in the front row of the visitor's section in the directors' box for the start of the game.

'Okay Mike?' said Graham, 'Flight okay?' Graham was about to sit down next to me when John turned on him and shouted, 'Is that the best you can do Graham? Mike's come all the way back from Spain to join us and the best you can do is to ask him what the fucking flight was like!'

I looked across at Jimmy Hill sat on the end but one seat on the opposite side of the box. His jaw had dropped which was something worth watching in itself! He had obviously heard John's outburst.

We watched the game. Graham sulked. John, with the flow of alcohol in his system now well and truly reaching the parts that matter, shouted out again at Mr Grumpy, this time it was, 'Go and sit at the end of the box if you are going to behave like a spoilt child'.

At that precise moment I desperately wanted to be instantly transported back to Spain! How could the new board work under these conditions?

Fulham looked the better team and John turned to me and asked me which one of their players I wanted for Reading. His hand gently removed his chequebook from his inside pocket suggesting that he was ready to do business. Now, I was not the most fervent supporter of old, worn out football etiquette. The age of no women in boardrooms, staff being treated like lap dogs, cosy director to director chats over lunch before a game. The modern game didn't need these archaic rituals just as it desperately tried to enter a new era, but to ask me in front of other directors and with second row Reading vice-presidents peering over his shoulder was way out of line. I was not qualified to answer and even if I was I would have suggested that we talk to our manager first. I felt that some form of response to his generous offer was needed. 'John, their number eight is a good player but the manager will know all about him,' was my weak response.

We went into the boardroom at half time and with a cup of tea in hand, John marched up to Jimmy and asked in a loud stage whisper, 'How much for your number eight Jimmy?'

Mr Grumpy put his cup of tea down and walked out of the boardroom. He was never seen again that day.

18

HARRODS SELL FULHAM

Ian Branfoot had been offered the manager's job at Fulham in 1995. He'd had a torturous spell at Southampton when death threats and personal abuse had become unbearable. After being paid off by the Saints, Ian managed to stabilise his life before seeking a route back into the game. Isn't it strange that the harder football people are hit, the quicker they want to return to the arena inevitably to be kicked even harder?

In his first season at Fulham as manager, he suffered yet another torrid time when the club hit absolute rock bottom. They were members of the third division and looked like prime candidates for the drop to the Conference. These were desperate days. Home gates were down to 4,000 and less than 1,000 season ticket holders bothered to commit themselves to the club. Behind the scenes the club was a shambles. It was down to seven full-time staff and morale was at an all-time low. In January 1996 they travelled to Torquay who were bottom of the entire Football League. Fulham had the distinction of being one place above them. Fulham lost. To many of their dwindling number of supporters, this was the blackest day in the club's history. It was not so much a case of dropping out of the League, but dropping out of existence.

Ian had recruited Micky Adams as a player. Micky was one of his former Southampton stars. In his wisdom, and presumably with gentle support from the board of directors, Ian eventually suggested that Micky should take over the reins as manager as he had all the qualities needed to take the club out of trouble. It worked and Micky steered the club to a position of safety.

Ian was appointed general manager and it was at this point that he asked me to visit him. I was working freelance at the time under the pretentious title of Soccer Doctor. Some people in the game might just suggest that the description Soccer Doctor is very apt as I have managed to put a club or two into a deep sleep. After four weeks of assessment I placed the cold hard facts in front of the Fulham board. There was hardly any marketing; no PR as such and the offices were a mess. Staff worked in small rooms that were far from conducive to good performance.

I was asked to do further work, but at that time I was completing the deal to put Hewlett Packard on Tottenham's shirts and had also committed myself to Millwall for a short period whilst they dealt with the massive problem of running the club under administration. Working with me on football projects was Annie Bassett. I first appointed Annie at Reading in 1985 as the first ever female marketing director in football. She was brilliant then and is still brilliant today. In my opinion, she was by far the best marketing person in the lower divisions. I suggested to Ian that Annie could provide assistance. He was delighted with that suggestion, as he had worked with her before. Part of the deal with Annie was that I should be given two days a week developing income areas and setting up a PR arm of the club.

Fulham directors Bill and Andy Muddyman had appointed Ian as general manager. They were very supportive of him, particularly at this time when the club looked dangerously over the precipice and stared down at the football Conference. Bill and Andy were responsible for the day to day running with Jimmy Hill as the figurehead. Credit must be given to all the directors for keeping the faith. They were to be rewarded.

It disappointed me to hear comments from staff at the club criticising Jimmy Hill. The remarks were more akin to the description of some buffoon and were well out of order. Perhaps the staff were too young to remember the man's tremendous contribution to the world of football. From those distant days of Jimmy's chairmanship of Coventry where he displayed an exciting brand of commercialism that was 10 years ahead of its time, to the ambassador's role at Fulham, the man deserved respect. He introduced the all seated stadium concept at Coventry, engineered sponsorship deals that were far ahead of anything else in the UK at that time and he carried this out together with a refreshing view that was to challenge many of the old traditions. In 1961, as chairman of the Professional Players Association, it was Jimmy who steered through the abolition of the maximum wage for footballers. I just wonder whether that achievement keeps Jimmy awake at night in these days of the £100,000 per week player. At the time, the PFA with Jimmy at the helm, managed to release hard working professionals from the chains of their employers, freeing them to negotiate their own entitlement. Yes, perhaps the pendulum has swung too far in the opposite direction, but Jimmy will go down as a players' man bringing some equilibrium to the business. Seen as a figure of fun by some observers, they should read about the evolution of the game before enjoying a cheap laugh at his expense.

In a very shrewd move, Ian Branfoot promoted Micky Adams from playing to managerial level. Micky led the team to promotion at the end of the 1997 season with the club finishing second to Wigan. Both clubs achieved 87 points but it was Wigan's superior goal difference that handed them the Championship. The season closed on 3rd May. Little did we know what the next four weeks would bring to Craven Cottage.

The Muddyman's asked me to take a more permanent role at the club, but I sensed that they were reluctant to hand me a contract. I was curious. I voiced my concern to Branny who responded by saying that he too felt a little uneasy as many other decisions were being put on the back burner. Micky Adams was scouring the lower divisions looking for players who would join Fulham and work for a reasonable wage. Branny was busy keeping the morale on a high after the glorious campaign of the previous season. Annie was creating mailing lists for distributing season ticket application forms to thousands of supporters old and new. She was also making new friends who were later to become major sponsors of the club due to her persistence and professionalism.

It was the middle of May when the rumours started that Mohamed Al Fayed was going to buy the club. They also came hand in hand with wild speculation: 'The club is moving to Chelsea and Fayed is going to build a bridge across the Thames.'

'A new stadium is going to be built on the other side of the river opposite the present ground.'

'We're going to play in Harrods Green and Gold shirts.'

As part of my wider role I was now handling all the publicity for the club so I suggested to Branny that we ignore all the rumours and get on with the job in hand on the basis of what will be will be.

On 22nd May 1997 Annie said that a certain Mark Griffiths was going to visit her the following day. I asked her why she felt that I should be made aware of his visit.

'He's from Harrods Mike. Perhaps all these rumours are true.'

Within 24 hours, Neil Rodford, another Harrods representative made a visit to the Cottage to see Ian and Annie. I was introduced to him; Neil seemed a young, bright and a very personable guy with an obvious penchant for football. We later discovered his undying love for the Hammers! I was told to liaise with ex-BBC man Michael Cole who was now Mr Fayed's media man. Michael asked me to let him know if any publications were due to leave the club in the near future. I explained to him that I was editing a celebration brochure covering last season's success and perhaps it would be appropriate to save a page in the brochure for any comments from the new chairman. My thinking was that if Cole gave me some copy then perhaps this would shed a little more light on these rumours. He was tight lipped. I also took the opportunity to add that it was frustrating not being able to refer to the rumours about Mr Fayed's intentions. Michael asked me to hang on for a few days and then he would be in a position to give me something positive to say. Now a nod is as good as a wink to a blind man, so I hurriedly prepared for a major announcement, crossed reference with Annie and in doing so she informed me that a press reception was being organised for Thursday 29th May. I was responsible for press packs and to ensure that the club extracted maximum publicity. How could we fail to do this? Helicopters were landing on the pitch, the Harrods' catering team in their magnificent chefs' outfits were laying out wonderful food in the adjacent room to the press conference. The place was filled to the brim with TV cameras, radio interviewers and newspaper hacks. Even the most cynical scribe could not fail to be impressed with the scene unfolding before them.

The top table included the old board and some new faces plus Micky Adams. Micky, looking rather pensive, nervously fiddled with his tie. Mr Fayed opened the conference by getting straight to the point, introducing himself as the new owner of Fulham Football Club. He added that he was a very busy man and would leave the day to day running of the club in a supervisory role to Bill and Andy Muddyman. Interestingly, he spoke of his long-term support for the club that he loved and had supported from the terraces. I quickly looked around the room and caught sight of some media men with raised eyebrows, others whispering comments behind closed hands presumably doubting Mr Fayed's allegiance.

With the superb confidence of a man who had seen life from the inside, outside and all four corners, he became vitriolic. 'This club will be in the Premiership within five years' (isn't it strange that the magical term 'five years' seems to appear in every new Chairman's opening speech). Well Mohammed delivered on his promises, although it took him an extra year to achieve Premiership status.

Then it was the turn of the media. With embarrassing shyness, some of the cub reporters appeared quite overawed by the occasion and their questions were muted as a result. Of course, the wiser and older members of the press held fire until the fledglings had paved the way for the 'heavies'. In came the boys from the nationals with obvious questions about investment, share-holdings, the management team, the stadium and one question directed at Micky Adams that for me sealed his fate as far as any long term relationship with the new owner was concerned. The question was a simple one, 'Micky, the most you have spent on a player is £5,000. The new Chairman has just informed us that he is prepared to finance the playing side to the tune of £8,000,000. Will you be able to handle that?' Micky floundered and honestly admitted that he was not experienced enough to handle transfers at that level, but that he would quickly learn. He never got the opportunity. By October of that year, Kevin Keegan was in control.

That day Fulham Football Club was reborn amid great anticipation of what might be. It was a certainty that the tight monetary controls suffocating the club would be more relaxed. Overnight, money was no object. I received a memo from Harrods reminding me that as the chairman of the football club *was* the owner of Harrods, it would be appropriate for any purchases of any equipment I might need to be made from his store. The appropriate store card was attached. Included in the same envelope was a seasonal pass for the Harrods' Car Park. 'How kind,' I thought. 'The next trip to Harrods with my wife and daughter will be so much more enjoyable not having to search London for a car parking space that didn't cost a mortgage.' Every daily visit to the car park was met with an invitation for me to have my car valeted. How different it was from my days at Newport County when it cost me ten bob to have a couple of apprentices clean my car. One week later came the news that we were moving out of the Cottage and were to be re-housed in Harrods (thus the car park pass).

Driving from Reading, where I lived at the time, to Harrods was a much easier journey than Reading to Fulham. Of course it depended when I timed my run. My view was that it was better to leave a little later, at 8.30 am and work later to avoid the massive congestion normally experienced coming in and going out of the city at peak times. Our 'new' offices were part of an annexe to Harrods in a building called Trevor House. Trevor House contained the editorial staff for *Punch* magazine. It was not unusual to see contributing writers wander through the corridors. The football department, as it became known, were even allowed to use the *Punch* boardroom with its fascinating table containing the carved names and initials of many famous visitors. Our office was a very pleasant area on the fourth floor. We took the eastern wing with the Harrods Product Development Department at the opposite end. Before too long we were accepted by the gorgeous ladies working in that unit as they saw these 'footie' people as fun. In fact, it came as no surprise during a coffee break to be confronted by a most attractive young lady proposing the following. 'I wonder if you could do me a favour.' Being 56 years of age at the time, I rapidly came to the conclusion that the favour about to be asked was purely professional, but we can all dream can't we? The favour requested was for me or other male staff to sniff 24 phials of men's aftershave and to identify the one that I would consider using. This cannot be done. After sniffing three I lost all sense of smell, so rather than disappoint the beautiful lady, I choose one at random.

'Well, how strange,' she said. 'That's my favourite too.' These visits became more regular as our expert opinion was much sought and valued!

Punch occupied the floor beneath. Their offices also contained a large area used for the setting of copy. I thought it was ideal for the production of a match programme for the football club. It came as no surprise to find that the creative lads in the *Punch* pre-production department liked to smoke, drink and do whatever else came naturally to these young and virile spirits. They were decent lads and were very good at their job. What I couldn't fully understand was the fact that on the occasion of 'putting the match programme to bed' (usually late on a Friday evening), I really felt on a high. Was it the euphoria of finalising the product that by now had become the best in the division by virtue of the vast amounts of dosh thrown at it? Or was it something else? Sharing this phenomenon with my colleagues I became acutely aware that they thought that I was taking the piss by asking the question.

'They're all at it down there Mike, whacky backy, powder, the lot,' said Ross our new marketing assistant.

The penny had dropped. My hours spent in the compositing shop breathing in this high octane air almost had the same effect as those indulging themselves! Those same lads, eager to please and help us to produce a great match programme were, I discovered, in fear of losing their jobs as *Punch* was going through a difficult time. No wonder they sought relief. Even the non-footballing 'compositors' (I haven't kept up with the new jargon) had new, fresh ideas. The drab 36-page programme had its re-birth as a spanking new 48 pager.

Nearly all the lower division clubs 'do their bollocks' with their match day programme and if it were not for the advertising element then heavy yearly losses would occur. But, here at old-fashioned ex-Cinderella club Fulham, money was no object. So I decided to really go 'gung ho' on the programme, sod the expense. My decision to throw caution to the wind was based on the premise that it would be easier to justify an overspend than to defend a poor product. First we hired a top photographic agency to cover both home and away games. The norm would be to scrounge away action pics from the local photographer in Darlington or Southend on a reciprocal basis. We had articles written by all the main soccer writers. The new Chairman had his own page, the copy for which had to be presented to me by the Thursday of the week of the home game. Michael Cole was responsible for the words after checking out the content with me to ensure that Mohamed was not using expressions out of synch with present day football terminology. I liked Michael because he was a true professional in an area that was completely new to him and he was eager to learn. He would ask me if the fans would understand what Mr Fayed was trying to communicate to them through his programme notes. I made some adjustments to the copy, faxed them back to Michael and without exception they were passed.

By now Trevor House was buzzing with football activity. Micky Adams was still manager and as such was writing his own programme notes that always included the immortal words, 'Think doubt and fail – think victory and succeed'. At the time I really thought that Micky should stay off the psychology cocktails, as all the fans wanted to see was the ball end up in the opponent's onion bag more times than ours. Then, one memorable Thursday afternoon, Micky came into my office and said that he was confident that I could write his programme notes on the proviso that he checked them before they were printed. What a breakthrough! Micky's a Yorkshire man. He does not easily dish out praise, as many a player dripping with sweat as they came off the park would testify. Not that I expected praise, despite the fact my article written on his behalf was a damn sight better than anything he turned out. I applied the personal touch that showed the fans a little about the man rather than a bald statement of facts. The deadline for copy was fast approaching and the lads downstairs in *Punch* were ready to wrap it up for the day and put the programme to bed. I rang Micky at home.

'Yes, it's okay Mike but listen you bastard, I would never use words like "Incidentally". I can't spell it for a start!'

I only had the opportunity of writing his notes for another three programmes before he was fired.

Eight weeks earlier I had 'borrowed' Dodi's office as a base for laying out our new generation business plans. Meetings were held there with prospective shirt sponsors, as our deal with GMB was about to run its course. The arrival of the deadly duo of Kevin and Al Fayed meant a renewed interest in all the club's commercial activities. Annie Bassett and I, ably supported by new boy Ross McIntyre, had spent many weeks before the previous season had finished, identifying a new major sponsor for the club in the knowledge that GMB were happy to stand down should the club receive a better offer. We took phone calls from big companies asking if *they* could meet with *us!* Demon Internet, a fast rising company, came to see us. We were in a particularly good position as Kevin promised that Adidas would stump up £100,000 per season if we were struggling to find a new sponsor. Demon brought their top marketing people to the meeting in Dodi's office. Annie and I had prepared a bullish presentation.

I am not sure that Annie was too pleased with my forceful suggestion that we should ask for £500,000 per year. I believe her feelings were that Demon might not be able to go that far. At the start of the meeting I watched with eagerness and anticipation the body language of the marketing director. As anticipated he went straight to the back page where the cost of the sponsorship was entered. 'What's this?' I asked myself. There was no blanch, grin or any reaction at all. 'He's playing his own little game perhaps.' I concluded to myself. His colleagues were pouring over the presentation with intense interest. I wondered where Kevin was. We had asked him to be here on the dot of 3.00 pm and now it was 3.20 pm. I looked at Annie and she gave me a wry smile. She too had followed the reactions of the marketing director. Then came a pregnant pause that is usually the precursor for sweaty palms. We waited for a response. Fortunately the silence was broken in a most fortuitous manner. In strode Kevin Keegan, all smiles, handshakes and a sincere apology for not being there when they had arrived. He explained that some transfer business had reached a crucial point and he needed to take an urgent phone call. No one else in football could use this as an excuse for being late and also have been believed. The lads from Demon stared opened mouthed. The marketing director happened to be a QPR season ticket holder so he was gob smacked that 'God' had joined us. His joy was almost orgasmic when Kev actually named the player we had just secured.

'I've just signed Paul Peschisolido for £1.1 million.'

It wasn't the fact that we had 'Pesch' for he was not exactly a top world stage player, it was simply that Kevin Keegan had rushed into Dodi's office and released the news first hand to them. He spent 10 minutes chatting to the guys, dropping in all kinds of 'hot news' that would quickly be doing the rounds back at Demon HQ. He helped our sponsorship cause no end. The job was done. They could not wait to sign the agreement.

Al Fayed's man, Neil Rodford, was running the club machine back at Harrods with style and panache. It was he who was given the responsibility of providing the helping hand to Kevin to guide him through some of the more tricky situations that might occur under new ownership. Kevin's relationship with Al Fayed sat well above any need for him to be looked after in this way, but Rodford, a football fan himself, cleverly nudged Kev safely down these potentially difficult paths. The media interest was at an all time high and left some of the old staff bewildered and lost. They could not cope with these fast flowing waters that this metamorphosis had brought in its wake and some sadly fell by the wayside. I needed to go head to head with Kevin about my own position. He listened and said that my role was to be extended and he wanted me to search for a Premiership standard training ground as well as carry out my normal duties. I found him a new training ground 50 yards away from the old one!

Money was poured into the team and signings were plentiful. Off the field we were in good shape too. New facilities were added, existing facilities modified and further appointments made in the area of marketing, sales, finance and security. Even the playing surface got a face lift. Frank Bohene looked after the pitch. I first met him at Reading when he was an aspiring youngster trying to seek a living as a pro. He was a decent player together with his brother Michael. They were both released as junior pros by Ian Branfoot. Franky went to work for Reading University as an assistant groundsman and his brother went into music. Before their release from Reading, we received a visit from their dad. He wanted to thank Ian Branfoot for the kind attention he had given his lads. On the same day, Ian called me from his poky office no bigger than a large cupboard occupying a space at the top of the director's box staircase. He liked it there because he was away from the noise and the bustle of the main office and dressing room area. I rushed upstairs and managed to squeeze my big frame into Ian's office. Frank's dad stood next to Ian's desk. I perched on a little landing that gave everyone entering this office a bird's eye view of the Gaffer's desk and its contents. Those reporters who had mastered the art of reading correspondence upside down had no trouble in obtaining hot news. Yet we still wondered why so much information leaked out of the club!

'Mr Bohene wants to show us something Mike.'

From his jacket inside pocket he produced a bottle of Bells Whisky, proceeded to pour most of it on the floor and then started chanting and dancing around the whisky sodden carpet. My first thought was what a waste of a good blend it was, but the fascination of the intricate movements of this tribal dance had me glued to the spot. The ritual lasted eight or nine minutes. Mr Bohene explained that the dance represented two factors – good luck and a blessing. He shook us both by the hand and left. I looked at Branny and he looked at me. He got in first with, 'What a bloody waste of whisky'. We won promotion that season.

Back at Harrods the marketing department was at full stretch. Propelled forward by the success of the Demon deal, we pushed forward on other major fronts. Anything that could be sponsored was. If a facility did not make money then we changed it until it did or franchised it out. Peterborough United was the original 'Posh'. Now it was Fulham's turn. Cutbacks on the agenda at most clubs were foreign to us. We were dynamic and the access to funds made things happen. One day, Pete, my main man in the programme printing department, rang me and asked if he could come upstairs for a chat. Looking slightly overawed by being in a Harrods office rather than the print room downstairs, he sat uncomfortably across the desk. He should not have worried as often my mind would drift back to the old days at Newport when my office was a converted player's toilet. Only no one bothered to tell the players that it had been converted. The occasion when our 6 feet 4 inches centre half Ron Walker backed into the room, shorts dropped, and backed his way towards where the toilet seat used to be will live with me forever.

Pete opened with, 'I've an idea Mike'.

'Go on Pete.'

'You know that thing that looks like a wart on Fayed's cheek?'

'Yep.'

'I can airbrush it out. In fact I've done it.'

He produced a picture of the new Mohamed. I couldn't help but be impressed. 'In fact Mike, I've dropped it into Saturday's programme. You said we should keep two pages for the Chairman and produce a full page-sized print of his face on one of them, well, there it is.'

'Okay Pete, leave it with me and I'll gently run that past Kevin.'

'Too late Mike, it's gone to the printers.'

Shortly after that, on one of his infrequent trips to see us, Mr Fayed headed straight for my desk. My first gutless thought was that I hoped that Pete the printer was downstairs in case I needed some support. Mohamed had a programme in his hand. Christ this is it. Goodbye Fulham. There have been a number of occasions in my life when I feared a P45 seemed to be winging its way to me. Once, when I was a licensed trade stock taker, I completely forgot to go down the cellar and count the barrels of beer. On another occasion when I was just 18 and working as a clerk in a builder's merchant's yard, I was asked by one of our sand lorry drivers to move his truck laden with sand from the hopper on to the weighbridge. I miscalculated the right hand turn that was needed and demolished the end of the weighbridge office. This was going to be another of those occasions, or so I thought. Could I immediately acquire the prowess of Alistair Campbell, the verbosity of Ken Livingstone and the ability to fib with such confidence that Mr Fayed would smile and walk away? There was not an ice cream's chance in hell. He gently put the programme on my desk. I remember thinking to myself as I looked at the back of his hand; I wonder how many famous hands that one has shaken. Then he opened the page where his photograph appeared. The page opened itself as he had obviously shown it to the many people and the crease was almost permanent. I felt the trickle of sweat run down the back of my neck.

'You did this?' He said pointing to the baby skinned area of his cheek where the blemish once resided.

'Well, actually, eh yes'

Looking down at me with those big brown eyes he said, 'Can you try and restore a little more hair on my head next time?' He turned and walked away. Kevin Keegan looked back and winked.

The same day Kevin asked me to slip into his office for a moment, as he had a concern. His problem was that he felt £500,000 per year was too much to ask Demon to pay. The club could not support the sponsorship, he added.

'Kevin, they are doing it because of you and Mr Fayed, it's as simple as that. I would love to think that my marketing skills were responsible for that success, but on this occasion, no way.'

He accepted this with some reluctance. At the same time he asked if we could mock up a Demon Internet shirt so that Mr Fayed could approve the design.

Young Ross, our marketing assistant, had worked hard on this sponsorship so we decided to let him take the mocked up shirt to the Chairman's office on the top floor of the store. Ross had reservations as he felt that as the junior member of the department, a more senior executive should undertake this duty. Annie insisted that the young, bright newcomer should 'cut his teeth' and at least make himself known to the boss. With some reluctance, Ross agreed. The day and time was arranged. Off trotted Ross wearing his best suit and sporting a special hair cut to boot. The sample Demon shirt was tucked well under his arm and we wished him well. He was a brave lad. He was gone three hours. On his way into the store he was stopped by a security man who asked him what he was carrying in his bag.

'It's a Fulham shirt for Mr Fayed.'

Mr Jobsworth smiled that knowing smile and proceeded to put our boy in a secure room. Ten minutes later he was interrogated. With the matter cleared up he went upstairs and waited to be called to the see the Chairman. Once inside this vast office he was made to feel as comfortable as possible. Mr Fayed asked to see the shirt. Holding it up he said that he was satisfied with the design. He then asked Ross to tell him how much Demon was going to pay for the privilege of having its name on a Fulham shirt. It was a surprising question as we fully believed that Kevin had already informed Mr Fayed.

With a cough and a splutter and a huge grin on his face, Ross blurted out, '£500,000 a year Mr Fayed'.

'£500,000 a year, is that all? Go and get me £1,000,000.'

To this day we have never established whether or not this was Fayed with his acute sense of humour at work. Did Mr Fayed know all along what the deal was and simply played games with our Ross? Or did he really believe that we could get £1,000,000?

By now Ross was somewhat bewildered and perhaps it was his state of mind at this moment that made him forget to put the shirt back in the bag. Yes, you are there before me. On the way out of the store he was stopped and put into a secure area and heavily questioned again. A call to Mr Fayed's secretary rescued the young man.

I bet he has dined out many a time on *that* story.

19

THE GAME GOES ON

It was 31st August 1997 and the day of my 56th birthday. I had breakfast in bed, a few presents to open from the family and a lunch planned at our favourite Italian restaurant. It sounded good to me.

As it was my birthday and as breakfast in bed was so welcoming I decided to go the whole hog and enjoy a little television whilst being propped up by four pillows. The pictures that appeared were unreal; a mangled Mercedes in a French tunnel. Diana and Dodi dead. Was I dreaming? Then Michael Cole appeared outside Harrods. His words echoed what the nation was feeling – utter despair.

For a totally different reason I was equally stunned 31 years earlier when I saw, on a black and white TV, Neil Armstrong planting his foot on the moon. Scenes such as these leave an indelible mark on a person's memory.

Because of recent links with the Fayed family through my involvement with Fulham, I felt as if I should be doing something. What I should do, I was not quite sure, but at least I had to make the journey to the Cottage. I was sure it would become a focal point for mourners together with the Harrods store. My family were sympathetic and wanted to come with me. On arrival at the Cottage, the sight before me was truly amazing. The main wrought iron gates leading to the Cottage were festooned with flowers. The floral tributes were beginning to stretch 50 yards down the pavement. Women were in tears and unable to speak. Grown men were silenced. Even at this early stage of mourning it was becoming obvious that it was the loss of Diana that received most attention. It was understandable, in those early moments I felt a huge sadness for Mohamed. This man had saved a football club from extinction and battled with government and civil servants over many issues through the years. He was not always popular and was seen by many as an undesirable character, financed it was rumoured by some dodgy middle eastern 'friends'.

'Speak as you find,' my adoptive mother taught me at an early age. It was that maxim that helped me deal with those who could not wait to tell me during the course of my duties how much they hated Fayed. I found him to be a delightful man who had invested his money in a no-hope football club and was in my opinion, a million miles away from the tyrant often portrayed by the media. I was not naïve enough to think that this very successful businessman always played a 'straight bat'. But who does at that level? My thoughts were with him at that precise moment.

Diana was worshipped by millions. She was stunningly beautiful, but I had a niggling doubt about her personality. Perhaps she was too good to be true? Prince Charles can do no wrong in my book. I like his style. I felt in union with the man, even if that bond came through our mutual love of the Goons. He possesses a great sense of humour that shines like a beacon in this dull old world, although there are occasions when the observer might just wonder exactly what planet he is on! Many a writer has given us their own versions of the split between Di and Charles. I took them all with a pinch of salt. Whatever the rights and wrongs, Charles was never given a chance of competing for the hearts and minds of his people. The beautiful Princess always had centre stage. And so it was proving to be the case with Dodi Fayed even at this time of tragedy. His father displayed dignity with a full understanding of how the loss of Di and Dodi would be perceived by the nation. Football, quite rightly, had to take second place in the shadow of these events. Nevertheless, the game had to go on. They would have wanted that, as some wag commented on our return to duty at Harrods the following day. How could this bimbo in the office have any idea what 'they' would have wanted?

The man that mattered was Al Fayed. We asked if the game should go on. The game in question was the home match against Plymouth three days after the tragedy. I took my hat off to the guy who had to ask the question. I imagine it was Kevin. The answer was a positive 'yes' and we were to dedicate the game to Dodi and Di. The programme was reprinted within 24 hours and contained delicate and sensitive references to the tragedy. The Chairman, having buried his son on the afternoon of the game, said he wanted to attend the match. I liaised with Michael Cole and we decided to have a simple ceremony of dedication in the centre circle before the game. Michael would take a radio mike with him and his dedication on behalf of the deceased would last for two minutes. After that there would be a minute's silence. My job was to organise the radio mike and 'balance' it with the very old public address system that at times seemed to have a mind of its own.

We rehearsed most of the day with club staff taking up the positions of Michael Cole and Mr Fayed. Everything worked perfectly.

At 5.30 pm, two hours before kick off, we tested the system again with a perfect result. The itinerary was as follows:

6.00 pm. Open gates.

6.00 pm to 7.15 pm. No announcements. Silence was the order.

7.15 pm. Michael Cole, Mr Fayed to go to the centre spot. Both teams to stand around the centre circle with the match officials.

7.20 pm. Michael Cole to speak.

I handed Michael Cole the radio mike at 7.14 pm. It was switched off and he would switch it on at 7.20 pm. I retired to the side of the pitch. The stadium was packed. As Cole and Fayed made it to the centre of the pitch, a silence engulfed Craven Cottage. Never before in my life have I experienced this sort of phenomena. A pin dropping would have sounded like a dustbin lid falling to the floor. I stood next to Janice, the club secretary, who whispered the immortal words, 'I hope that radio mike works because at the last match it let us down'.

Filled with smugness, I said, 'Not this time Janice, we've been testing it all day'.

It was 7.20 pm, and Craven Cottage stood in silence. Michael Cole lifted the radio mike to his mouth and quickly took it away again, placing it down by his side. The eerie silence continued, many believing that we were in fact observing two minutes silence.

After those two minutes that seemed like a lifetime to me, he raised the mike again and this time, signalled by a click through the PA system that could be heard all over the stadium, he spoke, his voice booming around the arena.

It was little David Hamilton, a Fulham fanatic, who sidled up

191

to me and said, 'You got away with that one Mike'.

I was devastated. 'What had happened?'

Janice came to the fore again. 'Didn't you know Mike that between 7.00 and 8.00 pm when Charing Cross hospital has a power surge if they are using all their operating theatres, that we lose our radio mike signal? I did try to tell you'.

'No you bloody well didn't.'

I spoke to Michael Cole the next day and he said that he knew there was no signal when he first placed the mike to his mouth. He was waiting for the audible 'click' when he pressed the on button but it never came. Rather than wave his arms in the air, hold up the mike and let 15,000 people know there was a problem, he waited. Sure enough, probably as operating theatre number three was being vacated, the signal returned.

'No problem Mike, if you pardon the pun,' was his final comment on the matter.

Even now I comfort myself in the honest belief that I could not have done more to make events go to plan. Fortunately I am never to be remembered as the man who cocked up the mike on this tragic occasion. Perhaps if I ran an insurance test that included checking with the London Electricity Board how many kettles and washing machines in the Hammersmith area would be switched on as well as contacting the local hospital to see if their operating theatres were going to be fully utilised at 7.20 that evening then I would have felt perfectly at ease.

The result of the game was immaterial.

The Fulham adventure was coming to a close. I was offered the job of delivering a new stadium in Swansea for use by the soccer and rugby clubs. Swansea City FC needed revamping having limped along for too many years. My package as commercial and marketing director was too attractive to turn down.

A new era had passed at Fulham and I had been fortunate enough to be part of the evolution at this one-time small club. I said my goodbyes and left with my going away present. It was a painting of Craven Cottage with signatures of all the staff and management filling the surround. As I type the pages of this book, I am aware of its presence just out of eyeshot hanging on the wall of my makeshift office in the spare bedroom.

The Fulham story is one that every aspiring chairman, with a few bob in the bank, should study carefully. Love him or hate him, Fayed has proved that throwing money at a club can work, but only if a brick on brick structure is put in place. Whether or not you agree with these sentiments is immaterial really as Mr Abromovich has proved beyond all reasonable doubt that a Premiership winning team can be cherry picked by virtue of the cheque book. Ask a Chelsea fan if he believes that the battle for supremacy is unevenly fought because of the wealth factor. You know what the answer will be. Football fans are notoriously fickle. From Gigg Lane, Bury to Goodison Park, Everton the clarion call is the same. We want a winning team. If it is going to take a massive investment from a consortium or individual to achieve that aim, so be it.

20

'NICE SWAN CYRIL'

Having joined the Swans in March 1998 as their commercial director I had high hopes of an upsurge in income from commercial sources. My first board meeting meant a journey to Henley. Neil McClure, the owner of the club lived nearby and, because of business commitments, decided to hold this particular meeting near his place of business in London's West End.

The meeting was held in the Phyllis Court Club overlooking the Thames. McClure, Steve Hamer (Chairman) Peter Day (chief executive) Carol Booth (PA to McClure) Ronnie Hamill (financial director) and I sat around a huge table that had been prepared conference style. At the far end of the room, the double doors had been opened to admit a refreshing flow of air on this balmy May day.

I have always held the belief, rightly or wrongly, that I can normally sum up people within the first two minutes of meeting them. This is not foolproof of course and mistakes can be costly. My view of the people sat around me was as follows. McClure I liked. He was larger than life both in personality and physical appearance, (weighing in at 20 stone). At times he behaved like a public school bullyboy leading to some of his contemporaries disliking him. Personally I enjoyed his zest for life and his great sense of humour.

Hamer I put down as a charlatan. In the short time I knew him I saw a man who could be funny, entertaining and charming one moment and then turn into a spoilt child, lashing out at all around him the next. He painted a picture of being a true Swans fan full of knowledge and on many occasions he would smother anyone who was prepared to listen with useless information such as, 'Do you know the name of the only goalkeeper under 5 feet 6 inches who played for the Swans and never conceded a goal?' His delight in informing the now bored to the hilt 'prisoner' was a joy to watch.

'Bert Jenkins, bloody Bert Jenkins played twice in the 1940s. I thought everyone knew that.'

Hamer publicly criticised me for being paid too much, although he was the chairman and board member sanctioning my salary. He criticised the fact that I drove a Jaguar exclaiming that the fans would take exception to it. The hypocrite drove his 4 x 4 to the club on match days and he openly admitted that it was the mileage allowance that the club paid him for attending matches that gave him the financial muscle to buy the machine. He charged 69 pence per mile to the Swans, along with bills for lunches, train journeys and any other expense he could claim.

The chief executive, Peter Day, was an old friend from my time at Tottenham. Peter was enjoying life at Swansea although there were early signs that his relationship with McClure was thinning at the edge.

Ronnie Hamill, the financial wizard whose first priority was to try and keep Ninth Floor (Neil McClure's company) in business, saw the football club as a drain on the holding company's finances. He was a nice guy, always helpful and supportive.

Carol Booth never left McClure's side and was an excellent PA. She was an attractive lady with good social skills and blended in well on the occasions she attended matches.

So that was the line up for my first board meeting.

The meeting was chaired by Hamer. It was more a reporting session rather than a hardnosed business meeting. This was probably due to the fact that the temperature was up in the 80s and the view through the large open double doors begged for us to step out and enjoy the weather. My report included reference to those areas where the club had not performed very well in the past. These areas included sponsorship, advertising and PR. In truth, when Swansea City was discussed at commercial managers' meetings in the past, the club was regarded as a joke. The Sharpe family, with Doug as chairman and son Robin as chief executive, had let the club rest on its laurels and had not moved forward since the Toshack era. So it was not too difficult to make instant improvements.

The meeting was about to draw to a close when Hamer looked at me and asked if I had any ideas of how to improve the image of the club. I responded by saying that my first priority was to establish tried and tested money making schemes. Then, instead of leaving matters there, I went a bit further and suggested that to improve the profile of the club we should have a club mascot.

Neil asked what kind of mascot and Hamer interjected by shouting out, 'A Swan I hope!'

I had given a little thought to the subject and really should have waited for the next meeting to fully outline my ideas. Now here I was dancing on my feet. Nevertheless I ploughed on stating that the bird would have to be of Disney standard, that it would be sponsored so there would be no financial burden on the club. I also stated that the bird would be different because of its size. It would be no pint sized bluebird like Cardiff's, but a big bird 9 feet tall. There was no opposition so far.

Then Hamer asked if I had thought of a name for the Swan.

'Yes Chairman. Cyril.'

'Why Cyril, Mike?' asked McClure.

'After Cyril Knowles, the famous Spurs player, Neil.'

There were stunned looks on the faces of those present until Steve Hamer, being one step ahead, said, 'Got it Mike, nice swan Cyril, nice swan son.'

He was spot on. Yes, I was going to convert the old Spurs song, 'Nice One Cyril' to 'Nice Swan Cyril'. Where this crazy notion came from I do not know but somewhere in the crevices of my mind I found this inspiration. McClure's face was a picture. I wondered whether or not at that precise moment he thought that he had made a grave error in appointing me! Neil's hate relationship with our new born bird started that day.

Having been hoisted by own petard, so to speak, I set about bringing the bird from an idea to reality. I was supported in this task by two colleagues at the club. Michelle and Dianne worked in the newly formed commercial department and were full of inspiration and vitality. They arranged for a theatrical costume designer to visit us and help bring Cyril into existence. The girls obtained a sponsor for Cyril so the two swan suits costing £2,500 each were covered. Two suits were needed because we planned to have Cyril get up to antics that would necessitate the need for a frequent costume change!

The North Bank at the Vetch accommodated the real die hard fans. I guessed that for the opening game of the 1998–1999 season when we entertained Exeter City would you believe, (similar coincidences seem to appear through my life) that the North Bank would be almost full with 3,000–4,500 in attendance. My suggestion that Cyril traverse the ground by 'flying' from the south west floodlight pylon to the north east pylon using a tight rope and harness did not go down too well with the safety committee. It was Mr Jobsworth at his best. Still, it was a good starting point.

Dianne, our commercial executive, knew of a couple of SAS soldiers who were fanatical Swans supporters. They offered their services should we need them. A decision was made to place Cyril in full regalia on top of a floodlight pylon from 2.00 pm until 2.50 pm when he would abseil down the pylon, run across the pitch to the north bank and perform a chest thumping gesture. When the decision was taken to perform this exploit it became obvious that we could not use our groundsman, Eddie, to pull on the outfit as there was an element of danger attached to this manoeuvre. Even the SAS guys seemed a little concerned.

Eddie had valiantly offered his services to become Cyril. He fitted well into the costume and immediately transformed into a manic bird. Remember, this bird was 9 feet tall with a huge neck and oversize clown-like black boots. No, this was a job for the specialists.

No publicity had preceded the arrival of the bird. As supporters came into the ground, it took most of them a few minutes to realise that a giant swan was perched on top of a floodlight pylon. The word soon spread and on this hot, sunny afternoon, resplendent in his brand new gear, Cyril was born. The sheer disbelief shown on the faces of fans, particularly the younger ones, was a joy to see. Cyril was waving, bowing and just as the PA man announced that a Swan had gone missing from the Swan sanctuary at Llanelli, Cyril started scratching his head. I pulled the directors out of the boardroom just as Cyril was about to descend the pylon. To the tune 'Nice One Cyril', slowly but surely he climbed down. There were now 10 minutes to kick off.

McClure had no idea that we had managed to organise Cyril in readiness for the first game, as four months had passed since the discussion at that first board meeting. He was truly shocked to see that the bird was perched 90 feet up in the air standing on flimsy iron framework that supported our floodlights.

'Christ, I hope nothing goes wrong,' bellowed McClure in my ear.

As Cyril reached the ground the crowd cheered. The bird made for the popular North Bank standing enclosure, stuck out his chest waved his wings in the air, followed by performing a series of sweeping bows that would have made the finest actor proud as he took his curtain call. He had become an instant hero.

If only Cyril had kept to the basics, then perhaps the club could have avoided a hefty fine and suspension from the Football

Association of Wales, complaints from visiting teams and the necessity to bail him out when taken to a police station in Huntingdon! Cyril, or more pertinently, Eddie our groundsman who was receiving VIP status in the city, decided that he would enlarge his repertoire at our home game against Norwich in the first leg of what was called the Worthington Cup.

A bad call from the linesman standing directly in front of the dugouts sent Cyril scurrying down the track from the corner flag where he had been entertaining some children. It was commonplace for mascots to parade up and down the touchline during the game. In fact his antics were enjoyed by kids and adults alike, much more than the events out there on the turf at times, especially when the Swans were in one of their less than exciting moods. His 9 foot frame brushed past Irishman Bryan Hamilton, the diminutive assistant manager of Norwich, sending him sprawling to the ground. Hamilton got up and faced Cyril (well his chest in fact) and made some threatening gestures. The crowd went crazy and Mr Hamilton did not enjoy the rest of the evening as he was constantly jeered.

Norwich City sent a letter of complaint to the club, the Football League and the FA. There was no disciplinary procedure this time.

This proved to be the first of many run-ins with the football authorities. By far the most hilarious, but in the eyes of the Welsh FA the most serious of offences, occurred some three months later when the Swans were drawn at home to Millwall in the FA Cup first round. By now Cyril had been warned time and time again by the club about his behaviour and he always promised to be a good Swan at the next game. I spent half an hour before the Millwall game lecturing Cyril and reminding him that the Millwall fans had a reputation for not suffering fools gladly, so he must not go down the Millwall end during the game.

Against our wishes, Millwall brought their mascot, Zampa the Lion, and suggested that if we held a half time penalty shoot out between Zampa and Cyril, this just might have the effect of keeping the Millwall fans quiet and peaceful, to say nothing of keeping a small section of our own fans away from their fans who were located a short hop over a perimeter wall. The teams marched off the pitch at half time and the Lion and the Swan entered the arena, patting each other on the head in a display of what seemed like mutual affection. Zampa took the first penalty in front of his fans and scored. Then Cyril took his first and scored. Zampa, by now encouraging Millwall fans to support him, tucked his second under the falling body of the swan. Then came the moment I dreaded. The lion, on his way to face Cyril's second kick took a swipe at Cyril almost dislodging his head. Cyril, who in his four months of existence had never lost his head, in a physical sense anyway, was so indignant that he wrenched the head off the unsuspecting lion and produced a perfect drop kick that would have made Jonny Wilkinson proud. It flew straight into the middle of the Millwall supporters. Hell, what would happen now? Then the Swans fans started singing the theme song, *Nice One Cyril* with the Millwall fans surprisingly joining in the fun and laughing, which went to show that even fans with a bad reputation can enjoy a moment of sheer pantomime!

McClure and the rest of the board were downing their chicken curry in the boardroom at the time. It was not until the end of the game that the events of half time became known to them.

The Swans went three up during the second half. The celebrations for the third goal brought Cyril onto the arena. With a tremendous leap he launched himself on to the shoulders of the Swans players. As he was dislodged he fell to the ground just as the ball, that seconds earlier was nestling in the back of the Millwall net, arrived at his feet. With a swing of his right boot (size 20) he sent the ball rocketing into the bread box of a Millwall player, despatching him to the ground. Cyril, unaware of the discomfort he had caused to the player, ran across to the linesman who was flagging to attract the attention of the ref and caressed his bald head. The official was not amused. The referee had seen most of the incident but wanted the linesman's input to include Cyril's actions in his post match report. The whole episode was caught on our own CCTV camera and was used at the subsequent hearing in front of the Welsh FA disciplinary committee. Requests made by me to 'edit' the film before release fell on deaf ears!

We waited for several weeks for the hearing date. I met one of the Welsh FA councillors at a friendly match and I asked him why it was taking so long for the hearing to be called.

'Can't get a committee together Mike. No one wants to sit on *that* panel.'

Eventually three members were press ganged into service. Cyril's adventures had by now become internationally famous. I had to appoint a specific member of staff to administer his bookings for birthday parties, weddings and TV appearances including doing the *National Lottery Live*. The fans loved him, much to the chagrin of Mr McClure, who would privately threaten me with statements such as, 'It will be you or that fucking bird Lewis.' Yet publicly he took some of the glory for the inventiveness of the club, particularly when entertaining in 'the Smoke' where I imagine his business friends, being made well aware of Cyril's antics through massive media coverage, had more to say about the bird than Neil's football team! He really was enjoying the limelight that Cyril brought to the club. Perhaps it was because on-field activities were mediocre to say the least!

Eventually we were given a date for a hearing to be held at the Posthouse Hotel in Cardiff. The charge was bringing the game into disrepute. Neil McClure insisted that we use a lawyer of repute. We certainly met that requirement. Only weeks earlier a famous Manchester lawyer managed to get Eric Cantona off a charge of physical abuse when the player kicked out at a spectator at Crystal Palace after receiving racial abuse. The lawyer in question was Maurice Watkin who, in November 2001, also played a major part in preventing a strike by players.

Maurice, a long term friend of McClure's, could not wait to take on Cyril's case. I briefed Maurice and I was instructed to stand at Cyril's side during the cross examination.

A nervy committee of three, not knowing whether to laugh or cry at this ridiculous situation, sat at a huge table in one of the hotel's conference rooms. Maurice sat to their left and Cyril and I stood to their right.

Cyril, being a mute Swan could not speak for himself! We were specifically asked that Cyril attended in his regalia so that the committee could see for themselves how he looked on the day of the alleged offence. How Maurice and I kept straight faces when Maurice was asked by the Chairman of the committee to put a series of questions to me and for me to repeat them to Cyril I will never know.

'Ask Cyril Mike, can he see a football at his feet when he is wearing his costume,' was Maurice's first question.

Cyril, bending down so that I could speak into his ear understood the question and shook his head.

'Ask Cyril Mike, did he intentionally kick the ball in the direction of a Millwall player?'

Once again a shake of the head.

The next question was put to Maurice. 'Mr Watkin, were you

aware that Cyril patted an official on the head shortly after Swansea had scored their third goal, this was after encroachment on the field of play?'

'Yes Mr Chairman, Cyril thought that he had seen a coin thrown at the linesman and went over to console him.'

Brilliant, Maurice, brilliant.

I was eventually dismissed. On entering the anti room used for witnesses, I was asked to go downstairs and give the media some idea of what was happening and how much longer the hearing would take.

Some five hours later the committee had reached their decision. There was a £1,000 fine and Cyril was banished to the stands for a whole season.

Maurice asked me to go down to the foyer and announce the verdict to the media. It seemed that every national and local newspaper, TV company and radio station had attended this bizarre hearing. When Watkin and McClure saw the plethora of cameras and reporters, I was banished from sight, leaving them to take centre stage. Speaking into a barrage of microphones, McClure said that the club would obviously abide by the decision. I stood back and let the opportunists have their moment of glory. For McClure, grasping this moment to talk to the media was nothing short of hypocrisy. For a man to say that he wanted nothing to do with this discredited mascot one moment and then thrust himself into the limelight the next did nothing for his credibility.

The Sun newspaper signed a contract with the club there and then. The next day Cyril was national news. The Welsh FA was ridiculed. Cyril appeared in *The Sun* dressed in a prisoner's uniform with a huge tag line stating, '*Save Our Swan*'. Desperate attempts by the media to unveil the bird's identity were unsuccessful.

Cyril was voted mascot of the year by *Four Four Two* magazine. Large amounts of money were thrown at the club to secure his services. His antics had drawn many admirers around the globe.

A very poor imitation of Cyril in a Weetabix ad filmed at QPR provoked me into contacting the advertising agency concerned. It was not that we wanted to complain about the bird being imitated, but the poor quality of the costume as it did a disservice to our beautiful bird. Weetabix offered us a year's supply of their brand. They were told where they could put it!

Cyril was invited to join the pantomime at the Grand Theatre in Swansea where Aladdin was on show. His part was to portray the Emperor of China's pet. The kids and perhaps some adults too, thoroughly enjoyed it.

A pop record was produced, alongside a very well written and illustrated book. The record sold 5,000 copies and the book sold 4,000 copies.

A fans' survey produced by the club revealed that 95 percent of the fans thought that his antics were great fun. It was just a pity that the Welsh FA couldn't find it in them to see the wider picture.

Many months later I met Alun Evans, the chairman of the disciplinary committee that handed the Swan his fate. I asked him how he felt about the hearing. His huge grin helped to confirm for me that the whole episode was a complete farce. Evans, a standalone rebel in his own right, had seen the entrepreneurial stuffing knocked out of him over the years and had become an establishment man, if for no other reason, than to keep his seat on the Welsh FA Council. I was well aware that the whole episode regarding Cyril caused embarrassment to the Welsh FA. Had they taken into consideration the huge pleasure the bird gave thousands of fans? I doubt it. Had they considered that the publicity, even if it did not always complement the game, had brought poor old Swansea City Football Club into the international spotlight? Probably not. Did they consider that this ungainly bird had become the hero of mascots throughout the world? Did they consider that the antics of Cyril at home games, in particular those where crowd problems were always a possibility (Bristol Rovers, Bristol City, Cardiff, Hull, Millwall) actually defused any potential problems? I don't think so.

When you are watching a 9 foot bird climb out of a small Robison helicopter in the middle of the pitch 10 minutes before kick off, then perhaps, just perhaps, those with any intention to climb fences and have a go at their 'enemies' might be distracted enough not to bother. I got a bollocking from the safety committee for not informing the prison service that a helicopter was flying into the Vetch to drop off Cyril. I was told that this event caused a security alarm to be raised at Swansea prison. The prison was adjacent to the ground. The pilot had to circle the prison several times before he could get his correct height before swooping over the main stand to glide into the centre circle.

Eddie (Cyril) was not at all happy about the helicopter ride as he suffered from vertigo. The distance from the airport to the club was four miles and the pilot had arranged for the passenger door to be removed for Cyril's wings were far too big to be contained inside the small cockpit. Left wing hanging out as the whirly bird came into land, Eddy could not wait to hit the ground. In his panic to get out of the machine he had completely forgotten the last warning I gave him before driving to the airport. 'Eddy, just remember that Cyril is 9 feet tall, and the rotor blades on the helicopter, although a few feet higher than that on landing, are very flexible so you must duck when jumping out.' Did he listen? No. With wings raised, not this time in celebration of welcoming his beloved fans but in relief because he had arrived safely, Cyril's head was no more than a few inches below the slowly turning blades. The pilot had been told not to cut his engines in case they could not be re-started. What a story that would have made. **'Helicopter prevents match being played. Swan decapitated.'**

Future pre match meetings with the safety committee were always a little sensitive. A permanent item on the agenda was *Cyril the Swan Activities*. I could appreciate their concerns, but in an age where 'officialdom' brings with it the arse covering syndrome, it is very sad that risk factors are so determining that many a good show has to be cancelled or re-structured to take into account the very slight possibility that something extraordinary may go wrong. When the committee heard that Cyril was arriving by helicopter they swept into action. A fire engine was parked outside the stadium in case the helicopter caught fire, an ambulance stood at the ready. Extra stewards had to be employed to keep any fans off the pitch at the time of landing. The fact that the strongest possibility of a disaster was the decapitation of Cyril seemed to have escaped their check list!

I was mildly surprised that the new directors appointed in 2002 had not put Cyril in front of a firing squad. The dying swan would have been further proof that these short sighted men wanted to rid the club of anything Mike Lewis had been involved with. Incredibly, the Football League brought in a code of conduct for mascots following a series of other misdemeanours involving animals and birds. This was after the Oldham mascot was sent off for confusing a linesman who kept flagging the 7 foot owl offside! A league spokesman stated, 'Mascots add a sense of fun and attract youngsters to matches, but there have been a few negative incidents'. The 'not in front of the children' attitude just doesn't wash. Watching a big furry animal trot around the pitch waving to the crowd is not half as much fun as seeing a swan decapitate a lion. Cyril the Swan is the Vinnie Jones of mascots.

The request to hold the National Lottery draw live at the Vetch, featuring Cyril was met with 100 percent enthusiasm. Cyril was to be portrayed as a bird under threat of extinction that would be replaced by a black swan should he not correctly predict whether the bonus ball would be odd or even. Cyril called the bonus ball number correctly, much to the approval of the 1,000 fans that turned up for the occasion. The black swan disappeared into the early evening mist never to be seen again.

The 2001 Mascot Grand National held at Huntingdon racecourse was a race designed to channel the energies from within the polyester costumes into a friendlier persona, ended in injury and shame. Wendy the Wolf left via a stretcher, Harry the Hornet cracked two ribs and police were left searching for a mysterious long necked figure after a woman claimed that she had been punched and pushed over damaging her wrist. 'I can confirm that Cyril the Swan is the main suspect,' a police officer said at the time.

I bailed the bird out of prison after his arrest. The matter was dropped by the police after investigation. It was a pity really as the thought of Cyril standing in the box in court unable to speak, with me by his side inviting him to shake or nod his head in response to questioning still brings a smile to my face.

John Batchelor, my wicked solicitor acting for me in the Exeter case, loosely suggested that I could turn up in court wearing a Cyril uniform.

Supporters of the Swans, if asked, will probably state that the only worthwhile action Lewis ever took whilst he was at the club was to invent Cyril the Swan. Well if that's the case then I am proud of it!

21

REGRETS? I'VE HAD A FEW

The offer to join Swansea City as their commercial director was too good to resist. The package reflected owner Neil McClure's ambitions for the West Wales club. My only slight concern was how the fans would react to a Newport County man taking a senior management role at the Vetch. I have never understood why fans consider that a player signed from another club can quickly be accepted as a loyal servant of his new club, yet in the case of an executive, they will constantly remind then that their loyalties are questionable because their affiliation must rest somewhere else. In my case the Swansea fans reminded me that I was a Newport fan.

I had a soft spot for Swansea over their rivals Cardiff City. Cardiff rejected me at 18 years of age and even today I still feel sore about them making this huge mistake. In doing this they overlooked the next Welsh international super striker. The Swans had never done me any harm apart from knocking Newport County out of the Welsh Cup on several occasions.

I was always fascinated by the appearance of the Vetch stadium. It never looked finished with its East Stand crying out for completion on its northern side. The main stand was well past its sell by date on my arrival in 1998 and needed constant repair work. One improvement that was high on my list (but never achieved) was the removal of half of the seats in the directors' box. My reasoning behind this was twofold. Firstly to give anyone like myself who happened to be over 6 foot tall enough room to sit with their legs in an orthodox position rather than at ridiculous angles that at times resembled prostrate chickens on a cool shelf in Tesco's! And secondly to reduce the number of people allowed in the directors' box. Over the years anyone who had done half a favour for the club was invited to sit in the directors' box to watch a game. There were 73 seats with 40 seats occupied by the do-gooders! Invitations to sit in the box and enjoy the hospitality in the boardroom should have been of special significance. I failed to push through my proposal at a management meeting after my appointment when it became obvious that the opposition to the removal of every Tom, Dick and Harry was going to cause huge problems. Some of these hangers on had enjoyed the privilege for many years. Normally I would have cut through that bullshit and faced the consequences. Unfortunately many of these pseudo supporters were owed money by the club and I was not ready to take them on when so many other pressing priorities were piling up on my desk.

The front of the main stand was no further than three yards from the edge of the pitch. Conversations with home and away managers and their coaching staff would often take place. If it wasn't directors spouting their advice it was the fans sat directly behind the directors' box. This 'facility' to debate the game with those in charge of players often provided light entertainment. I remember one of my fellow directors looking straight at the Doncaster Rovers' manager as he turned around, holding his head in his hands and crying out, 'Jesus, now we have conceded a bloody free kick on the edge the box'. The director, showing some sympathy towards Doncaster Rovers who had already been relegated to the Conference before they came to Swansea, shouted out, 'Don't worry mate we're crap at set pieces.' The Swans took the free kick and the ball shot into the top of the net only for the referee to award a free kick to Doncaster because of an 'off the ball' incident. The Rovers' manager turned around, looked at the Swans' director and with a broad smile on his face exclaimed, 'Christ, with that sort of luck I'm still in with a shout for the Manager of the Month award.'

Opposing team's players, who were warming up by sprinting down the track alongside the main stand, were so close to the spectators in the front rows that they simply could not ignore comments hurled at them. One loud mouth shouted at a sub as he passed by, 'Bloody hell mate, I can run quicker than that!' At which point the sub started to strip off and handed his shirt to motor mouth. Match officials also came in for almighty stick. Linesmen (I refuse to call them assistant referees) running the half of the pitch nearest to the main stand needed to have skin as thick as a rhinoceros.

'Hey mate, Specsavers are doing a good deal at the moment.'

'Why don't you stick that flag up your arse?'

'There's a job for you on Swansea station.'

'Keep your flag up you idiot.'

And should the official be follicly challenged the comments were, 'Get a bigger bed chum, your head's rubbing against the wall.'

On examining the books prior to my arrival, I found that little or no effort had been put in on the commercial side of the club. The previous owner had done a fair job keeping the Swans afloat, but never showed enough enterprise to push the club forward on the marketing front. From my perspective this was not necessarily a bad thing as it was going to be relatively easy to improve matters. I appointed two women to deal with commercial affairs. They were Michelle Carpenter and Diane Griffiths. They soon established themselves and the department really took off. They met a lot of resistance from business people in the city. Some suggested that giving money to the football club was a waste of time as the previous regime never seemed to appreciate any outside support. I told the girls to look for new customers and avoid those who had been approached in the past. Mind you, there were not many of those. Matches were now sponsored. New advertising hoardings appeared on the ground filling up the many gaps left by years of non activity. Player sponsorship, programme advertising together with the advent of Cyril brought a new respect for the club. I poached my lottery hero from Fulham. Phil Chant started out with me back in 1984 at Reading and was the finest operator in football in my opinion. Lottery income moved from zero to £140,000 net profit within 18 months. He was still the Lottery King.

As the commercial director, I was satisfied that the new department was making a big contribution to the club's funds. From a position of £65,000 being raised in the year 1997–1998 we increased that figure to £140,000 in the first year, £380.000 in the second and £600,000 in the third. I was aware that Peter Day the chief executive of the club was not particularly enjoying his role. We both worked for Spurs during the late 1970s and early 1980s. His relationship with Neil McClure, the owner of the club was beginning to be strained. He had a slightly better relationship with Steve Hamer the club chairman, but even that was tense at times. McClure's complaint made to me on several occasions was that Peter did not converse with him often enough. Peter's version of events was that he felt that McClure didn't really know football and was playing 'city games' with the club.

Anyway, as Peter kept reminding me, Neil was really a Norwich City supporter who watched Arsenal! The relationship was destined to fail. The pair reached a stage where they hardly ever spoke. McClure based in his London office would make decisions without reference to Peter. Peter would go his own sweet way. It was purely coincidental that I needed to see McClure about personal matters at a time when Peter had moved nearer the edge.

As I made the journey back to Reading on a Saturday night to spend a little time with my family on Sunday, it was convenient for me and Neil to meet as he also made his way 'home' to Reading for the weekend. Neil did not make all the home games leaving it to Hamer to provide the face of solidarity, giving him the opportunity to spend some time with his son at his Berkshire home. When I returned to Swansea quite late on the Sunday, I received a call from Peter asking me if I could meet him for a drink. He told me that he was required to attend a meeting with McClure in his office early that week. On his return from London he informed me that he had been sacked. I was horrified as only three days had passed since my meeting with McClure. To this day I feel that Peter held me partly responsible for his demise. Nothing could be further from the truth. At my meeting with McClure, Peter's name was never mentioned. In fact my major gripe with Neil was over the fact that they (McClure and Hamer) had decided to appoint John Hollins as manager without reference to the other members of the board. As I was a fairly new kid on the block I felt that it was important for me to take a stance on this matter. Hollins would not have been my choice of manager. His starting salary of £85,000 per year plus bonuses and an expensive 4 x 4 vehicle made me angry as a hungry for success young stallion would have fitted the bill far better and been a lot cheaper.

The club was not renowned for stability at managerial level. When Ninth Floor bought out Doug Sharpe before the start of the 1997–1998 season, fans expected some changes. What they were going to see over the next few months were changes that were completely unexpected. After the first six games away from home, the points' board showed zero. As a result the club dropped from fifth in the league to bottom. McClure and Hamer sacked manager Jan Molby and his assistant Billy Ayre. 24 hours later Micky Adams was appointed upon my recommendation after Peter Day rang me for advice. Alan Cork was appointed as his assistant. Then 13 days later Micky walked out claiming that the board had lied to him about the amount of money he could have for the recruitment of new players. Corky accepted the manager's role and appointed Alan Curtis as his assistant. Corky lasted until the start of the 1998–1999 season when Hollins was appointed and Curtis continued as a number two.

I joined the club in December 1998. The little I could see of Alan Cork's managerial skills suggested to me that he was a better number two and felt happier in that role. He appointed Alan Curtis as his number two. This was a safe appointment as Alan lacked the essential qualities to be a number one but he was knowledgeable in the affairs of Swansea City.

When John Hollins was appointed as a successor to Cork, Peter Day wasn't happy and it showed. For my part, as the club's commercial director, I was able to stand to one side and watch the dust settle between the two. It was not directly my concern. By the start of the 1998–1999 football season, relationships between Peter Day and John Hollins had deteriorated to the extent that Hollins ran the football side without reference to Peter. This was not acceptable to the CEO as his terms of reference included overseeing the football manager's activities. Hollins was far more at home speaking to Hamer, the man that had salvaged his career as a manager and given him the level of wages befitting a manager in the first or even Championship division. McClure, as owner of the club, effectively gave Hamer *carte blanche* with respect to the footballing side. This annoyed Day even more. He was feeling more uncomfortable as his role as chief executive was being usurped by the minute. Board meetings were torture for Peter as he was constantly derided over quite minor issues. As the commercial department continued to grow I was able to avoid any flack.

John Hollins engineered an amazing cup run that saw us dispose of higher division opponents in rounds 1 and 2. We drew Premiership West Ham United in round 3. Some 2,000 Swans supporters made the trip to Upton Park for the game. Jason Smith, a summer signing from Tiverton Town, headed the ball home to give the Swans the lead. Smith had been signed after a tip off from Phil Chant my lottery manager. As Phil was a Tivvy lad himself he knew Smith and spoke to Peter Day about him. Peter, always prepared to listen and act when new talent was mentioned, made the journey to Wembley Stadium to see Smith play in a non-league cup final. He was so impressed that he made an offer of £10,000 with follow on payments if Smith made 20 first team appearances. John Hollins, not one to spot talent easily as he didn't put in the travel and hours necessary to keep a finger on the pulse, reluctantly took Smith and, as they say, the rest was history. Smith became the regular right sided centre back for three seasons. Back at Upton Park, Julian Dicks fired home an equaliser giving West Ham an undeserved replay. For a reason that has never, to my knowledge, been made public, Julian Dicks never played again for West Ham after these two cup games. The Vetch was crammed full of supporters for the replay. They were to witness a giant killing with Martin Thomas, signed from Fulham 12 months' earlier, driving home the winner from 20 yards. In the fourth round, Swansea drew Derby County and went out of the Cup losing 1–0.

I was finding my personal situation tough. Having decided to live in Swansea it meant that the only time during the football season that I could see my wife and daughter was on a Sunday. This meant either shooting off from the ground at 6.00 pm on a home match day, or driving to Reading from wherever we played. The strain was beginning to tell and it was not too long before my wife Angela sent out quiet messages that she was not going to let this position continue. Sure enough another divorce was on its way.

After the cup run the Swans concentrated on the league and the club found itself in a play-off position at the end of the season. A 1–0 home win in the first leg against Scunthorpe United was followed by a 4–1 defeat back at Scunny, thus consigning us to another season in the lowest league.

Another unhealthy situation was brewing back at the club. Neil McClure wanted an experienced accountant to pave the way for an eventual floatation. Initially, via an agency but later to be put on the books, the position was taken by Martin Burgess. Day and Burgess did not hit it off. I was not sure about the man either. It's fair to say that most of the staff at the club felt that there was a dark side to the new man. I was to find out 16 months later that he was in fact a snivelling creep. Behind the smiling face was a calculating brain. Whether or not he was any good as an accountant was debatable. McClure certainly took the view after working with Burgess for a year that he was a prat. They too had reached a point where conversation dried up.

Burgess was put on a salary of £60,000 a year, once again a decision taken arbitrarily and without discussion with the board. His problem was two-fold. Firstly, at the first sign of any disruption at home we would receive a phone call to say that he couldn't come in. Disruption in this context was that the kids were sick. Where was Mrs Burgess you may ask? Well she had a well paid job as the only Welsh speaking psychiatrist in Wales and her appointment book was far more important that her husband's. The club got a part time accountant on a full time accountant's wage.

Hollins was doing a good job, a fact rammed home to me at regular intervals by Steve Hamer. I couldn't disagree. We had achieved nine consecutive wins and played 700 minutes without conceding a goal. This thrust us into a top spot. As I was the club's general manager (I was elevated into this position after Peter Day had been dismissed) I too was beginning to wonder if I had got it wrong with Hollins. Instinctively I was still concerned about the man. He hardly ever went scouting, either to look at new players or the opposition. When I examined his expenses on a monthly basis before signing them off, I could see that he never left Wales. John was quite happy to sit in his apartment in Caswell Bay overlooking the sea. As Curtis found it difficult to cross the Severn Bridge also, it meant that we never seemed to have the low-down on the opposition unless we used a scout. Some of the scouts we used would have been more at home with the 32nd Mumbles scout troop. Looking at some of their reports on the opposition made me cry out with laughter.

'*The blond boy at the back is good in the air.*' Bloody right he was for he was 6 feet 5 inches tall!

'*They* [the team we were due to play in a few days] *are good going forward but not so good going back. Try and keep them pinned in their own half.*' Hell, where would we have been without that piece of information?

Swansea won promotion to the Second Division after a 3–0 win against Exeter at home (yet another coincidence). Not only did the Swans gain promotion the day they beat Exeter, they won the championship thanks to a 1–1 draw at Rotherham on the last day of the season. A draw was sufficient. Strangely enough Rotherham needed to win that game for *them* to be Champions. The return journey from Rotherham to Swansea on the team coach was conducted initially in a party atmosphere, with players and management staff all having a ball. No sooner had we made our way out of Yorkshire when I received a call from the Swansea Police liaison officer informing us that Terry Coles, one of our fans, had been trodden on by a police horse and had died in hospital from his injuries. The remainder of the journey continued in a sombre mood. The planned celebration to be held in the Territorial Army HQ adjacent to the Vetch was cancelled as no one was in the mood to party.

The following day was Sunday. I arrived at the ground at 8.00 am as I felt that supporters would want to pay their respects to their lost friend. This might include opening the club gates. Sure enough not only were there dozens of fans when I arrived, some had obviously paid their tributes overnight by placing flowers on the main gates. Those that wanted to enter the ground were allowed in to do so. Some wandered across the pitch in a complete mental haze. Others went to the spot where Terry stood for many years. This was on the North Bank, the area where the diehards would stand. Sitting down was not for them. During the course of the morning, TV, radio and newspaper reporters descended on the ground. I managed half a dozen interviews with the media guys and left more personal questions to be answered by the Supporters Club representative who knew Terry very well. There was a high degree of anger amongst supporters too. They felt that the horse that had trampled this poor man to death had been allowed to lose control. It bolted down a narrow lane at the visitor's end of a ground that was a pure relic from the past. It was no better than the Vetch and was well past its sell buy date. An ever increasing lobby of fans demanded action. I had to take the middle ground as the police had promised a full investigation. My suspicions were that this bottleneck of a lane behind the away terrace was far to narrow to allow police horses to enter and canter down. At a subsequent inquest it was revealed that Terry had consumed more than an adequate supply of ale. Nevertheless I felt that he did not deserve to die in this way.

I was never comfortable with the role of police at football matches. Not only did they dictate the number of police they would deploy for a game but would sometimes demand that a very senior police officer should be in attendance. If that was the case the police bill would rise to an unacceptable level. Also I experienced some very poor police activity. I would have thought that with their superior communication aids nothing could go wrong. On numerous occasions I have witnessed the police going into the wrong areas in a ground, arresting the wrong set of supporters and generally cocking up. Police intelligence is often far off the mark and to cover their backsides they will, sometimes on just a sniff of potential trouble, increase their numbers. This costs the club at least £80 a man. Back in 1985 when managing director of Reading FC, we experienced a wonderful start to the season with the team winning their first 13 games. I met with the police to discuss arrangements for the 14th game at home to Wolverhampton Wanderers. We expected a full house of 11,000. Wolves have always been well supported away from home and the 2,000 capacity east terrace was going to be under a strain to accommodate all their fans. It was unfortunate that the police Commander for the game had just returned from a football crowd control seminar and was about to supervise his first ever match. My concern was two-fold. Firstly, if there was a 'lock out' of Reading fans, what would the police suggest? Secondly, and far more importantly, what if there was a 'lock out' of Wolves fan? The response I received from the Commander was earth shattering. He informed me that they would escort the overflow of Wolves fans back to the station (three miles away) and they would try to disperse the Reading fans quietly. As the crowd limit set by the local authority was, in my opinion, set too low, I felt that there was room for negotiation. Should there be in excess of 300 Wolves fans, then the escort plan was an option. Any excess number of Reading fans (realistically no more than 500) should be accommodated on the west terrace where the capacity had been arbitrarily reduced by 2,000. That was not acceptable to the Commander.

Quarter of an hour before kick off, we had no problem with home supporters but an obvious problem with Wolves fans. The club had shut the turnstiles on the east terrace leaving an increasing number of Wolves fans outside. At the 7.45 pm kick off time, the number of Wolves fans locked out had grown to 500. I was asked to meet the Commander in my office. I took him upstairs to the boardroom which had emptied as the match had started. I offered him a drink. He swallowed a rather large whisky and quickly explained that he had a problem with locked out Wolves fans who were reaching boiling point. He asked if I could rig up a commentary facility with loudspeakers directed at the Wolves fans stranded outside the main doors of the stadium so they could hear what was happening on the pitch. Was he being serious? At this point I started to press home my concerns and clearly reminded him that any disturbance outside the ground was his responsibility. I advised him to get the fans inside the ground and said I would take any grief from the local authority because of crowd limits being exceeded. His face, filled with anguish, brightened a little as he talked into his lapel radio phone and gave the instruction to let the Wolves fans into the ground.

Several years later, football experienced a disaster that to this day brings back images that can keep me awake at night. The sight of dead bodies being carried on advertising hoardings and taken to a makeshift mortuary at the Hillsborough ground still flashes through my mind at times and even more so at the moment of writing this particular chapter as I reflect on the decision I forced the police Commander to take at Reading that night. It was the right decision at the time as the locked out fans could have easily rioted and caused a mini Hillsborough. I appreciate that police knocking is an attractive pastime to some and I would certainly not want to be classed as a member of any group that derives pleasure from conducting attacks on the police. What does worry me however is the fact that the men in blue seemed to want to be protected at all times, even when they have made categorical mistakes. The police in charge of crowd issues at Hillsborough tried to place the blame firmly on the shoulders of Liverpool fans. They were no angels, but it was unfair to try and transfer all the blame upon them. History has taught us that blame rested just as much with the police as with the fans. Eight years earlier than the Hillsborough tragedy I attended a cup semi final there between Tottenham Hotspur (my club at the time) and Wolves. There were problems that day that lead to an apology being printed in the home programme for the Tottenham/Liverpool game some 14 days later. The apology read as follows:

SHEFFIELD
It has been brought to our notice that many supporters holding terrace tickets were caused a lot of inconvenience and discomfort at our FA Cup semi final tie at Sheffield a fortnight ago. The incidents described to us have caused us considerable concern and we have every possible sympathy for the supporters so affected. As supporters will surely understand, we had no responsibility whatsoever as a club for the crowd arrangements made for the semi final, and it is our earnest hope that spectators travelling to watch our team in the future will not be the victims of any similar circumstances.'

For legal reasons I cannot speculate as to exactly what those circumstances were, but I imagine that the same set of conditions that caused the disaster in 1989 pertained in 1981 with overcrowding the main reason for these incidents.

The Swans won promotion in the 1999–2000 season with John Hollins at the helm. John had taken the Swans from the foot of the football league to the Third Division championship within the space of two years. During the summer of 2000 he was invited to London to see Neil McClure and Steve Hamer. By now I had been promoted to managing director. McClure, conscious of the fact that any movement to increase Hollins' package would have to be run past me in my newly elevated position, made contact and said that he had wanted to secure Hollins' position at the club as his contract was up. The threat of him being offered other jobs in football seemed to be a reality. I was not convinced however that McClure wanted to break the bank to secure Hollins. Hamer, Hollins' best friend, wanted Neil to offer Hollins £115,000 per year with a three year contract. My stance on this matter was simple. Give him a rise by all means but not the equivalent of 33 percent *plus* a three year contract. McClure was in turmoil. He saw the element of blackmail creeping in to these negotiations. Hollins was threatening. Hamer was desperate to see his man get the proverbial bag of gold. Hamer, the same man who sat in my office overlooking the club car park a few weeks after my promotion and asked who the new Jag belonged to was now trying to 'sell' a package for Hollins worth £345,000 without even flinching! The Jag by the way was mine. I was offered an upgraded car by Neil McClure on my promotion. He said it was justified on the grounds of the vastly improved balance sheet of the club, in particular from the commercial income which had increased 500 percent over two and a half years. Hamer then made a comment that made my blood curdle. 'The fans won't like that.'

The Jag was part of a deal I did with a local dealer. The car was an ex-demo and was valued at £22,000. The club leased it.

Neil McClure was rapidly becoming disenchanted with Hamer, who by now was issuing his own threats. 'If you don't give Johnny Hollins his deal I will resign.' Little did Hamer know how near Neil came to taking him up on his offer. Relationships between all three parties were never to be the same. Hollins got his deal. Hamer had secured the manager's position and put his own in grave danger.

The new season in a higher division was greeted with a mixture of optimism and caution. Optimism because the team had performed so well in the previous season, caution because the club had said goodbye to two of its strikers and only recruited one new forward in the shape of Tommy Mutton. Tommy was a non league player from Aberystwyth. With little money in the coffers it was a case of sell to buy should the team need new faces.

The early games provided some hope. Two goalless draws against Wigan and Brentford and a worthy effort was shown before going out of the Worthington Cup to West Brom. Luton Town was beaten 4–0 at the Vetch and the club looked skyward rather than downward to the Third Division. But I was beginning to feel uneasy about Hollins' commitment. I felt that he was being carried away on the back of last season's success and complacency had set in. Strangely enough, it was our visit to Reading, my old club, and a 5–1 thrashing that made me shudder, as the gap between the two teams on that day appeared to be enormous. I pleaded with John to find fresh blood but I bottled out of an idea that I felt would have brought a new dimension to training ground activities. Through a contact I had made at Fulham several years earlier, the name Roy Evans was mentioned. Roy, the ex-manager of Liverpool, was doing very little in the game at that time and his spokesperson suggested to me that he only wanted to play a part with a smaller club and had no pretensions to become a manager again. Could I put this to John? On balance I decided not to. On reflection it was a classic mistake on my part and one I regret to this day. With a little arm twisting I convinced John that we had to find new blood. I agreed with a French agent that we would look at several players keen to launch into the UK soccer scene. Initially we signed a midfield player called David Romo. Another agent representing South American players asked if we could take a look at the Venezuelan striker Giovanni Savarese. He and Romo were initially successful and seemed to fit the bill. As they were both signed on short term contracts and were free transfers I felt that we had attracted a good package.

In his first game Savarese scored twice against Stoke City. After half a dozen games Romo proved to be too lightweight for the hurly burly of the Second Division. Walter Boyd, a signing from Jamaica, appeared to be conspicuous by his absence as the winter came upon us. My flat was 50 yards from his and one night he appeared at my door with his arms crossed across his chest mumbling, 'Mr Lewis I'm freezing'. Poor Walter didn't know how to turn on his central heating. After fixing it for him I went around his flat turning all the thermostats up to maximum. My everlasting memory of Walter was seeing him jump up onto a double radiator in order to get as much heat as he could into his frozen body.

Results deteriorated. We were not up to the job in hand and relegation to the third division seemed inevitable. During that forgettable period in the club's history I witnessed a display from a Chairman that will stay with me forever. Hamer now had to eat humble pie. His choice of Hollins as manager was under serious scrutiny. McClure was gunning for him. It was no excuse however for Hamer to enter the manager's office after the Oldham game and one by one select individuals enjoying an end of the match sandwich for his special brand of verbal treatment. I was walking past Hollins' office when I heard through the open door Hamer screaming at Paul Morgan the kit man, 'You are a fucking disgrace, a lazy bastard'. Then he turned to the physio Richard Evans, 'I'm not fucking sure about you either'. Then it was the turn of Glan Letheren the goalkeeping coach, 'What the fuck do you do?' He kept his real venom for Alan Curtis. 'You have never liked me and I have never trusted you.'

Bloody hell! I know that he liked his white wine and it was not unusual for him to 'entertain' the guests in the boardroom with some witty remarks about the state of British football and the individuals involved. He would use some words that are taboo with most men never mind women, but he carried it off more often than not. I would like to point out at this stage that I was not exactly holier than thou at home matches either. My weakness for the amber nectar often led me into tirades with staff. On a match day I would get fuelled up after a game and have fun, but never, to my knowledge anyway, have I sunk to the depths that Hamer did that day.

Neil McClure rang me the following Monday and informed me that he was at the end of his tether with Hamer. He felt that Hamer was undermining his efforts in every direction. I felt obliged to tell Neil exactly what I had witnessed at the last home game. I told Neil that I needed to speak to Hamer about his outburst, also to tell him that I was not happy paying out his expenses that included first class travel, meals and a 60p per mile petrol allowance. He really was taking the club for a ride. McClure asked me to wait a few hours before contacting Hamer. I was curious as to what was going on between the two. Perhaps I had misread the whole situation. Was this simply a 'lover's tiff' and was I going to feel the backlash? Just two hours later Neil rang me to say that he had organised the hand delivery of a letter to Hamer asking for his resignation as Chairman.

Neil made a rare visit to Swansea in June 2001. He had become so exasperated by the city council's apparent apathy towards the new Morfa Stadium deal that he arranged to see the CEO and the leader of the council to express his feelings for the last time. Several years earlier it was McClure and Keith Harris, an investment banker and later to become the Chairman of the Football League, who jointly put up a scheme for a new stadium in Swansea. The council farted around for years trying to string a deal together that would utilise the Vetch and St Helens which were both council owned, into parcels of land that would help to finance a new stadium. I should say that the reputation of the City Fathers over the years did not augur well for any rapid movement on their part. Their inferiority complex would often come shining through when big decisions had to be made. Politically the area had been served by the Labour Party for too many years to remember. They had gained a reputation of not only being ditherers but also control freaks. With some little legitimacy Swansea councillors would bang the table every time Cardiff or indeed Newport seemed to receive preferential treatment from Whitehall. They had little vision and hardly any ambition. Cardiff and Newport, and to some extent the valley towns, got on with the job of obtaining grants and central government help. Swansea always seemed to lag behind. So it was not surprising that McClure decided enough was enough as talk and more talk coupled with potential new problems on funding drove him into the ground.

The owners of the rugby club were playing a cagey game too. For some reason, which I never discovered, they had a strange hold over the elected members and senior officers. This was manifested by the fact that their ground at St Helens seemed to avoid the immense hassle that the Vetch was subjected to. Council officers swarmed over the soccer club at regular intervals demanding that upgraded work be carried out whereas St Helens was left to deteriorate.

On the same day as Neil McClure's final meeting with the Council, he asked me to meet him in the Swansea Hilton Hotel. The meeting was quite short and to the point. His opener was, 'Mike, I'm trying to do things with Ninth Floor that are going to take up all my time. My plans for Swansea City Football Club have not materialised. You are the only person I can trust at the club and I want to offer all Ninth Floor's shares to you [they represented 9 million shares equal to 96% of the club]. You can have the shares for £1 and I will leave £200,000 in the bank. I suggest that you get rid of Burgess as soon as you can because he is up to no good and anyway how can I trust a man whose bloody wife wears the trousers?'

He gave me a week to think it over. I didn't need that long. I rang him two days later, confirmed my interest and we met at a solicitors in Reading to sign the deal. My relationship with McClure was generally a very good one. We shared the same sense of humour for a start and that is a vital attribute when dealing with a soccer club. He was described to me before my appointment as being a bully who was sometimes petulant and dismissive. He was a bully to a point. He did sack me over the phone on two occasions. He was certainly petulant when confronted by buffoons inside and outside of the club. In particular he found several members of the Swansea establishment a real pain in the arse. He did not disguise his feelings. Underneath his thick skin I believed there to be a softer side to Neil. I wondered because of his huge frame (22 stone I would guess) if he found himself alone at times in the city of London whereas Hamer and Harris could use their charms to entertain and had comparative good looks to boot.

Having acquired the club I now looked around to see who I could trust and who I could not. On the board I could only trust Professor David Farmer. The jury was out on Martin Burgess, the financial director. Mel Nurse the ex player was new to the board and I needed a little time to suss him out. Some minor indiscretions in the boardroom made me feel a little nervous about Mel. Socially he was a gem if you could listen for the hundredth time about his exploits as a player.

My commercial team were still pulling up trees so Michelle Carpenter and Diane Griffiths were first on my team sheet together with Phil Chant the lottery manager. Don Goss the stadium manager was another good man I was happy to keep. Club secretary Jackie Rockey was someone I had worked with three years earlier when I did some consultancy work at Cardiff City. She makes no secret of the fact that she still has a soft spot for the Bluebirds, but I felt that she would be loyal to me when I decided to poach her from the capital where she was the assistant club secretary. When the Trust eventually took over the club some time later, it was Jackie who was told that her job was secure when others from my regime perished. On the playing side I was concerned about John Hollins. He needed to pick up the team after the previous season's disaster and do it quickly. Unfortunately this didn't happen.

Gaining control of the club was only the beginning of what was to be a tortuous six months. The club held a golf day at Clyne Golf Club in July 2001. A good turnout meant 18 teams of four took part on a sunny day. This event was a regular one organised by the Vice-Presidents. After golf we sat down to dinner and were entertained by a local comedian or singer. Just before dinner, Mel Nurse approached me and asked how I was getting on with finding possible new investment in the club as I had gone public a few days earlier and warned the City of Swansea that we might run out of money by Christmas unless I could find some financial support. I couldn't be sure whether or not Mel was on the back end of his favourite tipple of Bacardi and coke as he had not been playing golf that day. This gave him ample opportunity to 'get comfortable'. His outward appearance certainly suggested that he was well in command of his actions but what came next was a complete surprise to me.

'How are you getting on Mike, are you still talking to those foreigners?' By that he meant was I still talking in serious terms to two Americans and an Aussie. My endeavours to interest local businessmen during the initial period of my ownership were leading nowhere.

During the time of the takeover I was promised by all and sundry that they would do all they could to assist me. They felt that the club had suffered from being owned by a London businessman. In reality, anyone with substantial funds in a position to help hid for cover when the moment of need arrived. I should have known better than to expect a queue of investors to be banging down the gates of the club eager to help. Excuses given to me by local businessmen when asked to help the Swans were wide ranging.

'My company's going through a rough patch at the moment.'

'We're poised for a takeover and I dare not make any investment at this time.'

'My wife hates football and she will kill me if she sees me investing in the Swans.'

'Most of my customers are rugby supporters not like me so I have to be careful.'

Then there was Mel. Just before we sat down for dinner he said to me, 'Mike, forget these foreigners, I will provide the money necessary to see the club through. I don't want to be Chairman just a majority shareholder. How much will that cost me?'

'I'll sell you 51 percent of the shares for £400,000. The money from the sale will go to the club. I will get the legal eagles to prepare the paper work and ask their advice about the transferring of shares.

Mel extended his hand and we shook on the deal.

I could hardly conceal my excitement at the thought of Mel saving the club from a stormy few months of financial insecurity. Indeed, I really could not see a way forward after Christmas and my thoughts were turning to a Creditors Voluntary Agreement as an escape route. I told Mel that we could sit down and discuss the details within the next 24 hours. He happily agreed and we proceeded to enjoy the rest of the evening.

As Mel was embarked on his own project inside the football ground he was, up to this point anyway, very easily contacted. He very kindly asked if he could erect a bar on the North Bank side of the ground so that the standing spectators could enjoy a drink at the game. This venture had taken him several weeks already and by the time he had made the gesture in connection with shares, he had another four weeks of work to conduct. Mel was a hands on man and he loved nothing more than having a hammer and nails in his hands, joining in with the 'boys' to help construct the bar. It was not unusual for him to be seen constructing the roof, painting the walls and laying the floor. He was at the ground at least four days a week.

Having struck the deal with Mel I now had to put the American and Australian interest into the sidings for a while until I could firm up Mel's deal. I became worried when Mel went missing. He was not seen working on his project over the next few weeks and I could not track him down at his B&B 400 yards from the ground. When I questioned his friends about his whereabouts, I could detect reluctance on their part to give me any indication where Mel might be. I asked the ground staff to let me know the moment they saw him enter the ground. Sure enough, five weeks after we had shaken hands on the deal he appeared at the Vetch to put the final touches to the bar. On this occasion it was the signage 'The Mel Nurse Bar' that was due to be put in place. Sprinting around the ground to catch him before he disappeared again, the mounting fears that I had experienced since the handshake swelled into reality when I saw him on top of the roof of his building. He immediately put his head into his hands and started shaking his head. By the time he had descended the ladder I was confused as to whether I should be angry and have a go, or be sympathetic to whatever story he was about to spill out. There were no surprises. He explained that he had gone to his bank manager with a view to re-mortgaging 18 of his many properties in the Swansea area. Apparently his manager had refused him the facility.

'Never before Mike have I been turned down by the bank,' was his curt riposte.

'You have really put me in the shit, Mel,' was the only response I could find before walking away from the man.

To this day I am still peeved about Mel's turnabout because it was the precursor of torrid times ahead. Australian Tony Petty came in. Petty cocked up. I cocked up by selling to him. On taking over, Petty asked me if I would remain at the club and guide him through the increasing paperwork that was being generated in relation to the new stadium. I agreed to stay on four days a week. For this I was going to receive a consultancy fee of £25,000 paid at a rate of £2,083 per month over the next 12 months. A contract was signed and I placed myself in a little office once occupied by accountant Burgess to concentrate on the new project.

Because of his total lack of knowledge of the football industry it wasn't too long before Petty was standing at my door asking for help on a series of matters. These matters included the transfer of players, a run down on the profile of staff, how to deal with the Welsh FA and how to deal with the FA and the Football League. It was his desire to capitalise on the sale of any player worth a bob or two that made me suspicious of his motives. On one occasion he asked me to speak to John Dennis the Chairman of Barnsley as they had made an enquiry about Mama Sidebe our tall striker who was attracting attention from other clubs. Petty felt that I was better placed to negotiate with Dennis as I knew the man. So I did. My lack of enthusiasm for the transfer of the player plus an over value must have shone through as the Barnsley Chairman backed off. I couldn't stop the transfer of Stuart Roberts though. Wycombe Wanderers had shown an interest. Their manager at the time was Lawrie Sanchez who I knew quite well from my Reading days when he was a player there before being transferred to Wimbledon. Petty, once again used his, 'These people don't know me Mike,' approach and asked me to speak to 'Sanch'. My valuation of the player was £200,000. In the conversation with Lawrie it became obvious that Wycombe were not speaking the same language and £100,000 was nearer their estimate. Sanchez asked me to speak to their Chairman and that conversation only confirmed my belief in the value they had placed on Roberts. Nothing moved on this issue for a few days until I walked into a meeting that Petty was having with an agent. The agent represented Stuart Roberts. Petty asked me to sit in. What happened next horrified me. Successive calls from the agent to the Wycombe Chairman, Sanchez, the player and his father were made with Petty coming in on the end of these conversations. I was only getting one side of any of these conversations. Petty, walking across to the big double windows that covered the whole of one wall that once was my office, put his hand under his chin and said, 'Okay, we'll do it'. The agent picked up his mobile, spoke to the Wycombe Chairman and confirmed the deal. '£100,000 it is Ivor [Ivor Beek was Wycombe's Chairman]'. I was gob smacked. Given another half an hour to work on the deal I would have at least reached a figure of £150,000. This was a sell out.

Petty and his sidekick John Shuttleworth started to apply some of their own business 'expertise' to the club. Unfortunately they seemed to ignore the fact that players not only had watertight contracts, but had an excellent trade union. His attempt to rip up 17 player's contracts and start again was laughed at by the relevant football bodies to say nothing of his causing anger and frustration amongst the fans that quickly turned on him. I stayed at the club for eight weeks until it became impossible to work with the man, who incidentally never honoured the agreement put in writing to the effect that I would deliver the new stadium project over the course of the following 12 months. His refusal to honour that agreement gave him great amusement. I was made aware of this by one of his so called inner circle friends. He enjoyed informing listeners that Lewis would not see a penny from the agreement. Petty comes a very close second behind Geller as someone with whom I have an old score to settle.

Pettty's appearances at the club were becoming less frequent. Shuttleworth was left to sort out the mess that Petty had created with his flash ideas of how to run a football club and in doing so showed complete disregard for football etiquette. Stories told by

Petty of how he was followed after a home game and nearly chased off the road had to be taken with a huge pinch of salt and were some distance away from reality. What was real was the lump on the back of my head after being attacked by supporters after the Carlisle home game on 15 December 2001. What were real were the death threats I received on my mobile phone. What was real was the junk mail coming through my letter box at my flat on the marina. Somebody somewhere was writing to the suppliers of wheelchairs, stair lifts, incontinence pads and any other aid for disabled people and giving my address for forwarding purposes. The receipt of these gave me cause to chuckle. The complete video collection of *Agatha Christie Murder Stories* was delivered to my front door by the lovely old lady living across the corridor from my flat. She allowed the postman to bring them into the foyer of the flats after he rang the front door bell earlier in the day when I was at work. The receipt of these videos did make me wonder if some twisted mind was at work. What were real were the gestures and the bad mouthing that occurred when I was recognised in my car whilst pulling up at traffic lights. I received V signs, and the words, 'Fuck off Lewis,' (and worse profanities) were mouthed at me. What was real was the request by the police to be informed of my movements if I was to venture out to the city centre at night. What was real was the disappearance of so called friends at the club. Their loyalty was worth no more than the majority of footballer's loyalty to their clubs. Through it all, the person I despised more than anyone was me. How could I be such a fool as to not see what was happening around me? My marriage was coming to an end. My rolling contract with the Swans was almost worthless due to the club entering into a CVA in early 2002. The 5 percent creditors' pay out meant that the £83,000 owed to me by the club resulted in a magnificent £4,100 settlement. Some fans would take the view that I should have received nothing. I would remind them of the previous two years when the financial fortunes of the club were dramatically improved.

Petty, having been run out of town by fans, sold the shares that I handed over to him for £1 for £25,000. How the bloody hell can you sell a business losing £250,000 a year for £25,000? Somehow he managed to get the Supporters Trust to cough up their hard earned cash to pay for the shares. In the process, Petty tried desperately hard to convince people that he was doing it for the benefit of the club. In the land of arseholes they don't get any bigger than that! Mind you, some would say that my backside equals his as it was Mike Lewis who invited him to buy the club. I can't disagree with that.

The earlier demise of John Hollins was no surprise. He told the media that with eight games to go we stood a chance of staying up. His state of mind was of concern to me as we needed to win *all* those eight games to creep out of the relegation zone. Inevitably, relegation was 'achieved' long before the season had ended.

The new season started with two wins in the first seven games. We were playing without commitment and direction. Effectively we had run out of new ideas. Our 3–1 defeat at Plymouth on that fateful day of Tuesday 11 September 2001 proved to be fateful for Swansea City Football Club too. Perhaps it was the scenes on TV of the destruction of the twin towers that put my mind into a, 'Let's not put off breaking the bad news mindset'. Instinct told me clearly to relieve John of his duties. To some extent I fully believed that I was doing him a favour. Surely he could see that the fight to save the cause was a futile one? Sometimes what appears to be an insignificant gesture or action can motivate me into taking action. As the third Plymouth goal was swept in I saw Roger Freestone, the Swans' keeper, kick the ground in disgust. It was not so much that gesture as the one that immediately followed. John Hollins turned with his back to the playing field, looked up to the clouds, caressed his chin with his hand and gave that wide eyed look of a man who knew that his only hope was to come from the man up in the sky. Having travelled down to the game with Ray Trotman, a loyal friend of the club, I was spared the long coach trip back to Swansea with the players. Travelling with the team is fine when they've won away, but a loss where the team played badly is a completely different kettle of fish. My travelling companion kept asking if I was okay (the silence from behind the wheel had made him wonder). I couldn't tell him what my plan of action was going to be.

Early the next morning I called John Hollins and asked him to come to the club for a meeting at 9.30 am. Being a sensitive person I knew that he would be thinking the worst and it gave me little comfort to make the call. I asked him to bring Alan Curtis along too. I had called together all the board members at 9.00 am and put it to them that I felt a change was essential. I got unanimous agreement from my colleagues, in particular Nurse who felt that Hollins should have gone long ago. Professor Farmer, Burgess and Nurse gathered with me in the boardroom for the 9.30 meeting. John was ushered in and sat at the far end of the table holding his mobile phone in his hand. I explained to John that the team's performances were giving us all some concern and that I felt we needed a change. I made that statement in the singular as I wanted to give the other members of the board a chance to explain their thinking. Hollins simply said that we would be hearing from his solicitor and proceeded to throw his mobile phone on the table. 'Do you want to see Alan now?' was his final remark as he left the room. I asked him to tell Alan that we wanted a few minutes together as a board and that I would collect Alan when we were ready.

The sacking of Jimmy Scoular as the manager of my home town club in Newport was not pleasant but overdue to the extent that he really got six months more employment with the club than he deserved. I certainly didn't lose any sleep over that one. At Reading I had to terminate Maurice Evans as manager. It was not easy but again essential. I did stay awake at night over that one. Coping with the responsibility of hiring and firing managers was nothing new to me, although it was not a pleasant experience. Back in West Wales, Alan Curtis entered the boardroom shortly after Hollins had left. He was probably aware of his fate and my heart sank. Alan was, and still is, a local hero. He is a likeable man with the looks of a film star and a soft and gentle nature. This sacking was going to be uncomfortable and unpopular but we had no choice. He wasn't up to management and had not made a tremendous impression as the head of youth development. Under normal circumstances he would have had a future role in the club. These were not normal circumstances however. We could not afford to find Alan a job. I put the position to him and with the good grace I expected, he simply got up from his chair and wished us all the best. As he was leaving the boardroom, he turned around, looked straight at me and said, 'Mike, you're right you know. We have lost our way'. The following Saturday after John Hollins' departure saw us play Halifax at home. We lost 2–0. It was time to find a new manager.

A man I knew would keep us out of trouble and would provide the spirit and enthusiasm for the fight for a brief period was Colin Addison (known as Addo). I recruited Colin back in 1977 to save my beloved Newport County. Addo had worked wonders. He turned the club around on the pitch whilst the commercial team was improving matters off the pitch. He was my choice to take the place of John Hollins at the Swans. The other board members agreed for me to talk to him. Colin was doing some media work at the time having recently left Yeovil Town. Together with Mel Nurse and Burgess, I met with Colin at a hotel in the Vale of Glamorgan.

My reasons for taking Nurse and Burgess along were purely selfish. They were different reasons, but still selfish. I knew that Nurse would curse any appointment that did not have his endorsement and Burgess would spread poison should the new manager lose a few games. He was inclined to panic as most accountants do when they see the pendulum swing the wrong way. I had enjoyed the moment on 20th June when Burgess panicked. The occasion was a trip to Charleroi for the European Cup. England was due to play Romania and courtesy of Carlsberg, the beer supplier to Swansea City Football Club, Burgess and I were invited to fly out to see the game. After a champagne reception in the executive lounge at Stansted airport where some 40 guests were assembled, we were led out to a Fokker F27 aircraft. I have always enjoyed flying, but Burgess made it quite clear that he was a 'white knuckle' flyer. As this trip was before I became chairman and owner of the club, my relationship with Burgess was steady. I needed his accountancy input on a daily basis, even if his figures were often wide of the mark. Other senior members of staff were more wary of him and made their concerns known to me. We took our seats on board the plane with Burgess sitting in the window seat. As he looked out through the small window he could see the starboard turbo prop engine. The ageing stewardess went through the necessary safety procedures. As the assembled guests were club stewards, restaurant owners or company directors linked to Carlsberg, it was no surprise that the stewardess' message was not given full attention. Events over the next 10 minutes were to prove that our lack of attention to the safety procedures could have proved fatal. The noise from the turbos as the pilot prepared to taxi down the runway was almost deafening. Burgess gripped his seat rests like a man clinging on to a precipice. As we moved down the runway, a severe shuddering and rattling ran through the framework of the aircraft. As the plane must have been 20 or 30 years old, I put these vibrations down to wear and tear. Suddenly the plane started to brake. Ceiling panels started to dislodge themselves and fly through the cabin. Two of these panels came close to decapitating passengers. I looked around to see a man sat two seats behind on the opposite side of the plane gripping his neck with blood spurting through his fingers. I was clipped by one of these flying panels, but fortunately my wound was nothing more than a flesh wound as the cowboys used to say. The smell of fused electrical cables and burnt rubber filled the cabin. The stewardess was frozen to her seat. The aircraft slowly but surely came to a halt. Silence, rather than panic reigned as we all sat in complete disbelief. From the cockpit the captain emerged, I would guess that he was a senior pilot of about 55 years of age. His once crisp, beautifully ironed white shirt was drenched in sweat. No sooner had he entered the passenger cabin than foam wagons, police cars, and ambulances appeared alongside the aircraft. Paramedics attended to any injured passengers and the remaining passengers were asked to stay in their seats for a moment. The captain, having left the plane for a few minutes, returned and asked us all to walk off the aircraft. As I descended the steps I looked around and to my amazement I saw that the complete front wheel nose cone had sunk itself into the runway. We were taken by bus back to the terminal (what an unfortunate description that is) and returned to the VIP suite. The Carlsberg staff left behind had replenished the stock with a huge pyramid of Carlsberg cans used as the dominant feature. The brewery rep informed us that another plane was on its way and those who wanted to 'try again' were welcome to climb aboard. Bravado took over. We talked in little groups about the incident after making calls to our loved ones as the media had already blasted news of the mishap to the world. To their credit, no one ducked the trip and we all had a great time in Belgium. Even the result went my way with England beaten by Romania. Diolch.

Meeting Colin Addison at a hotel in the Vale of Glamorgan brought back memories of an early meeting with Colin when, back in 1977 I introduced him to Ron Warry the Chairman of Newport County. Mr Warry sat at the driving wheel of a huge Mercedes and repeatedly turned to me on the short journey from Somerton Park to the hotel on the outskirts of the town to ask me about Colin.

'Mr Lewis, is this Mr Henderson any good?'

'No, Chairman, it's Colin Addison, not Henderson, he's an ex player from Arsenal, Sheffield United and Nottingham Forest. He managed Hereford United to the historic cup win over Newcastle United and is just the sort of guy we need to lift the club.'

'What's the deal with him Mr Lewis?'

'£80 per week plus £10 petrol money Chairman.'

'Do you think we can get him for £60 per week?'

'Chairman, I've spent the last two days looking for a new manager. This man is right for us. Let's go and get him.'

Colin, looking dapper as ever was waiting for us in the foyer of the hotel.

'Colin, this is Mr Warry the Chairman of the club,' I said.

'Pleased to meet you Chairman.'

'Shall we get down to business Mr Henderson?' were Mr Warry's first words.

'The name's Addison, Chairman, not Henderson.'

What a bloody start! The rest is history as they say.

I wanted Colin's appointment at Swansea to be unanimously agreed by the board. With the support of Nurse and Burgess together with Professor Farmer (who was not a well man and quite happy to go with the flow) this was easily achieved. Addison's managerial record spoke for itself. He had been Ron Atkinson's number two at Athletico Madrid eventually taking over from him in 1988. He had managed Celta Vigo, Cadiz, Deportivo, not to mention his Svengali role at Newport County on two occasions.

In horse racing terms I knew that Colin was a sprinter not a three miler. He hardly ever stayed at a club for a long period. I believe that his style of management, plus living on his nerves, led to a situation where Colin would eventually burn himself out having used all his guile and energies to steer respective clubs out of trouble. Those energies and enthusiasm sometimes led to confusion in his mind. Occasionally in the company of others he would repeatedly get names wrong, even if he had known them for years. Regarding Colin as a long term friend I am still amazed at his ability to retain this feature. Endearing is the only word I use to describe this facet particularly when he is in full flight. His 100 percent enthusiasm added to that smiling, happy disposition, meant that Colin would always be on the 'wanted' list.

Colin asked if he could have an assistant. Normally the answer would have been a definite 'no' as our precarious financial position left no room for number twos. When he said that Peter Nicholas was the man he wanted to assist him I was happy to put the matter to the board as Peter had shone as manager of Barry Town taking them into Europe on two occasions. This was, in my opinion, going to be the dream team. The fans immediately took to Colin and Peter as both were refreshing characters embracing the fans with their thoughts and plans. Incidentally, Peter Nicholas was born and grew up just a mile from my home in Newport. He lived within a stone's throw of my first ever girlfriend. I wonder if he ever saw me say goodnight to the lovely Gaynor Sage on her doorstep.

In fairness to John Hollins he was also an engaging type of manager but was not the finished article. He certainly lacked the verve and energy that came in abundance with Addison. Unfortunately Colin and Peter having led the team to league safety by mid March, were dismissed by a new consortium led by, 'In Mel we Trust' Nurse. Their dismissal, made on the grounds of cost cutting was, in truth, more a case of sour grapes on behalf of the new owners. Any connection with Mike Lewis was regarded as poisonous and should be removed even if it meant getting rid of a pair of decent and successful people. In addition to the two coaches, Phil Chant the best lottery man in the football league was also given his marching orders.

The new board installed club captain Nick Cusack as player-manager with Alan Curtis returning as his assistant. This was a bad appointment by any stretch of the imagination. Nick was not even a leader on the field of play. The 2001–2002 season ended with the Swans finishing 20th in Division Three.

The following season saw the consortium's judgement come apart with Nick Cusack being sacked after nine games. His demise came after a 4–0 defeat at the hands of Wrexham. Whether it be by luck or judgement you have to admire the way these amateurs have steered the club into what is now called division one. They have also managed to move into the new stadium and improve the financial state of the club. Missing out on promotion to the Championship in seasons 2005–2006 and again in 2006–2007 was in no way a disaster. The club appears to be in a stable condition with every hope of going forward in the 2007–2008 season.

22

GREAT EXPECTATIONS

Having departed Swansea early in 2002 I was anxious to get back into the only business I really knew. Stuart Dawe the Exeter City director first made me aware of John Russell's existence. He met John Russell some years earlier at a match at Carlisle when John was Chairman of Scarborough FC. I called Dawe whilst he was on holiday in Austria to talk to him about some consultancy work at Exeter as I was keen to get back into football. Dawe showed me some operating figures for Exeter and asked me to report back to him with my comments. I did this sending him a rather gloomy report. It contained reference to a commercial department that was costing the club money, a lottery that was operating at a loss and a travel club that was losing money. Rather worryingly some gate figures did not seem to truly reflect the level of attendances they were attracting. Putting it kindly my report suggested that there was seepage! Heavy loans over the years from directors were a millstone around the club's neck totalling some £750,000 at the time. Most of the loan was owed to Chairman Ivor Doble.

As Russell was going down to see the board at Exeter with his own ideas of how to raise funds, we decided to meet there and exchange views. The meeting with the board was non productive to the extent that Russell and myself said that we would look around for other clubs who might be interested in our respective services.

I then received a phone call from Ivor Doble during February 2002. He came straight to the point and said that the club was a few months away from extinction. None of the directors wanted to put more money in and he, as the major investor over the years, had come to the end of his tether. He also felt that the chief executive had lost the plot and was allowing the club to stagnate. He asked if John Russell and I would consider returning to Exeter to meet again with the board. We were not exactly excited about the prospect as we both felt that the club was being badly run, possibly beyond redemption. It was when we took control several months later that we found out just how badly the club had been run.

Together with Russell I prepared a document that outlined how we, if invited, would set about dealing with the debt load. This document included a payback of director's loans from a pool of money that would be generated from new income. New income was not too difficult to generate on the back of the club's poor commercial performance for many years. In return the board would hand over the day-to-day control of the club. The key to the success of this proposal was the willingness or not of Ivor Doble to relinquish control, hand over the Chairmanship of the club and promise to hand over his majority shareholding of 67 percent to Messrs Russell and Lewis for £1. This would be after a sum of £250,000 had been paid off Doble's loans. In addition, other director's loans were to be paid back over a period from any surplus income generated from player transfers, cup runs, TV appearances and any surplus generated by over the average home match gates. Peter Carter a director of many years standing studied the proposal and immediately threw his arms up in the air shouting, 'I couldn't possibly sign this'. Doble looked stunned. I looked at John Russell and intimated to him that enough was enough. We had made a second visit to the club and were once again led up the garden path. Was it any wonder that the club was incapable of running its affairs when they couldn't even come to a consensus on how *their* loans were going to be repaid? John and I walked out of the meeting and returned to our respective homes (John returned to West Yorkshire and I returned to Swansea).

Doble rang me several days later and said that he wanted to do a deal on his own. He asked if I would put down on paper some benchmark ideas for a deal that could be encapsulated in a legal document drawn up by his solicitor. Doble's solicitor drew up the agreement that Doble insisted should be a secret deal. As his solicitor was responsible for the wording of the document, we were happy to comply with the requirements of the deal, excepting a few minor amendments.

The third visit to Exeter to meet the board was definitely going to be our last. This was communicated to Doble in no uncertain manner. Should any prevarications take place at the board meeting then we would leave instantly. It is my belief that Doble had threatened his colleagues on the board that if they turned down the opportunity to hand over control of the club to Russell and Lewis, he was going to 'pull the plug' and put the club into administration for the second time in a decade. Chief executive Bernard Frowd had already remarked to us on more than one occasion that the club was not in a position to see its way through the summer of 2002. This was hardly surprising given some of the contracts that they had entered into. A £2.4 million project to build new stands on a fixed price basis eventually cost the club £3.3 million. They also had a 10 year lease for a ticket machine at £15,000 per annum!

At the meeting I detected a completely different attitude from the same directors who had previously poured scorn upon us. Indeed, even Frowd and Carter were wearing smiles on their faces, which was a little bit worrying. What we didn't know was the answer to the important question as to whether or not Doble had indicated to the other members of his board just what the deal was with Lewis and Russell. Had they had serious doubts about the deal then they certainly didn't show concern at the meeting. The vote was unanimous and we were voted onto the board of directors.

I covered the ground with John Russell on the question of Chairman/Vice-Chairman positions. I wasn't keen to take on the Chairmanship having just relinquished a similar position at Swansea City where the muck and bullets scenario during the last three months of my tenure had spoiled for me what was mostly an enjoyable experience. John Russell on the other hand had stepped down as Chairman of Scarborough some years earlier and was, to my understanding, keen to have another go. However, he was insistent that I should be Chairman as I had had far more experience at all levels in the game over my 30 years of involvement. I was not too sure. We decided to spin a coin. The winner could choose which of the positions he preferred. I won the toss and elected to be Vice-Chairman. With hindsight this was probably the most important decision I have taken in recent years. It meant that as Chairman, John would be seen as the figurehead of the club and as such would have to sign important legal and financial documents. Having spent many hours with legal eagles and accountants trying to save Swansea City only months earlier, I was in no hurry to take on that level of responsibility again. That factor was to be vital in the examination of our activities by the police after our 11 month tenure.

Our arrival as the 'saviours' of the club did not exactly set the West Country on fire. It did not come as much of a surprise to walk into the club on the first day to be greeted more by sympathy rather than excitement. The club had been run into the ground. Bernard Frowd its chief executive officer (also former chief executive of Exeter City Council) had taken the club from crisis to crisis. My early opinion of the man was that he could hardly run the Pick 'n' Mix counter at Woolworths and much of Exeter's demise seemed down to his incapability. The club had committed to a massive spend on the new stands, one of which was never completed, leaving areas such as changing rooms, officials rooms, medical and media rooms remaining in the old 100 year old stand opposite the new stand.

The truth of the matter was that Russell and Lewis were never really accepted by the cautious footballing public of Exeter. As for the Supporters Club, Dave Bennett, their Chairman was always evasive but never had the bottle to tell us what he was really thinking. No support came from that quarter.

The introduction of Uri Geller and his son Daniel to the boardroom was generally seen as being nothing more than a publicity stunt. This assessment was unfortunately re-enforced by Geller who would make statements about the club without reference to John or me. Some of these statements were embarrassing to say the least. The planting of crystals for instance on the pitch at St James' Park seemed to give the opposition more of an advantage than the home team. His behaviour at the Wrexham away game on Tuesday 18th September 2002 when we were humiliated, losing 4–0 showed a poor image indeed. He pulled John Cornforth, the manager, to one side after the game and began a one-sided diatribe that was nothing less than a teacher-pupil lecture on how to run a football team. Cornforth reacted angrily in full view of the media. We were subsequently confronted by the scribes asking if the board were behind Cornforth or Geller. The writing was on the wall for Cornforth who had lost the dressing room. He only gained some last ditch support from his cronies such as Sean McCarthy, Kwame Ampadu and Andy Roscoe. I was not always John Cornforth's biggest supporter but on this occasion I was four square behind him. Geller was out of order. Remarks such as his should be reserved for the privacy of the boardroom.

When I saw Geller behave this way, it made me regret inviting him and his son Daniel to join us at Exeter. At the time it made sense for sleepy Exeter City to be associated with a world wide celebrity. His son was a fanatical Grecians fan illustrated by the 'shrine' to the club he had in his bedroom. My extended invitation for Daniel to join us also made sense. His father, prone to mood swings with previous interests in football clubs, needed the guiding influence that Daniel might be able to bring. The media backed the involvement of Uri and Daniel with certain reservations. Their concern was that he would probably generate interest in the club but only if he gained an equal amount of publicity. Within a few months the football club was to witness an event that would silence Geller's critics for a while.

Six weeks after our take over, St James' Park, Exeter was host to a remarkable occasion. Michael Jackson, David Blaine, Patti Boulaye and support acts took to the stage and entertained 6,000 spectators. Fellow directors who secretly despised Geller fell over backwards to be at the event. Some brought their families too. It was hypocrisy at its highest level. This was the biggest event to hit Exeter since the Beatles appeared in the Odeon Cinema for a live show back in 1965!

Wacko Jacko's visit to Exeter coincided with the scandal of him dangling his baby over the balcony. Even Geller was stuck for words on that subject. Uri was in his prime. On the day he stuck to Jackson like glue. I was introduced to Michael and he asked me about the stage lighting. His question concerned the colour of the lighting. He wanted to know if it was white light. Well it certainly wasn't green and I replied accordingly. My impressions of the man were mixed. I could detect a tortured soul underneath the fancy clothes and make up, yet, he seemed very happy, was only too ready to meet people especially the young handicapped children he had insisted attend the event. The executive box we used as his dressing room was festooned with flowers with rose petals scattered on the floor. His managers had also insisted on the room temperature being at the right level. The show was an amazing success and is still talked about today in the sleepy hollows of Devon.

During the fateful 2002–2003 season a total of 42 players pulled on the red and white shirts for city. This was far too many players and both Russell and myself have to take the blame for some of that excess. One of the 'failures' was Lee Sharp who joined us on

11th August 2002, played four times and took his £2,000 a game. He looked so disinterested out wide on the left that he would have been better used selling programmes.

The signing of Don Goodman on John Cornforth's advice heralded to me the possibility that the club could really make an impact in the football league's lowest division. I had seen Goodman play at various levels over the years and he was a class act. Was, being the operative word. He made 12 appearances all season and turned out to be another who was there for the ride. Accepting that he had a run of bad injuries that slowed him down, he never showed the form that was his trademark when playing for West Brom and Wolves.

John Cornforth's reign came to an end after 12 games in the 2002–2003 season. It was apparent to John Russell and me that he had lost the dressing room and his promise that we would not be in any danger of struggling to keep our league status was beginning to look an empty one.

The six signings I was involved with during that season, turned out to a mixed bag in terms of success. I was seriously involved with the signing of the following players: Sean Devine, who turned out to be the club's leading goal scorer in season 2003–2004; Santos Gaia who played 38 games in his first season; goalkeeper Kevin Miller played 51 games in season 2002–2003; George Pilkington, a loan player from Everton played 12 times and would have been retained for a further season had he not wanted to return to the north. Martin Thomas played 30 times in season 2002–2003. My pride and joy was the signing of Chris Todd from Drogheda United in the Irish League. I was at Swansea City when Chris was coming through the ranks and it was devastating news when I heard that the new board of directors had let him go. He went back over to Ireland playing part time football. Then his father rang in late February 2003 to say that Chris wanted another stab at the Football League. Neil McNab was the manager of Exeter at the time and I will always be grateful to him for acting quickly on my recommendation to bring Chris over. I was also grateful to him when he eagerly told me after the first day that Chris had trained with us that he was good enough to put straight into the first team. He was rarely absent from the team after that and gained the captaincy in 2006 before signing for Torquay.

Unfortunately one or two of the players at that time were inclined to be selfish and disloyal when the club needed them most. For example Kevin Miller who was mighty quick to leave the club on its relegation in May 2003 commented, 'These two [Russell and Lewis] ran the club like a circus. They were spending money on players when the existing squad were not getting paid'.

This was absolute bollocks! The players never went without pay, something that could not be said during the reign of the previous regime. Then the Professional Footballers Association came to the rescue of the club by loaning them money to pay players. Miller was always a grumbler who put himself before anyone else, including his team mates. He seemed to relish criticising management at a time when we all needed to pull together. What a pity such a fine keeper had to resort to bad mouthing. His short stint at Torquay United at the back end of the 2006–2007 season did little to save them from the ignominy of relegation to the Conference.

Exeter also had a few decent guys such as Barry O'Connell, Chris Curran, Scott Hiley, Santos Gaia and Sean Devine. The appointment of Neil McNab as the new manager of Exeter City on the recommendation of the late ex-World Cup hero Alan Ball, came initially by route of his friend and Exeter director Stuart Dawe. John Russell, Stuart Dawe and I interviewed several candidates for the post including Jan Molby, Graham Rix and Neil 'Razor' Ruddock. The criticism that came our way after a disappointing tenure by McNab should be put in the context of what would have happened should we have appointed one of the other 'high flyers'. Jan Molby was sacked by Kidderminster, Graham Rix was sacked by Oxford then went on to manage Hearts (he was then relieved of his duties from Hearts) and Neil Ruddock is still out of the game to my knowledge. My personal choice that day was Molby as I found him personable and enthusiastic. Neil McNab was a close second on my list as he was hungry for the job. The endorsement by Ball was enough to make me lean towards McNab when the vote was taken. Unfortunately the new manager went 23 games, winning only six games, drawing eight and losing 11 which left us in a perilous position at the bottom of the Third Division.

Neil McNab privately made it known after departing Exeter City that he did not want Sean Devine to sign for the club. He admitted that he had not seen him play. When asked on many occasions what he wanted, McNab made it clear that a striker was his first priority. When asked who he had in mind his expressionless face told me all I wanted to know. He did not have any particular player in mind. Devine scored three times in his first four games! He went on to captain the club and was without doubt a huge success.

There was not time for the interviewing process to take place after McNab's departure. I looked around for guidance. Dawe kept quiet as his previous choice had backfired on him. John Russell was still reeling after his selection of Gary Bennett as McNab's assistant had failed badly. The club needed stability and discipline on the field of play if it were to be saved from the perils of relegation to the Conference over the next 13 games.

I blew the whistle on Geller after a senior first team player admitted to me that he had taken cash off Geller, albeit through Shippy his manager. Graham Bean, who at the time was the FA's compliance officer, filed his damning report that included affidavits from several first team players. All those interviewed 'coughed' as Bean made it quite clear that if they did not tell the truth then not only would the suspects be punished but all the first team players as well should his investigation prove that players did take money outside of contractual arrangements. What a shame that this issue raised its ugly head just at the time that the Grecians had a remarkable turn of fortune.

Having navigated their way through to the third round of the FA Cup, the draw paired Exeter with Manchester United at Old Trafford. But the fairy tale does not end there as the Grecians held the mighty United to a 0–0 draw thus sending their team of all-stars to St James' Park for the replay. Not surprisingly United won the replay 2–0 but in the process, the Devon club netted £800,000 and in the process wiped out a huge chunk of debt.

In April 2004, Bean's successor, David Lampitt, wrote to Geller and confirmed that the payments made to players by Geller did constitute a breach of FA rules and warned him of his future conduct. So our spoon bender was capable of bending rules as well!

23

SO NEAR, YET...

During my eight years at Reading, one player stood out in terms of being head strong, disciplined and single minded. He had made his way up the managerial ladder through stints at Cambridge United as number two to John Beck. He then had his own success at Preston where he helped the club gain promotion from the Third to the Second Division in 1996 and in the process gave David Beckham his first run out during his loan spell from Manchester United. Gary Peters then went on to run a very successful youth academy at Preston.

I learned that Gary was out of the game in 2002 and was doing some scouting for David Moyes at Everton. I asked Gary if he would come and see us play at Bournemouth in late February 2003. Gary stayed the night after the game and together with John Russell we struck a deal to bring Gary to St James' Park.

The fans were not that appreciative of his efforts initially as they saw the appointment of Lewis and Russell origin. They thought perhaps he would eventually go the same way as McNab. However, after six unbeaten games they started to get behind Gary and the team. Come the last game of the season we were placed four points above Shrewsbury who were already relegated to the Conference, and we were one point behind Swansea.

As I am writing this book I am overwhelmed at the number of links and coincidences that have occurred during my travels through the game. We had to beat Southend in the last game of the season and Swansea had to lose against Hull City, as one point separated the clubs. The 'losers' would find themselves playing Conference football the next season. Shrewsbury was the next club that Gary Peters was to manage and Swansea was the club I sold for £1 in 2002.

The build up for the last home game of the season against Southend was nothing short of manic. We engineered a situation that reminded every football loving fan in Exeter and its environs that this game was the most important in the (mostly sad) history of the club. The media hype was supported by constant reminders that it would be necessary for fans to get to the ground early to ensure a place in the stadium. The capacity of the ground at that time was 9,036. The police, once again pushing their authority to the limit, tried to reduce the capacity by taking out a whole section of the main stand for segregation purposes. We reminded them that it was Southend who were the visitors who occupied 14th position in the league. Their small band of fans was hardly likely to cause problems. In fact I was able to demonstrate to them that so few Southend supporters were coming to the game based on the number of tickets they had sold, that it would be a good idea to put all the Southend supporters in the old Grandstand where 450 seats were reserved for away fans. This would release the standing terrace behind the goal for our fans. They reluctantly agreed with my proposal.

I was filled with excitement and anticipation. I could envisage Gary Peters motivating the team to win this all important game. This was his ideal arena. I could not see Brian Flynn, the struggling Swansea City manager, being successful in his efforts to motivate a poor team, a team that Exeter had managed to beat both home and away in this season by the same 1–0 scoreline. Swansea's visitors on this all important occasion were Hull City, a team that had not made the necessary progress during the season to put themselves into a play off position, but they had several highly paid players I believed would be playing for new contracts. Nevertheless I had a strange feeling that they might just lie down and die.

Normally I would arrive at the ground at about 11.00 am. On this particular morning I walked into my office at 8.30 am. My early start received the following comments:

'Wet the bed Mike?'

'Do you know what time it is Mike?'

A cheeky, 'Is that a mirage I see walking across the room,' was uttered by one of the main office staff. This drew chuckles from his colleagues.

Fair play to the staff, they made these remarks in the knowledge that on a match day I was unlikely to be seen at that time in the morning.

I could not get the thought of Swansea taking on Hull at the Vetch out of my mind. Could the magnificent support from those diehards in West Wales carry the team through? Or even worse, could it cause a riot if they were losing to the extent that the match had to be abandoned? I knew enough about the 'hard boys' on the North Bank at the Vetch to know they were quite capable of prematurely bringing a game to an end. The Vetch was a typical old style stadium where the fans were in very close proximity to the players, often causing problems for the club. Assistant referees too were intimidated. It can never be proven, but the general consensus in football was that putting these factors together was worth a goal start for the home club. Should the game not be completed and Exeter was to win against Southend, Swansea would have to win their game whenever it was played. This would give Swansea the advantage of knowing exactly what they had to do to secure their league place. They could prepare accordingly perhaps playing four up front and only three at the back.

As the thoughts of our relegation battle were racing through my brain, yet another coincidence sprang to mind. Back in season 1998–1999 the Swans were scheduled to play Hull City at home in the last game of the season. This was a vital game for the Swans as they needed a win to secure a play-off place for promotion to the then Second Division. Anyone who has spent some time on the delightful West Wales coast will say that when it rains it bloody well pours. In my humble opinion meteorological abnormalities occur on this coastline whereby the rain clouds seem quite capable of going around in circles for a week at a time and not venturing east into England. The Severn Bridge almost acts like a weather wall! Heavy rain on the Friday night meant that the poor Vetch playing surface resembled a paddy field. I received a call at 8.00 am from the stadium manager to say that we needed an early referee's inspection. I disagreed with his suggestion on the basis that I knew that the League would insist on the game being played. The reality was that at midday there was no way a game of football could have been played on this surface. The ground staff were sweeping water off the pitch only to find that the continuing deluge of rain sweeping in from the coast put them one step forward and two back.

The match referee arrived at 12.30 pm. His first visit on to the ground was a short one. Wearing rain beaten, mud covered wellies and looking as if he had just stepped out of the sea he came up to my office and asked if he could use the phone. He wanted a private conversation with Jim Ashworth, the official at the Football League responsible for liaising with referees regarding match day pitch inspections. The poor man came out of my office, pulled me to one side and said that the League was insisting that the game go ahead. This decision gave the ref a huge problem as his first consideration had to be for the safety of the players followed by the entertainment value for the fans as the match could easily turn into a farce. The Football League's reasons were understandable and I imagine that they did take into account the referee's concerns, but this was the final day of the season and all fixtures needed to be completed. To compound their dilemma the result of this game had a bearing on the play-off positions. Hull City had nothing to play for other than pride as they were in a mid table position.

Vain efforts to clear the pitch meant that as we approached kick off time the surface was unplayable. The ref (now constantly on the phone to the league official) was in a right old 'four and two'. The League official became insistent and directed the ref to get the game started. Fortunately there was a break in the weather and the game started 20 minutes late. This meant that the result of other games that had a bearing on the play-off positions would be known 20 minutes before the Swansea game finished. Still, this was far better than a period of 24 hours or more, but it nevertheless gave Swansea a marginal advantage.

The Swans won the game in 1999 2–0 thus confirming their play-off spot.

The pitch at the Vetch was always likely to cause a problem with fixtures due to the lack of any real investment in the playing area. It was also susceptible to postponements due to frost. One third of the pitch on the main stand side of the ground never saw the sun. On many occasions two thirds of the pitch was perfectly suitable for play with soft, lush grass presenting the players with a perfect playing surface only for the other third to be bone hard and encrusted with frost. On Saturday 31st January 2001 we were due to play Peterborough United at home. There had been a hard frost the night before and I was fearful that the match referee would take the view that it would be dangerous for the players to play on a surface that was two thirds okay and one third dangerous. They could use footwear that would compensate for the pitch inconsistency, but that would have still left a doubt as to their safety should they be heavily axed on the frozen area. I asked John Hollins for his opinion. Trying to be less than forceful, I wanted the game played as gates had slumped by 25 percent over the last two months and we were under severe financial pressure. John Hollins asked Ryan Casey one of the fringe players to put on a long studded boot and run up and down the frozen section of the pitch turning at each end of the run to see if he could stay on his feet. Now Ryan at 6 feet was a gangly player not noted for his centre of gravity but the experiment was partly successful.

The referee that day was a Mr David Crick, a referee I had not met before. He arrived at 11.30 am and immediately carried out a pitch inspection. John Hollins accompanied him and I decided to walk quietly behind them in order to hear what they were saying. I did not wish to get involved at this stage. Hollins was laid back and was obviously listening intently to the referee who, with repetitive shakes of his head walked up and down the frozen section. He decided to go back to the dressing room and change his normal footwear for his match boots. Back onto the frozen section he repeated what the player had done earlier. His athleticism was to be admired. Unfortunately for him, but much to the amusement of those watching, which included members of the media wishing to get a verdict on whether the game was on or not, he slipped and fell over as he negotiated one of his 'turns'. I couldn't join in the hilarity as his fall probably meant that he would render the pitch unsafe. Hollins was as much use as an ashtray on a motorbike at this moment and did nothing to encourage the ref to wait and see if the pitch improved over the few hours before kick off, or to suggest that different footwear could be used by both teams. I followed the ref back to his changing room by which time his assistants had arrived. I decided to appeal to the ref's softer side. I explained that the club was in severe financial difficulties and should the match be postponed then the 'lost' £35,000 from the gate receipts would place the club in jeopardy as we did not have another home game until 11th February. I asked him if he was undecided to the extent that he could wait until 2.00 pm before making a final decision. His response only confirmed to me that most referees could not care a piggy's dicky about the financial state of a club.

'I cannot take into account Mr Lewis any other matters other than the state of the pitch and the safety of the players.'

'Even if it is marginal Mr Crick?'

'No, Mr Lewis.' At which point he turned to his assistants with a self satisfying look on his face that suggested to me that he was playing this situation to the book in order to impress his junior colleagues.

'What I am prepared to do Mr Lewis is to explain my reasons for calling the game off to the manager of Peterborough when he arrives.'

No sooner had Mr Crick made his 'generous' offer of explaining his decision to Barry Fry, than the man himself strolled into the ref's room.

'What the fuck's happening ref?'

'Um, um, I'm calling the game off Barry.'

'I've just walked on the pitch ref and it seems okay to me.'

'Shall we go out and look at it together Barry?'

I called John Hollins out of his office to accompany us. The following dialogue that took place on the pitch should be placed for posterity in the annals of the Football League as a guide to common sense.

Barry Fry as he steps onto the frozen section: 'Yeah it's tight ref but with the right footwear it's not a problem. What do you think John?'

With his hand placed under his chin, pursed lips and a glancing look at the ref without comment, Fry got no response from John.

'What footwear do your lads have Barry?' asked Crick.

'Fucking footwear ref? In the back of that coach parked out there I have got every type of footwear. Pimples, dimples, long stud, short stud, bars, blocks, sandals, ice skating boots and fucking wellies. Come on ref let's have a game of football.'

It worked and to this day I will be ever grateful to Barry Fry.

In fairness I could understand John Hollins' reluctance to play the game as his record over the last 13 games did not put him in good shape for this one. I imagined that he would have been quite happy for the season to finish there and then. The game ended in a 2–2 draw and left the club three off the bottom of the league.

At St James' Park on Saturday 3rd May 2003, so much depended on the result of the respective two games. I did have feelings for many friends I had left behind at Swansea. I imagined that they were experiencing the same anxiety as any Exeter supporter. I wish that I could say that part of my heart was still in Swansea, but it wasn't. I had moved on and still bore the scars of that final period in the West Wales City. The fervour that accompanied support for the Swans through the years was most definitely going to reach its highest peak on this day. I knew that the more laid back approach by Exeter fans would give the Welsh club a distinct advantage. I was informed by a fan who made his way up to the directors box just before kick off that they were playing the Welsh National Anthem at the Vetch just before kick off bringing watery eyes to the many inside the ground. His information came via his radio tuned into BBC Wales.

Having spent endless hours over the last 11 months trying to breath life back into Exeter City on the back of it having been ravaged by years of neglect, there was no way could I hang on to old allegiances. The Devon club had been nowhere, was likely to go nowhere, and on this day I could see the real possibility of the club going out of the football league and consigning itself to football oblivion. The day meant as much to me as the successive visits to Wembley with Spurs, avoiding the 'drop' with Newport County and that wonderful occasion at Newport when Reading created an all time record achieving 13 straight wins from the start of the season. I had already felt the hurt of seeing Newport County, my home town club going out of the Football League in 1988. Football pundits say that it is almost impossible to regain League status once it has been lost. The history books tell a different story with the promotion of Darlington, Barnet, Doncaster, Colchester, Chester, Carlisle, Shrewsbury, Lincoln and Macclesfield from the Conference rising like a Phoenix from the ashes to regain Football League status. Unfortunately I cannot see the County returning to the Football League, certainly not if their current form is an indicator of their capabilities. Languishing in the Blue Square Conference South does not provide a very strong springboard for a return. Those heady days of 1980 when they gained promotion from the Fourth Division of the Football League followed by a sensational run in the European Cup Winners Cup after winning the Welsh Cup seems like light years away. The County went out in the quarter final to Carl Zeiss Jena FC of West Germany. Having drawn the first leg in Germany, the County lost the return leg 1–0 at Somerton Park in front of 18,000. My dad would have been ever so proud. If the opportunity presents itself for me to drive past the site of their old ground at Somerton Park memories come flooding back even if the trains don't stop there anymore.

Exeter City had a poor pedigree and honestly could not compare their relative successes even with humble Newport's successes. That made little difference to the stark reality that on this day they too could lose their league status and I would be held responsible. Apprehension and fear was sketched on the faces of the fans as they descended on St James' Park for the kick off. The fans I spoke to were sympathetic to the cause and said that even with the events of that day making or breaking their club they bore no resentment towards Russell and Lewis. I wondered if that was the general view.

In the boardroom it was business as ever with John Russell, Ivor Doble and me trying to put a brave face on matters as we greeted the visiting Southend directors. Remarks such as, 'May the best team win', or 'Let's hope it's a good game', seemed rather futile on this historic occasion.

As the players came out for their warm up they received a great reception from the burgeoning crowd. Hundreds of fans clasped mini radios to their ears in readiness for the kick off. Those with a more sophisticated receiver were able to pick up Radio Wales as the signal only had to travel across the Bristol Channel and down a bit. I had stood at the back of the directors' box all season, positioning myself against a wall. I made sure that my left foot was six inches from the side of the step and my right positioned half way along the concrete plinth (old habits die hard), I realised that this was going to be 90 minutes of hell.

Within five minutes of the kick off, the news from Swansea was devastating. Swansea was awarded a penalty which James Thomas converted. The groans from the capacity crowd were obviously transmitted to the Exeter players but it did not stop them from taking the game to Southend. Then, 11 minutes into the game, as if we needed to be reminded that there was always the possibility that Southend may score, their lively winger Brett Darby was upended in the penalty area and referee Fletcher pointed to the penalty spot. Tes Bramble took the spot kick and rolled, rather than kicked the ball straight to Kevin Miller in the Exeter goal. Had Geller visited the away dressing room before the game? Then on 25 minutes, a huge cheer went up as the news filtered through that Hull City had gone 2–1 up. I turned around to see the expression of John Russell's face. He was in such a state that he seemed incapable of showing any emotion. His eyes were fixed and his crimson face expressionless. The euphoria lasted until just before half time when Swansea was awarded a second penalty and Thomas converted his second to take the teams in level at 2–2 at half time. If matters stayed that way in Wales and we could find the net, then Swansea City would be playing Conference football next season and Exeter would retain their league status.

John Russell watched all the home games whilst pacing up

and down the boardroom. The club doctor raised concerns with me at the start of the season and suggested to John that he calmed down during games. So what he was thinking now as John wound himself up for the second half I had no idea. Perhaps an appropriate pill from his bag was the answer.

On the basis of what I had seen in the first half, it seemed unlikely that we could make a breakthrough. We had most of the play but looked fragile the moment we got anywhere near Southend's goal. Flack and Devine who were supposed to spearhead the attack looked uncomfortable playing together. With the score at Swansea still standing at 2–2, survival for the Grecians was very much on the cards but we didn't have to wait long for bad news to descend upon us. Three minutes into the second half at the Vetch, a scrambled goal put Swansea 3–2 up. Then the knife was twisted in the back. After 60 minutes of play, the Swans went 4–2 up. Thomas scored his hat trick and in the process sent their 9,566 fans into ecstasy. The news was greeted with an eerie silence at St James' Park. The fans knew that the game was up for The Grecians. Two minutes into injury time, Cronin found Flack in space and the burly striker rounded the Southend keeper. With some panache he rolled the ball into the net. Why couldn't he have done that three weeks ago at Cambridge? Some of the crowd had left the ground by then as the Swansea result was confirmed 15 minutes before the game at St James' Park had finished. This was due to the fact that we had kicked off 15 minutes late because of crowd congestion. There were accusations emanating from Wales that Mike Lewis had pleaded with the referee to kick off late so that Exeter could gain an advantage. Heaven help us! Who are these morons that come up with these suggestions?

Returning to the boardroom was an unpleasant experience. What could be said? We had won the game. Manager Gary Peters had put in a magnificent effort and nearly pulled off a miracle to keep us in the league. Surprisingly, no blame was openly placed at the door of Russell and Lewis albeit we invited comments by going straight to the clubhouse after saying goodbye to the Southend directors. There was a very subdued atmosphere in the bar. All I could do was apologise to the supporters and tell them that if it was their wish I would stay next season and do all I could to pave the way for the club to return to the Football League. I was walking around in a complete daze. I decided to go to the boardroom and see if Gary Peters had come up from the dressing room. Indeed he had and was accompanied by his wife. Words stuck in my throat. The best I could manage was, 'Thanks Gary, no one could have done more'.

John's wife Gillian came into the boardroom and we shared a couple of drinks in an environment that was hard to describe. It was like attending a funeral without a corpse. John had been Chairman of Scarborough when they lost their league status in 1999 after a heartbreaking finale to the season when Scarborough, having finished their season, needed Carlisle not to beat Plymouth in order to secure Scarborough's League status for another season. Who would have guessed that Jimmy Glass (the on loan Carlisle keeper) would come up for a corner in the fourth minute of stoppage time and prod the ball home? Here again was John Russell going through similar emotions only this time the fate of his club was known at 4.30 pm not 4.50 pm as was the case at Carlisle. John unfortunately had created his own record in football as the first Chairman to steer two clubs from the football league to the Conference.

Following on the sequence of remarkable coincidences, who was it that Exeter beat in their last but one game in the league at home in the 1989–1990 season? Can you believe it was Scarborough? Those lost three points helped to put the final nail in the Scarborough coffin. As for Exeter, well they won the fourth division title by 10 points. It's a funny old game!

Back in the boardroom at Exeter the gathering black cloud had already descended. The reality that Conference football was on its way to St James' Park next season was hard to accept. Fortunately the budgets, drawn up well before the end of the season when it was a fair guess that relegation was on the cards, didn't necessarily spell disaster. Ten player contracts were not being renewed. This gave the club a saving of £275,000 and in turn reduced the playing squad from 32 to 22. Developing financial performance of the commercial department through Annie Bassett's leadership headlined by her recruitment of FlyBe, an up and coming airline flying out of Exeter, to become the sponsors for the new season, we stood a chance. Incidentally she has never been credited for that deal that is still in place. Little did I realise that as the sun went down on that fateful day of 3rd May that within 11 days my world was to be turned upside down and brought to a crushing halt never to be the same again.

Since my arrest in May 2003 and the publication of this book, over four years have elapsed.

24

TIME TO REFLECT

Exeter, the sleepy University City has a fascinating history. The last execution of a witch took place there in 1684. If some of the present day supporters of the football club had their way then the market place could yet again witness the burning of witches. John Russell and Mike Lewis would be strung up on gallows and a bigger attendance than that attracted to football matches would look on in eager anticipation. There would be no shortage of volunteers to light the taper!

My philosophy on life is a simple one. Having crammed so much into my three score years and five, I am eternally grateful for my lot. I've had two divorces, death threats, a possible jail term and a cancer scare. These have all helped to make me more resolute. These bad experiences will not prevent me from firmly shaking the hand of my maker, whoever he or she might be, and thanking them for more than a fair share of the good life. I only hope that should that great person upstairs adopt a plan of equalisation that my share of good fortune in terms of a life fulfilled has not deprived anyone else of their share of good fortune.

In December 2005, I received a phone call from an old and dear friend. Earlier in the book I referred to Ernie my school mate. We shared a desk in secondary school from the age of 11 through to the age of 15. Our friendship was never one where we lived in each other's pocket as my travelling prevented any regular contact. Nevertheless our friendship survived intact. We kept in touch by telephone over the years and had the occasional get together. The fateful phone call was, in typical Ernie style, made in a very serious and controlled manner. There was no obvious panic, just a down to earth statement of the hard facts put before him by his doctor. Ernie had felt unwell for two months with back pain, when he decided to visit his doctor. After being sent for tests, he was told that his pain could be linked to a diverticular problem. The pre-Christmas news from his doctor after his tests was earth shattering. He was suffering from an advanced form of pancreatic cancer and was given at best, a few months to live. His tendency to take control of all matters included now, in his last hours, issuing final instructions to all his family, doctors and nurses and to a lesser degree his friends. But it was his bravery in the face of hopeless odds that, if I am honest, surprised me a little, as I had known Ernie complain about aches and pains over the years and rightly or wrongly I would take the piss as he had cried wolf far too many times before.

Cometh the hour cometh the man. Ernie was nothing other than dignified as he stared death face on. He pleaded with the medics to let him die at home where he was so proud of his obvious material wealth. He had a beautiful house adorned with classic paintings, antique furniture and so tastefully furnished that it was a testament to his and his adorable wife Annette's efforts over the years to make it a perfect haven.

The inevitable came at 10.10 am on 12th March 2006. He quietly passed away just 20 minutes before I could get to his house in Cowbridge, South Wales. There was no specific reason for me travelling from Swansea to Cowbridge *that* Sunday morning. I was due to visit earlier the next week. During life I've found there are times when I'm motivated to act on instinct. This was one of those times.

Life is full of regrets. One of my sincere regrets was that fateful morning. How I wished that I had not stopped for petrol and a Sunday newspaper on my way to see him. The need to look at the football league tables shamefully took precedence over the need to see Ernie as quickly as possible. The doctor present when he passed on said that it was possible that just prior to his death he might have been able to hear what was being said around him. I wish that I could have been there in time to say goodbye. Shit! Why couldn't he have hung on a little longer? Perhaps it was his way for getting even with me for cribbing his music exam paper all those years earlier!

25

BACK TO NORMALITY?

During the search for a barrister to present my defence after my arrest in 2003, I perhaps mistakenly once again followed the advice of John Russell my former partner at Exeter City and now one of the co-defendants. He suggested that we seek a preliminary meeting with Guy Kearl QC who was head of St Pauls House Chambers in Leeds. Mr Kearl had achieved notoriety through representing defendants in high profile cases. He was at the RAF base in Northolt in May 2001 waiting to represent the infamous Ronnie Biggs on his return to this country.

My first meeting with Mr Kearl together with John and Gillian Russell was informal to a point, but nevertheless I had the distinct impression that Mr Kearl was sizing us up as we responded to some of the gentle questions put by him. Imagine my surprise some two weeks later when one of his solicitors rang me to say that Mr Kearl had decided to take on my case, but was not happy to represent John and Gillian. The following months and years saw the advent of dozens of meetings with the legal eagles held either in Leeds, Exeter, Swansea and London. The amount of paperwork generated would have seen the demise of dozens of trees!

On 16th April 2007 came the advent of trial proceedings at Bristol Crown Court. For the next three days there was furious activity on the legal front with barristers and solicitors representing all three defendants scurrying across the floor outside courtroom 7. It seemed they were oblivious to the desperate needs of the defendants to know what was going on.

Deals were being done. For my part it meant that if I put up my hand to the charge of fraudulent trading (trading whilst insolvent) for the nine week period from 3rd March 2003 to 14th

May 2003 then charges relating to obtaining a pecuniary advantage, giving financial assistance to myself and conspiracy to defraud, would be dropped. I accepted the deal and had to return eight weeks later to receive my sentence. What I have promised myself is that I have a score to settle with the people who made a complaint against me in the first place. How this score settling will manifest itself I am not sure, but I have promised myself that before I go to my grave, those who cast the first stones will regret the day they trotted off to the Devon & Cornwall Constabulary to file a complaint. I am not a vindictive person. Too often I have turned the other cheek. Not this time. It seems that the initial complaint was made by spoon bender Geller. He is my main target for revenge. My proof positive that Geller was behind the handing out of payments to players is evidenced by the letter from the FA to him stating that he was guilty of misconduct and should he ever repeat the felony he would be very severely dealt with. During March 2007 his beloved Israel hosted the England team in a European Qualifying match. Predictably, Geller, having already failed to impress the England fans over the years that he could provide psychic assistance now turned his attention to his home country. Several Israeli players claimed that he had helped them through this encounter. How the man contained himself when a resurgent England team beat Israel 3–0 in the return leg at the new Wembley I cannot imagine.

I was relieved that I had avoided a nine week trial thanks to the supreme efforts of my legal team and to my pleading guilty to the offence of Fraudulent Trading. But imagine my disgust at the activities of Boston United and Leeds United during May 2007 when they decided to manipulate the timing of their entry into a Creditors Voluntary Agreement to satisfy their footballing needs. Boston held a meeting with their creditors on 26th April 2007 and decided to wait until they could ascertain what their league status would be before entering into a CVA. On Saturday 5th May they lost their league status and the club entered administration. Their Chairman stated that, 'The club has lurched from crisis to crisis. We just couldn't make the repayments to the Inland Revenue. If you look at the level of debt to the Inland Revenue it's not a lot bigger than it was three or fours years ago'. Hold on a minute. Was he saying that three or four years ago they were more or less in exactly the same position? If so, they were trading whilst insolvent and three or four years is a damn sight longer than *nine weeks!*

Leeds United was pushed into administration because of a £5,000,000 tax bill. The big question to ask here is this. Had Leeds gone into their last game of the season with half a chance of survival from relegation to the First Division, would their owner and Chairman Ken Bates have found the £5,000,000 thus avoiding the penalty of a points deduction for a club entering into administration? Of course he would.

I carry the regret that the absence of a trial meant that Geller would be spared the embarrassment of having to explain away his actions at Exeter whilst trying to convince a jury that I had been corrupt. They would have seen the man for what he is – nothing more than a showman with a tired act and an oversized ego. If only I had recognised the true face of Geller some 20 years earlier.

I tried on several occasions to warm to Bernard Frowd who I believe was Geller's cohort in complaining to the police. I tried on many occasions to give him the benefit of the doubt when it became obvious to all around that he was incapable of running a pick 'n' mix counter at Woolworth never mind a football club. As the club's chief executive officer prior to my arrival in Exeter, Frowd had gained a poor reputation to say the least, yet he had the audacity to point the finger at me and the Russell's for what I consider to be at worst, minor breaches of certain Company's Acts.

Prosecution and defence proceedings cost the tax payer £1,800,000. On the third day of the hearing when all the deals had been done, the judge declared that he felt that it was not in the public interest to have a nine week trial. Why didn't the prosecution accept that fact four years earlier?

John Russell and I stayed in a Bristol hotel the night before sentencing. I found it rather odd that John's wife was not accompanying him. My partner would have definitely been there had it not been for the fact that she was visiting the USA to see her first grandchild born just four weeks earlier. John was very worried because of his previous and the fact that he pleaded guilty to two charges whereas I had pleaded guilty to one.

After four years and two weeks of wondering what the end result might be I decided to enter the Crown Court with a smile on my face and my head held high. This was despite the fact that I was filled with anxiety about the outcome. Inside the court room I could see that there were two rows of press and several

Exeter City supporters sat in the public area. My thoughts raced to a gladiatorial scene in ancient Rome when the Emperor (or Judge on this occasion) gave the thumbs up or thumbs down depending on whether or not he wanted the prisoners to live or die. Here we had the press on the one hand looking for a juicy conclusion to this long running saga and the supporters on the other baying for blood. They were not to be disappointed.

Over a cup of coffee in the Court cafeteria shortly after the prosecution had delivered their case opening which had taken two hours, I sensed that John was beginning to realise that there was a real prospect of him being sent down. At 2.20 pm Derek Duffy QC spoke on behalf of John. He was on his feet for two hours. He did his very best to draw out any good points in John's favour. Guy Kearl QC acting for me took slightly less time in mitigation. What was surprising was that within seconds of Kearl sitting down, the judge asked John to stand and proceeded to state his reasons for passing sentence. I sat within two feet of John as the judge in summary stated that he was going to sentence him to 21 months imprisonment. The severity of the sentence openly shook John to the core to the point where I thought he was going to collapse. I wondered what the judge had in mind for me. When he called my name I stood trembling at the knees hardly able to comprehend anything that he was saying. I do remember his final words however.

'In view of your previous clean record, your age and the lesser involvement in the activities at Exeter City Football Club, I am prepared to accept the pre-sentencing report with its conclusion that a custodial sentence would not be appropriate. Therefore I am sentencing you to 200 hours of unpaid work and a disqualification from being a director of a company for five years.'

The pre-sentence report was drafted by a probation officer in Swansea who was not very sympathetic at the time of my interview. She openly declared that she was aware that most people in football were corrupt and that included fans, players and directors! On reading her report two weeks later imagine my surprise when I could only see supportive comments and her recommendation that unpaid work should be my sentence.

I sat down in the dock after the verdict and turned to look at John who was in a sea of sweat. I asked him if there was anything I could do and he suggested that I ring his wife Gillian and tell her the outcome. As I didn't have her number John reached inside his jacket pocket to extract her number from his mobile. Before he could open up his phone he was grabbed by two court officials and taken away through the back door in the dock. I was led away in the opposite direction leaving the dock by way of the front door. As I walked past the three Exeter City supporters sat in the public gallery I heard one of them shout out, 'Justice has been done Lewis!' Under normal circumstances I would have turned around and confronted these saddoes, but I was weary and could not be bothered.

Outside the court there was a plethora of cameras. I was invited to give an interview. What could I say? There I was in the sunshine in the knowledge that John was being 'processed' before being banged up and my thoughts were with him. There were times during our 11 month reign in Exeter when I seriously fell out with him. On one occasion I openly accused him of being a compulsive liar. Generally we had a good relationship and experienced laughter and tears in equal quantities. I feel guilty that he is suffering a greater penalty than me but I have to remind myself that John, in order to get his wife off the hook, pleaded guilty to other charges that carried with them higher sentencing levels.

Did any good come out of the four years of turmoil? It made me appreciate those people who stepped up to the plate when it mattered: my partner, Glenys was solid as ever in her support; my dear friend Ray Trotman was a great support; my daughter Faye provided strength (to name only a few supporters). To those who decided to keep a distance yet still claimed to be friends I would simply say, 'I understand'. As for Mike Lewis, well in the words of Del Boy, 'What a plonker'. I just hope that I have learned important lessons; refocused on my priorities and can spend these remaining years surrounded by people who really matter. One thing is for certain, as the egg timer of life speeds up and the grains in the lower half start to heavily outweigh those in the top, I will make bloody sure that I treat every Wednesday with extreme caution, even it that means staying in bed all day!

My unpaid work began in a charity shop. My first job was to sort out all the various clothes hangers and put them on racks. This was followed by a stint of steam cleaning, a highly dangerous task when a clumsy sod like me forgets that burning hot steam spreads over an area far in excess of the small nozzle used to slide up and down the clothes. This was the repayment of my debt to society.

By the time this book is published I will have completed my sentence, John Russell on the other hand will still be imprisoned and Uri Geller will undoubtedly have offered his mystical advice to the Israeli footballers for their European International game against England at the new Wembley stadium. It didn't work this time Uri!

Sadly we are normally judged by how successful our lives have been. Financially secure, happily married, good job and so on. In my case when I look back at my life I see a genuine patchwork quilt of vivid colours and depressing shades of grey. Through it all I have tried my very best to be philosophical and to that end I would totally agree with the sentiments of Orison Swett Marden (author 1850–1924) 'Success is not measured by what you accomplished but by the opposition you have encountered and the courage which you have maintained during the struggle against overwhelming odds.'